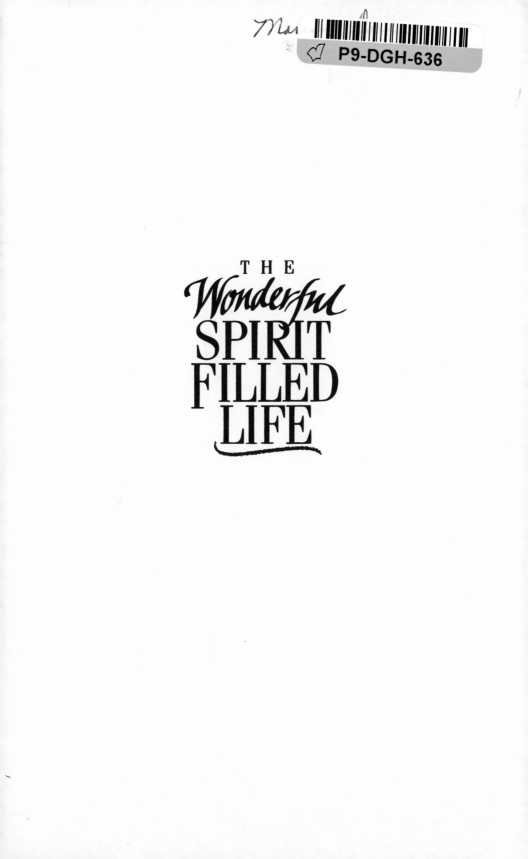

THE

Wonderful

SPIRIT
FILLED
LIFE

THE
Wonderful
SPIRIT
FILLED
LIFE

CHARLES STANLEY

OLIVER
NELSON

THOMAS NELSON PUBLISHERS
Nashville · Atlanta · London · Vancouver

Published in Nashville, Tennessee, by Thomas Nelson, Inc.

Unless otherwise noted, the Bible version used in this publication is the New American
Standard Bible, © 1960, 1962, 1963, 1968, 1971, 1973, 1975, 1977 by The Lockman Foundation. Used by permission.

Scripture quotations noted NKJV are from THE NEW KING JAMES VERSION. Copyright ©
1979, 1980, 1982, Thomas Nelson, Inc.

Scripture quotations noted KJV are from The King James Version of the Holy Bible.

Scripture quotations noted NIV are taken from the HOLY BIBLE: NEW INTERNATIONAL
VERSION. Copyright © 1973, 1978, 1984 by the International Bible Society. Used by permission of Zondervan Bible Publishers.

Some names have been fictionalized for protection of privacy.

Library of Congress Cataloging-in-Publication Data
Stanley, Charles F.
    The wonderful spirit-filled life / Charles Stanley.
        p.   cm.
    Includes bibliographical references.
    ISBN 0-8407-9141-0 hc
    ISBN 0-7852-7747-1 pb
    1. Spiritual life.   2. Holy Spirit.   I. Title.
BV4501.2.S7194   1992
248.4—dc20   92-15404
                                                            CIP

Printed in the United States of America.

23 24 25 QPV 02 01 00 99

*This book is lovingly dedicated
to the members of the
First Baptist Church, Atlanta*

Contents

ACKNOWLEDGMENTS

I am grateful to my son, Andy, and his wife, Sandra, for their editorial assistance.

Introduction

The Wonderful Spirit-Filled Life. I didn't like the title the first time I heard it. After all, life isn't always wonderful. And life for those who are filled with the Spirit isn't always wonderful, either. The apostle Paul is proof of that. But the Spirit-filled life *is* wonderful—especially compared to the alternative.

I know all about the alternative. I spent the early years of my Christian life struggling. Call it carnal; call it fleshly; call it whatever you wish. It was anything but wonderful. In fact, my experience on the other side of the equation motivated me to write a book about the Spirit-filled life.

In preparing for this project I read everything I could get my hands on that had to do with the Holy Spirit. You will find several of these sources noted throughout. Books on the Holy Spirit generally fall into two categories. They are either highly experiential —with great application—or purely doctrinal with little to carry with you on Monday morning.

This is not a criticism. These writers have accomplished exactly what they set out to do. Praise God for the motivation we gain through the testimony of others! And where would we be without the men and women who thrive on minutiae, those who labor diligently to discover how all the parts fit together?

The Wonderful Spirit-Filled Life is a literary attempt to wed experience with doctrine. That is nothing new. Luke did that when he wrote Acts. There we find the experience of the early church supported by apostolic sermons, quotes from the Savior, and references to the Old Testament. It is a lesson in theology presented in the form of narrative.

You will notice that some of my conclusions are slightly out of the mainstream of evangelical thought. I have done my best to support these conclusions textually without turning this book into a commentary.

I'm not sure what role this book will play in your pursuit of the Spirit-filled life. I do know that many years ago a man wrote a book about his quest, and it turned me upside down. After I read only a portion of his testimony, God opened my eyes to the reality of the Spirit-filled life. I haven't been the same since.

I write with the hope that this book will do for someone what that book did for me back in 1964. If that is the case, it will have been well worth the effort.

The Adequate Christian Life

---◆---

Dennis chuckled to himself as he read the bumper sticker on the car in front of him: HE WHO DIES WITH THE MOST TOYS WINS. He had seen and heard the expression plenty of times, and he always got a kick out of it. As he sat there staring at the bumper in front of him, the irony of his own situation began to sink in. At no point in his life had he ever consciously subscribed to the philosophy represented by that popular bumper sticker. On the contrary, as a Christian, his belief system was diametrically opposed to everything that statement stood for. But if he was honest with himself, an outsider who simply watched him for any length of time might conclude that his ultimate pursuit in life was the accumulation of the newest and most high-tech toys. That was not to say that he didn't want to be a good father and husband. But somehow those values were not the driving force in his life anymore—not the way they were in the beginning. In fact, lately he had noticed that several areas of his original belief system had taken a backseat to the priorities set before him by his world. What was happening?

Making his way up the exit ramp, he thought back to that night on the beach when, as a college student, he trusted Christ as his Savior. It was so real, so significant. His decision that night affected every facet of his life. He remembered the intensity with which he communicated his newfound faith to his fraternity brothers. Church was not a duty then. It was a joy. It was something he looked forward to each week.

Everything was different now. His faith hadn't changed. He still believed all the same things. But something was missing. His whole Christian experience could be summed up by, "I'm doing the best I can."

Cheryl plopped the groceries down on the counter and looked at her watch. 5:15. Dennis would be home in thirty minutes, and she hadn't even begun to prepare supper. As she grabbed her apron, she heard something fall out of the pocket. It was a refrigerator magnet that had somehow found its way into her apron pocket: IF LIFE GIVES YOU A LEMON, MAKE LEMONADE. She smiled and stuck it back on the refrigerator.

There sure have been a lot of lemons lately, she thought to herself. *But you've got to keep going. You can't let it get you down.* She rehearsed the argument she and Dennis had the night before. He always called them discussions. But in her book it was a good old-fashioned argument. She couldn't remember what the issue was or how it started. *It was always something petty—something he thought I meant by something I didn't say or something like that. It seemed like there had been a lot of "discussions" lately. But you've got to make the best of things; you've got to keep going.*

She walked back over to the refrigerator and looked at the plastic lemon. As tears welled up in her eyes, she thought, *Wow, my whole life boils down to taking an endless supply of lemons and doing my best to make lemonade. What has happened? It wasn't supposed to be this way.* She sat down at the kitchen table with her face in her hands and began to really cry: *I can't let this happen. I've got to keep going. Things will get better.* She attempted to pull herself together. Her eyes focused on the family Bible leaning against the toaster on the end of the table. *Dennis must have left it there after family devotions this morning. Family devotions, ha! What a joke.*

When they were first married, Cheryl had been a leader in a neighborhood Bible study. She lived to study and share what she learned with others. The Scriptures were alive back then. That was then. Her Bible reading had become little more than a dry ritual. There were mornings when something would jump out at her. But by lunchtime the insights were swept away by the cares of the day. *What has happened to me?* she thought. *Where is the joy? Where is the peace? Where is the love?*

Just then the door slammed. "Hi, Mom."

"Hi, Jodie. Dad should be here in a few minutes."

"I'm not staying for dinner. Grace is coming by to . . ."

Cheryl didn't hear the rest as Jodie scampered up the stairs. It didn't matter. At seventeen Jodie was in a world of her own, a world that was closed to Cheryl and Dennis.

Jodie slammed her door and checked the messages on her answering machine. "Jo, it's Randy. Everything is set for Sunday. Richard got his dad's boat, and my parents said we could use the lake house. Have you asked your folks yet? If not, find out tonight and let me know." Click.

Sunday. Mom will have a duck . . . but she will recover. Besides, I've been in church for the last two Sundays in a row. That's two more than most people. As Jodie brushed her hair, she paused to look at the bulletin board hanging next to her mirror. FRIENDS ARE FRIENDS FOREVER the pin read. That had been their theme at church camp last summer. She was overcome for a moment with a wave of emotion. She thought back to that last night at camp when she and her friends had rededicated their lives. They told the whole group that they were going back to their homes and campuses to make a difference for Christ. *Some difference,* she thought. *It's nothing more than a distant memory now. Good intentions but no follow-through. That's the way it always was at camp.*

Friends forever. *Some friends. We barely speak. Besides, I'm not really into the church thing much anymore. It didn't really work for me. I got tired of being good all the time. Other than camp, the whole thing was really pretty boring. I'll take another shot at it when I'm older.* Jodie shook her head and finished brushing her hair.

The doorbell signaled the arrival of Grace. Jodie galloped down the stairs and out the front door just as Dennis was pulling into the driveway. Jodie glanced over her shoulder at her father's car. For a brief moment they made eye contact. And both thought to themselves, *Good timing.*

PART ONE

Looking Up

My personal journey into the Spirit-filled life

I called out of my distress to the LORD,
And He answered me.

—*Jonah 2:2*

CHAPTER 1

The Wonderful Spirit-Filled Life

For too many believers the Christian life boils down to simply doing the best they can. There is no dynamic, no power, and there is no real distinctive that can be attributed to anything other than discipline and determination. I meet believers all the time whose doctrine can be summed up in two statements:

1. Nobody's perfect.
2. God understands.

For them, life is a long string of joys and sorrows with the promise of heaven at the end.

There is often a deep chasm between what they sing on Sunday and what they actually do on Monday through Saturday. They would be quick to argue that there *should* be a meaningful relationship, that somehow the truth they hear on Sunday *should* seep into their daily lives. But somehow the details of life are void of the divine. After all, business is business. Boys will be boys. Everybody is doing it. We have to be realistic. On and on it goes. These pithy statements serve as the foundation of their Monday-through-Saturday theology.

To an outsider looking in, there is often little or no difference between the life-style, thought life, and habits of the Christian and those of his "uninformed" heathen neighbor. Oh, there may be a foreboding sense of what ought to be done and what ought to be said. But change is usually motivated by guilt and consequently short-lived.

3

The divorce rate for Christian adults isn't far behind that of the rest of the world. The percentage of Christian adolescents who are involved in premarital sex rivals the statistic for those kids who say they have no strong religious beliefs. Christian counseling services are increasingly in demand. And not a month goes by that a major evangelical church or organization isn't rocked by a moral scandal of some kind. Statistically and observationally, there seems to be little difference between the life-styles of the saints and the sinners. *That should be!*

A View from the Pulpit

This situation is a constant source of frustration and concern for me as a pastor. I am driven by a desire to get the truth to people; the more people who hear, the better. Nothing thrills my heart like watching men and women grasp the goodness and grace of God. And nothing motivates me like seeing people integrate the principles of God's Word into their lives.

On the other hand, nothing is more frustrating than watching people listen week after week, oftentimes write it all down, and then do nothing with what they have heard. Evangelical America is note rich and application poor. As a result, there is little difference between many of us and our lost neighbors.

The real tragedy is that we have lost our ability to function in our society the way God originally intended. We were left here to be a light to our world. As my friend Tony Evans is fond of saying, our lives are to be a commercial announcement of a coming kingdom. People should be able to look at us and know there is something different about us. Not our clothes or our hairstyle. US! What is on the inside.

There should be something different in the way we do business. There should be clear distinctives in the way we raise our children. Our marriages should be testimonies of the love of Christ. Those who choose to remain outside the church should be enamored by the unity and love they see among believers. Unfortunately, that is rarely the case. Consequently, our society has a warped perspective on the person and work of Christ.

We cannot expect them to embrace a Savior they know nothing of. We certainly cannot expect them to surrender to a Lord whose servants can't even get along. As ambassadors for Christ, believers have the responsibility of living in such a way that others see

Christ in us.) As the body of Christ, we are His hands and His feet. We are His mouthpiece. Pardon the cliché, but we are the only Jesus most people will ever know. That being the case, it is no wonder that so many non-Christians want nothing to do with Christ or His church. They know too many Christians!

A View from the Pew

To make matters worse, most believers are convinced that it is the pastor's responsibility to bring people into the church as well as into the kingdom of God. Nothing could be further from the truth. The Scripture is clear on this point. Pastors were given by God to the church to equip the people to do the work (see Eph. 4:11–12). Sermons are not God's primary method for reaching people. People are His method for reaching people. What kind of people? Men and women whose lives and life-styles have been deeply affected by the truths of Scripture, people who have discovered the wonderful Spirit-filled life.

God is looking for imperfect men and women who have learned to walk in moment-by-moment dependence on the Holy Spirit. Christians who have come to terms with their inadequacies, fears, and failures. Believers who have become discontent with "surviving" and have taken the time to investigate everything God has to offer in this life.

God's method for reaching this generation, and every generation, is not preachers and sermons. It is Christians whose life-styles are empowered and directed by the Holy Spirit. Statistics push us to the same conclusion over and over again. Somewhere around 85 percent of all Christians came to Christ through a friend or family member. People are the key to reaching people!

My Concern

There are times when my frustration mellows to concern. I am troubled on behalf of those who have prayed a salvation prayer in the past but have reached the conclusion that Christianity just doesn't work. I am equally concerned about the believers who have not yet given up, but their lives are characterized by defeat and discontentment. I am concerned about men and women who are simply going through the motions—going to church, reading their Bibles, saying prayers, confessing their sins.

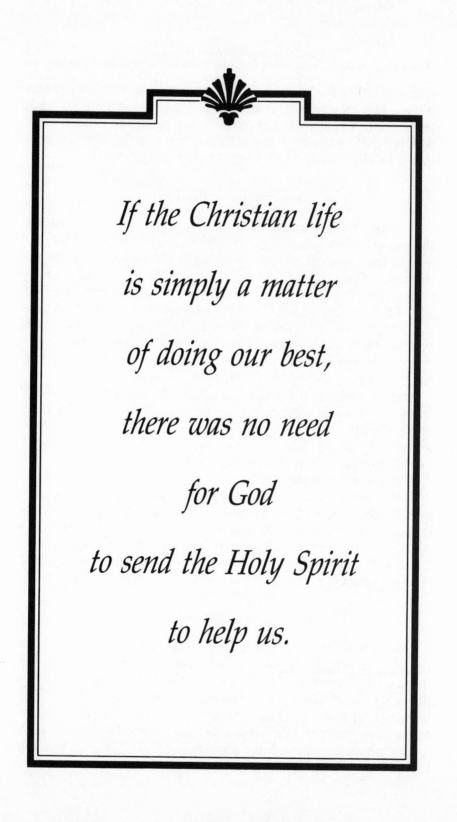

If the Christian life

is simply a matter

of doing our best,

there was no need

for God

to send the Holy Spirit

to help us.

I am concerned about the Christian couples whose marriages are filled with everything but the Spirit. Relationships where there are little or no peace, joy, and love. Relationships in which both parties have begun looking elsewhere for the satisfaction they assumed would come with marriage.

I am concerned about their children. Our children draw their conclusions about the viability of Christianity from our experience. If it doesn't work for Mom and Dad, why bother? Or worse, if it doesn't work for Mom and Dad but they try to convince everybody at church that it's working, you can really forget it!

Teenagers, college students, and singles all over this country are struggling every day to make the Christian life work. They live with the illusion that once they get older, get out of school, or get married, things will get easier. They think, *If I can just hold out, it will be worth it.* Years later, however, as the pressures of life continue to pile up, the internal battles intensify, and their youthful drive and determination wane, they, too, will wonder if the Christian life is all that they were promised it would be.

When I was younger, I can remember thinking, *Being a Christian is hard now, but when I'm on my own, it will be easier.* Nothing could have been further from the truth! You know as well as I do that growing up never solved anything. Life gets increasingly more complicated with time. The pressure of added responsibility makes the thought of running away a real temptation. All of us at one point or another have longed for the simplicity of childhood.

Occasionally, I meet single adults who blame their lack of spiritual vitality on their singleness. "When I get married, things will be different," they say. But every married person knows that marriage is not designed to be a problem solver. Marriage enhances problems. Besides, if a dynamic Christian life is dependent on marriage, God has certainly played a cruel joke on widowers and widows and people He has called to singleness.

Growing up, graduating, marriage—none of these good things serve as the key to the abundant life we all long for. Yet many well-meaning believers have set their hopes on them as the cure-all for their spiritual ills.

Maybe now you can understand why I am so concerned. Maybe you identify with those I am describing. If so, read on!

A Necessary Promise

There is hope for Christians who have given up as well as for those who are contemplating raising the white flag. Our hope springs from a promise Jesus made at a time when His closest followers were about to give up hope. He said,

> I will not leave you as orphans; I will come to you.
> —*John 14:18*

And then strangely enough, not too many days afterward, He returned to His Father in heaven. Hmm?

I don't think I'm stretching it to say that a good many followers of Christ feel like abandoned orphans. Directionless, unmotivated, discouraged, looking for a cause to attach themselves to, they simply do the best they can. And yet Jesus promised that this would not be the case.

If the Christian life is simply a matter of doing our best, there was no need for God to send the Holy Spirit to help us. After all, our best is our best. How do we improve on that? Since God is omniscient, as we certainly believe He is, He knows when we have done all we can do. Why complicate matters?

Jesus let it be known, however, that God was looking for more than *our* best. He was looking for a life-style and attitude that superseded our best, a life-style and attitude that we could never attain through our own efforts. And so He said,

> But I tell you the truth, it is to your advantage that I go away; for if I do not go away, the Helper shall not come to you; but if I go, I will send Him to you.
> —*John 16:7*

Think about this. If we don't need any help, why send a Helper? The promise of a Helper presupposes that we need help. The promise of a Helper was Jesus' way of tipping us off to one of the most profound truths concerning the Christian life—it's impossible! The quality of life Jesus expects from His followers is unattainable apart from outside intervention.

The Christian life is not simply difficult. It is not something that gets easier with time. It is not something you grow into. It's impossible. You can't live it. I can't live it. God doesn't expect us to live it. He knows it's impossible. Jesus knew it was impossible. It is time that we come to grips with this liberating truth—*it is impossible.*

"Liberating?" you say. "Why is this liberating? It sounds depressing to me." It is liberating because you may be on the verge of understanding why you have failed in your attempts to live the Christian life. It is also liberating from the standpoint that now you know there is nothing wrong with the system, either. I meet people all the time who say something to the effect of, "I tried to live the Christian life, but it doesn't work."

I've got some good news. Christianity is not the problem. More than likely, the problem is that you have been trying to live it apart from the help of the Holy Spirit.

Wait!

If there ever was a group who should have been able to live a consistent Christian life by just doing their best, it was the apostles. Think of all their advantages. They had been trained by the Master. They had seen lame men walk, blind men see, and the dead rise. They were privy to the inside scoop between the Son and the Father. They had even performed miracles themselves! Nobody could have been more convinced. Nobody could have been more motivated. Yet in their last encounter with the Savior, He let them know that they were still missing something.

> And gathering them together, He commanded them not to leave Jerusalem, but to wait for what the Father had promised . . . He said, "For John baptized with water, but you shall be baptized with the Holy Spirit not many days from now . . . you shall receive power when the Holy Spirit has come upon you; and you shall be My witnesses both in Jerusalem, and in all Judea and Samaria, and even to the remotest part of the earth."
>
> —*Acts 1:4–8*

Even after all they had seen and experienced, they were not ready. There was something, or rather, Someone, missing. I can only imagine what some of the apostles were thinking: *Wait? Wait? Wait for what? We have already been His witnesses. We have performed miracles. We have the power. Why do we need to wait?*

Jesus knew they were not yet ready for the task to which they had been called. They would need more than their human spirit to carry them. They would need more than sheer determination to fulfill their task. All that they had witnessed and learned was not enough. They needed help. They needed the Holy Spirit.

You already know what I'm going to say, don't you? If eleven men who had walked and talked with Jesus needed the Holy Spirit, how much more do we need Him? If they dared not make a move until they were assured of His presence and power in their lives, how foolish we are to charge out of the house every morning without giving Him a thought. No wonder our lives are characterized by defeat rather than victory; sorrow rather than joy; frustration rather than peace. Apart from the Helper, life is reduced to doing the best we can. And I don't know about you, but for me, that's not very good.

What Is Standing in the Way?

I believe there are two primary reasons so many Christians have failed to take advantage of the help afforded by the Helper. First of all, many preachers neither model the Spirit-filled life nor teach on it. What comes through from the pulpit week after week is, "Do the best you can, and remember, God understands." How tragic! No wonder so many churches are powerless and dead. We shouldn't be surprised that the majority of churches in this country go for months at a time without seeing one person come to faith in Christ. When pastors operate in their own power, they have no choice but to transfer to their people an incomplete and inadequate model of the Christian life. And so on those rare occasions when outsiders stick their heads in the church door to take a look around, what they find is oftentimes anything but inviting.

On the other hand, men and women who are walking in the Spirit don't waste their time arguing over who is going to chair this committee or what color to paint the children's department. They are too busy exercising their gifts for the common good of the church. Spirit-filled believers are given to prayer. Pastors who are filled with the Spirit don't simply use the pulpit to entertain and comfort their people. (I call that kind of preaching "sermonettes for Christianettes.") They equip and challenge their congregations to do the work of the ministry. And they teach and model how God's work can be done in His strength.

The other reason so many believers miss out on the Spirit-filled life concerns their early days as Christians. Generally, when people are born again, an excitement about their newfound life manifests itself by way of a whole lot of activity. This is especially true of people who are saved during their teens or later. This burst of spiritual energy makes it thrilling to spend time with new believers. They can't get to church early enough. They can't pray enough. They show up at every Bible study. They witness. They attend seminars. They carry their Bibles everywhere. They are unstoppable. The same is often true of a believer who comes back to the Lord after a prodigal son–type experience.

Well, all of this is fine except for one small detail. The energy source of all their activity is usually their own human strength—which, of course, is being fueled by the genuine joy that accompanies salvation or restoration. Don't misunderstand me. I am in no way criticizing the zeal that accompanies faith in Christ. We would all benefit from spending more time with new Christians. The problem is that they usually assume that what they are experiencing will last forever. If no one instructs them on how to walk in the Spirit, they will continue in their own strength—doing the best they can, which for a while is really pretty good! Eventually, however, they run out of steam. They grow tired of the activity. The emotional high subsides. And they wonder what the problem is. Determined not to regress, they dig in their heels and, you guessed it, do the best they can. And who can blame them? What choice do they have? After all, anything worth having is worth working for, right?

In his book *The Key to Triumphant Living*, Jack Taylor relates the thought process that brought him to this same conclusion:

> My father was a farmer and a very good one. I suppose that I simply deduced that if my father could become a good farmer by hard work, I could become a good Christian in the same manner. I do not ever remember not wanting to be a good Christian. So I set out *trying* to be what I had become. A sandy-land farm is not exactly the shortest route to becoming a millionaire, but my dad made it do. He had a few washouts, blowouts, hail-outs, some straight out crop failures, and every now and then a fair crop. So I figured this was what I would have to settle for in the Christian life. Thus, for almost two decades, my Christian life was like that of a share-cropper on a sandy-land farm. I tolerated it simply because I didn't know there was anything else. Nobody ever told me what the Christian life was all about.[1]

Nobody told me for a long time, either. And in the next chapter I'll tell you all about my pilgrimage into the Spirit-filled life.

NOTE

1. Jack Taylor, *The Key to Triumphant Living* (Nashville: Broadman Press, 1971), p. 19.

———— THINK ABOUT IT ————

- Is there a vast difference between what you experienced as a new believer and what you are experiencing now?
- Do you know Christians who just seem to have something or know something you don't?
- What makes you different from your unsaved friends? Peace, joy, and love? How you spend your Sunday mornings?
- What can you attribute to the power of the Holy Spirit in your life today?
- If someone asked you, "What does it mean to be filled with the Holy Spirit?" what would you say? Does the answer come easily?

CHAPTER 2

My First Encounter

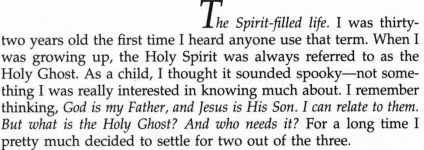

The Spirit-filled life. I was thirty-two years old the first time I heard anyone use that term. When I was growing up, the Holy Spirit was always referred to as the Holy Ghost. As a child, I thought it sounded spooky—not something I was really interested in knowing much about. I remember thinking, *God is my Father, and Jesus is His Son. I can relate to them. But what is the Holy Ghost? And who needs it?* For a long time I pretty much decided to settle for two out of the three.

There was another reason I shied away from the Holy Spirit. I grew up in a church where He was never mentioned. My pastor didn't explain who He was or preach sermons about Him.

The Christians I knew who did talk about Him were so strange that I assumed getting involved with the Holy Ghost meant I would have to be like them. I wanted no part of that. So I was content to worship the Father and pray to the Son—and leave the Holy Spirit for someone else to worry about.

It wasn't until I was in seminary that the Holy Spirit became a recognized factor in my life. I say "recognized factor" because as I look back, it is clear to me that He was definitely there all the time. I can remember several occasions when the Holy Spirit revealed things to me without my knowing who He was.

Preacher Boy

I was fourteen when I felt the call to preach. It couldn't have been any clearer if Gabriel himself had appeared and told me personally. I just knew in my heart I was to preach. That was the Holy Spirit. I didn't know it at the time, but in later chapters you will understand why I am so convinced He was at work.

My approach to the Christian life from that moment on was simply to do the best I could and hope God would forgive me when I messed up. I say "hope" because at that time, I didn't believe in eternal security (once saved, always saved). So there was a great deal of insecurity in those early days about where I stood with God. I was sure He loved me, but I wasn't convinced He liked me all that much.

God was very faithful to me. My father died when I was a baby. Several years later my mom married again. That was probably the worst mistake of her life. My stepfather made life miserable for all of us. As bad as things were, I didn't become bitter. I hated the way he treated my mother, but I didn't internalize my anger. I knew we weren't his real problem. He was mad at his father for keeping him on the farm and not allowing him to attend medical school. Understanding that gave me the freedom to forgive him and move on.

As I think back through those challenging years, I have no doubt that the Holy Spirit was at work in my life. I believe He was protecting me from the bitterness that destroys so many people who grow up in dysfunctional families like mine. Again, I didn't recognize His presence, but He was there.

Working Behind the Scenes

This is as good a place as any to let you in on something. The Holy Spirit is working in your life this very minute. You may not be aware of it, but He is.

"What is He doing?" you ask.

That is what the remainder of this book is about. Suffice it to say that a big part of the Spirit-filled life involves learning to recognize the fingerprint of the Holy Spirit. In fact, *learning to recognize the Holy Spirit is the first step in learning to live the Spirit-filled life.* After all, if we are supposed to be led by the Spirit (see Gal. 5:18), it would certainly help if we could recognize Him! It is difficult to follow someone whose identity is unknown. Anyone who has been given the task of picking up someone he has never met from the airport knows that.

As you read this book, you may find yourself thinking, *Oh, so it was the Holy Spirit who did that. So that is where those thoughts came from. So that is why I felt funny. So He brought that to mind.*

The Holy Spirit is not as mysterious and illusive as some would have us believe. The Holy Spirit is an integral part of our Christian experience. But because we are so unfamiliar with His ways, we miss Him. As long as we miss Him, we certainly can't follow Him. And, you guessed it, as long as we can't follow Him, we can't experience the wonderful Spirit-filled life.

To get us thinking in the right direction, I have listed a few tasks the Holy Spirit endeavors to accomplish in your life on a daily basis. We will look at each one in detail later on. But take a minute now to familiarize yourself with this list. Next time you experience one of these things, stop and thank the Holy Spirit. In doing so, you will develop a heightened awareness of His activity in your life. And at the risk of sounding like a broken record, the greater your awareness, the easier it will be to recognize Him and follow Him.

The Holy Spirit . . .

- convicts (see John 16:8–11).
- illuminates (see John 16:12–15).
- teaches (see John 16:12–15).
- guides (see Rom. 8:14).
- assures (see Rom. 8:16).
- intercedes (see Rom. 8:26).
- directs (see Acts 20:22).
- warns (see Acts 20:23).

My First Introduction

Another reason for some of the confusion regarding the Holy Spirit is that believers do not know who or what He is. His identity remains a mystery to a large number of those whom He indwells. Ironic, isn't it? Some think of the Holy Spirit in terms of a power or force—something like what we saw in the Star Wars series.

It is not unusual to hear Christians talking about "getting the Holy Spirit" or "tapping into the power of the Spirit." Such phrases leave the impression that the Holy Spirit is some sort of divine energy source that Christians are to live in harmony with, thereby increasing our personal potential and power.

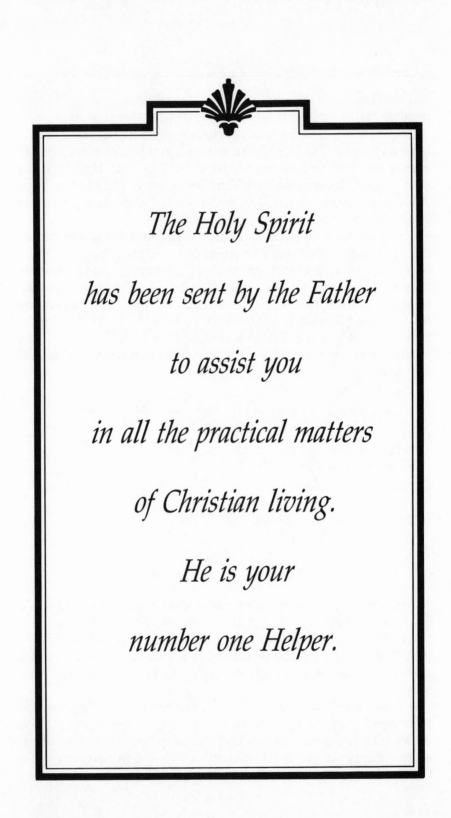

The Holy Spirit

has been sent by the Father

to assist you

in all the practical matters

of Christian living.

He is your

number one Helper.

I have heard New Age supporters talk about the Holy Spirit in a similar way. From their point of view, the Holy Spirit indwells all humanity. Our responsibility is to develop that Spirit within us and thus move toward a greater understanding of our personal deity and oneness with all people.

The Bible, however, does not present the Holy Spirit as an impersonal force or power. The Holy Spirit is not an "it" or a "something." The Holy Spirit is a "He."

As I mentioned earlier, I was in seminary before I began my formal education in the ways of the Holy Spirit. I was sitting at a table with several buddies, and during our conversation, I said something about the Holy Spirit and called Him an "it." I didn't think anything about it. Having been raised in a Pentecostal Holiness church, I had always heard the Holy Spirit, or Holy Ghost, referred to as "it."

When our conversation came to a close, one of the fellows asked me if I would join him in his room. It just so happened that he was a doctoral student, so I felt honored by his invitation. When we walked into his room, I was overwhelmed with the number of books he owned. They covered every inch of his walls and floor. If I wasn't impressed before, I certainly was then. After a few minutes of casual conversation, he reached over to his desk and pulled out his Greek New Testament and handed it to me.

"I noticed that tonight when we were talking about the Holy Spirit, you called Him an 'it.' "

"Yeah," I said. "Why?"

"The Holy Spirit is not an 'it,' " he said.

From there he proceeded to take me on a tour of the New Testament. We explored all the key verses where the Holy Spirit is mentioned. To my surprise, I discovered that the New Testament was consistent in its presentation of the Holy Spirit as a "He" rather than an "it."

One verse that particularly caught my attention was John 16:13:

> But when He, the Spirit of truth, comes, He will guide you into all the truth.

I knew just enough about the Greek language to know that the term translated "He" could not be translated any other way. John meant "He," not "it." Further study revealed that John went out of his way to use the masculine form of the pronoun.[1] I was convinced.

I had been raised on the King James Version of the Bible. It's a wonderful translation, I might add. But the King James Version translates the third person singular as "it" rather than "he." Romans 8:26 is a good example:

> Likewise the Spirit also helpeth our infirmities: for we know not what we should pray for as we ought: but the Spirit *itself* maketh intercession for us (emphasis mine).

If you are like I was, you may be a little uncomfortable about changing your references to the Holy Spirit from "it" to "He." As we look at other biblical support for this view, however, I hope you will see why such a change is necessary.

The Personality of the Holy Spirit

The Bible not only refers to the Holy Spirit as a "He," but it also ascribes to Him all the distinctives of personality. Specifically, the Holy Spirit is described as having (1) knowledge, (2) will, and (3) emotion.

The apostle Paul certainly believed the Holy Spirit was knowledgeable. He wrote,

> For who among men knows the thoughts of a man except the spirit of the man, which is in him? Even so the thoughts of God no one knows except the Spirit of God. Now we have received, not the spirit of the world, but the Spirit who is from God, that we might know the things freely given to us by God.
>
> —*1 Corinthians 2:11–12*

The Holy Spirit *knows* the thoughts of God. And the Holy Spirit imparts *knowledge* to believers. The Holy Spirit, then, is not simply an impersonal force. He has knowledge, and He has the power to impart knowledge.

The Holy Spirit has a will as well. In his discussion of spiritual gifts, Paul referred to the Holy Spirit's responsibility of distributing gifts at will:

> But one and the same Spirit works all these things, distributing to each one individually just as He wills.
> —*1 Corinthians 12:11*

The Holy Spirit makes decisions. He is not a power to be harnessed and manipulated. He has a mind and will of His own. To tap into the Holy Spirit is not to enhance one's ability to carry out one's will. Oh, no! On the contrary, the power of the Holy Spirit is available only to those whose intention is to carry out His will.

Good Intentions; Bad Theology

Several years ago a woman walked up to me after our Wednesday night prayer meeting and said, "I just want you to know that I am praying for you to get the Spirit." I told her how much I appreciated it and didn't think anything else about it—until the next Wednesday night when she did the same thing. That went on for several weeks. I had a feeling I knew what she was getting at, but I never had a chance to talk to her. She would just walk up, tell me she was praying, and walk away.

Then one Wednesday she took me by surprise. She said, "Well, did you get the Spirit this week?" I said, "No, ma'am, I didn't get the Spirit that you're talking about. But I have been filled with the Spirit."

"Have you been baptized by it?" she said.

It was clear to me at that point that she wanted to know whether I had spoken in tongues. So I said to her, "I know what. Why don't you pray that the Spirit will give me whatever gifts He wants me to have, and we will let Him decide from there."

"All right," she said. I never saw her again.

She had overlooked that the Holy Spirit has a will. He, not we, decides who gets what in relation to spiritual gifts. He is not our servant. As we will see later, He is our guide.

A third aspect of personality ascribed to the Holy Spirit is emotion. The Holy Spirit has feelings. Paul instructed the believers in Ephesus not to "grieve" the Holy Spirit (see Eph. 4:30). In his letter to the Romans he referred to the "love of the Spirit" (Rom. 15:30). *Love* and *grief* are terms associated with emotion. The Bible portrays the Holy Spirit as One having all the characteristics of personality. It makes sense, then, for us to think of Him as a person.

The Works of the Spirit

Another line of evidence pointing to the personhood of the Holy Spirit is His work. Throughout Scripture, we find Him performing duties normally associated with a person. For instance, He *prays* (see Rom. 8:26). He *searches* the mysteries of God and then *reveals* them to the saints (see 1 Cor. 2:10). He *teaches* (see John 14:26). He *reminds* (see John 14:26). He *talks* (see Acts 13:2). And He *guides* (see John 16:13).

The Holy Spirit is clearly not a force. He is a thinking, feeling, active person working with God the Father and God the Son to affect our lives according to their collective wills. But He is more than a person. He is part of that mysterious entity we call the Trinity—an entity we will take a closer look at in the next chapter.

Shifting My Paradigm

Discovering that the Holy Spirit was a "He" rather than an "it" was very disorienting for me. I didn't know exactly what to do with the new bit of theology. I was accustomed to talking to God and Jesus. I remember wondering whether or not I should talk to the Holy Spirit. The first time I tried it I was really uncomfortable. It sounded funny. But I felt like it was something I needed to do.

I was embarrassed by the fact that I had been treating Him like an it. Furthermore, I was convinced I owed Him an apology. After all, I had basically ignored Him for over twenty years. It took me awhile, but I finally grew comfortable addressing the Holy Spirit as a person. I quit referring to Him as a ghost. He is not a ghost any more than God the Father and Son are ghosts. The Bible does not instruct us to pray to the Holy Spirit. But since it doesn't forbid us to, I thought I would be safe.

As I grew in my understanding of the roles the Holy Spirit played in my life, I began asking Him to assist me in those areas. When I didn't know how to pray about a particular matter, I would ask the Holy Spirit to help me pray. When I needed insight into the Scriptures, I would ask Him to enlighten me. After six months or so, it felt natural to talk to the Holy Spirit. He has been a major part of my Christian experience ever since.

Do you talk to the Holy Spirit? Or have you been ignoring Him? He is a person just like Christ. The difference is that He never took on human form. And He didn't die for your sin. But

He has been sent by the Father to assist you in all the practical matters of Christian living. He is your number one Helper. In light of that, I would suggest you get to know Him. Talk to Him. Thank Him.

Why is this so important? It goes back to what I said earlier. The Spirit-filled life is a life characterized by keeping in step with the Holy Spirit. It will be much easier to follow Him if we know Him, if we have a relationship with Him, and if we can recognize His fingerprint in the daily affairs of our lives.

Take a few minutes to acquaint yourself with the Holy Spirit. If you feel uncomfortable talking to Him, tell Him so. After all, He already knows. If you feel a little embarrassed for ignoring Him all this time, tell Him you're sorry.

Take some time to look back over the verses I listed earlier. As you read each one, thank the Holy Spirit for fulfilling those responsibilities in your life. Ask Him to make you more sensitive to His promptings.

When my son, Andy, turned eighteen, he bought a brand-new Toyota. He was so proud. One day he came home and in a despondent tone of voice announced that everybody on the road had a car like his.

"What are you talking about?" I asked.

"Everywhere I look I see Toyotas like mine."

What had happened, of course, was not that everybody ran out and bought a car like Andy's. They were out there all along. He just wasn't as aware of them as he was once he owned one. The only thing that had changed was his awareness.

The Holy Spirit is doing His work in your life day in and day out. He doesn't need to change a thing. What needs to change is your awareness of His presence and activity. When you know *what* to look for and when you look for it, you will be amazed at how real the Holy Spirit will become to you.

These discoveries were the beginning for me. I share them in hopes that the Holy Spirit will take them and prick your curiosity to make you want to know more. We are blessed to live in a day and age in which we are no longer required to wait for the Holy Spirit. The truth is, He is waiting on us.

NOTE

1. For an in-depth explanation of the grammar of this passage, see A. T. Robertson's *A Grammar of the Greek New Testament* (Nashville: Broadman, 1947), pp. 708–9.

─────── **THINK ABOUT IT** ───────

- Have you been guilty of ignoring the Holy Spirit?
- Do you find it difficult to relate to the Holy Spirit as a thinking, feeling, and active person?
- Do you have difficulty identifying the Holy Spirit as a "He" rather than an "it"?
- Have you been reluctant to acknowledge that the Holy Spirit has attributes such as knowledge, will, and emotion?
- Can you identify things the Holy Spirit has done in your life in the past that you have not given Him adequate credit for?

CHAPTER 3

The Indwelling Spirit

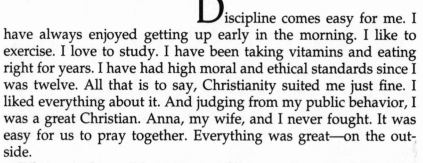

Discipline comes easy for me. I have always enjoyed getting up early in the morning. I like to exercise. I love to study. I have been taking vitamins and eating right for years. I have had high moral and ethical standards since I was twelve. All that is to say, Christianity suited me just fine. I liked everything about it. And judging from my public behavior, I was a great Christian. Anna, my wife, and I never fought. It was easy for us to pray together. Everything was great—on the out-side.

When people would come to me for counseling, I had the same answer for everybody. Whether it was marital problems, moral problems, spiritual problems, it didn't matter; I had the cure-all answer: "Just confess your sin and get with the program!" After all, what else is there to the Christian life? God has made His plan perfectly clear, hasn't He? Now all we need to do is to get out there and make it happen. So I graduated from seminary in May of 1957 and charged out into the world to make things happen for God (I'm sure He was quite impressed and very grateful).

A "Wonderful" Opportunity

In August of 1956, several months prior to my graduation, I was invited to preach for two Sundays at Fruitland Baptist Church, just outside Hendersonville, North Carolina. Anna and I were vacationing in the area at the time. After the second Sunday a group from the church asked me if I would be interested in being their pastor. I graciously informed them that I had another year of seminary to complete. They didn't take no for an answer. The following December they contacted me in Ft. Worth, where I was in school. They told me they had prayed about it, and I was the man for the job. The church was willing to wait for me to graduate.

I can't tell you how good it felt to know where I was going after graduation, especially that far in advance. Anna and I had peace that this was from God. We loved the area. We loved the church. It was perfect.

In April, one month before graduation, the director of the Fruitland Bible Institute called me. FBI was located directly across the street from the Fruitland Baptist Church where I was to pastor. The school was established as a training center for pastors.

"Charles, we are looking forward to having you in our area. The board of directors wanted me to call and see if you would be interested in teaching at the Bible Institute," he said.

I didn't know what to say. I hadn't even graduated from seminary yet, and they wanted *me* to teach? I knew enough about the school to know that it was full of men who had been pastoring and preaching for years. They hadn't had the opportunity to get much formal education, but their hearts were pure as gold. Most of them were in their forties and fifties. Several of them had been in the ministry longer than I had been alive! "What in the world could I teach them?" I wondered.

"We need someone to teach preaching and evangelism starting this next fall," he explained.

Preaching, I thought. *I haven't preached but a half dozen sermons in my life. These men have been preaching for years. And evangelism. They probably know more about evangelism than I will ever know.*

"We need to know as soon as possible," he said. "Think about it and give us a call as soon as you know something."

Well, I already knew one thing. He was asking the wrong man. I didn't even want to pray about it for fear that God would say, "DO IT!" Anna just smiled when I told her. "It's a great opportunity," she said.

To make a long story short, I agreed to teach.

We arrived in Fruitland in June of 1957, and I went to work as pastor. I loved it. Anna and I would have been content to spend the rest of our lives ministering to those dear people. It was a great place to begin a ministry. I had to do everything: unlock the doors, clean the commodes, print the bulletin, and take out the trash. But I didn't mind a bit.

The only thing that robbed me of my joy was knowing that fall was approaching. I felt totally inadequate. There wasn't a day that entire summer that I didn't want to walk over to the school and resign. The very thought of walking into a classroom and facing those men was nerve shattering. I was in over my head, totally out of my league.

In the back of my mind (and I mean way back) I knew that if teaching was really of God, He would give me the strength and insight I needed. My problem was that I had no idea how to tap into His strength. I felt adequate to pastor but not to teach. I needed something more.

Toward the end of the summer I picked up R. A. Torrey's book on the Holy Spirit.[1] I had read it once before while I was in seminary. I remembered how frustrated it made me. When Torrey talked about being controlled and empowered by the Holy Spirit, he made it sound so simple—too simple.

I was convinced I had to *do* something to receive the empowering of the Holy Spirit. For the past couple of years I had done everything from fasting to begging. I knew there was something more. But I didn't know how to get it. I believed there was some sort of secret I needed to discover. Up until then I had been casual in my pursuit of the Holy Spirit. But I was desperate. It was August, and September was approaching like a runaway train. So I devoured his book in hopes that somewhere in there I would find the secret. Looking back, I know that God had clearly engineered my circumstances to bring me to a point of desperation. It was time for another major lesson.

Back to School

If you had asked me during that time whether I believed the Holy Spirit was God, I would have answered yes without any hesitation. If you had asked me whether I believed the Holy Spirit was living inside me, I would have said, "Yes," and I would have quoted you a verse to prove it:

> Or do you not know that your body is a temple of the Holy Spirit who is in you, whom you have from God, and that you are not your own?
>
> —*1 Corinthians 6:19*

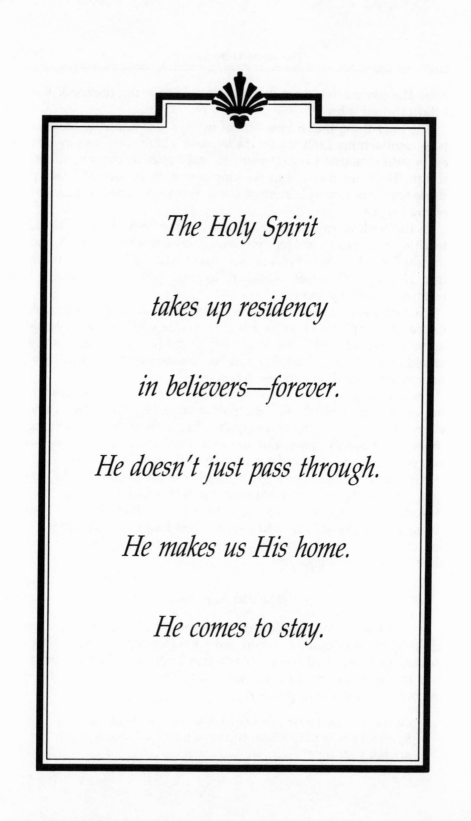

The Holy Spirit

takes up residency

in believers—forever.

He doesn't just pass through.

He makes us His home.

He comes to stay.

But if you had asked me what difference all of that was supposed to make on a daily basis, I would have been hard-pressed to give you a good answer. Oh, I would have come up with something but nothing very definitive.

There I was pastoring a church, and the life-changing implications of those two truths still had not sunk in. *The Holy Spirit is God. The Holy Spirit lives in me.* In a period of about two weeks those two statements took on incredible significance in my life. I will tell you more about that later. For now, let's take a closer look at the two statements.

The Holy Spirit Is God

The idea of the Trinity has been a point of confusion for many people throughout church history. Scripture clearly teaches that there is but one God. Yet, God is presented in the form of three distinct persons: God the Father, God the Son, and God the Holy Spirit. The formula adopted by the early church is as follows: one essence, three persons.

For many people, that distinction may not be helpful in the least. That is all right as long as one's inability to understand the full extent of this wonderful truth does not impede the willingness to put faith in it.

"But wait," you say. "How can I be expected to trust something I don't fully understand? Is intellect the enemy of faith?" Absolutely not! God has given ample information to support our faith. There are, however, a few things that will always remain a mystery to us this side of heaven (see 1 Cor. 13:12).

We frequently put our faith in things we don't understand. Every time I get on a jet I place my life in the hands of people I have never met and at the mercy of machinery I do not understand. That is not to imply that nobody understands it. Simply because *I* don't have an explanation for how it works doesn't mean there isn't one. In the same way, just because the idea of the Trinity is confusing to us doesn't mean that it doesn't make sense. It only means that it doesn't make sense to us.

The Holy Spirit and the Trinity

The Bible teaches that the Holy Spirit is part of the Trinity. The first reference to this relationship is found in the story of creation:

In the beginning God created the heavens and the earth. And the earth was formless and void, and darkness was over the surface of the deep; and the *Spirit of God* was moving over the surface of the waters. Then God said, "Let there be light"; and there was light.

—*Genesis 1:1–3*, emphasis mine

Notice how the author refers to God and the Spirit of God without making any distinction between the two. No explanation is necessary; the two are one! The God who created the heavens and the earth is the same as the Spirit who moved over the surface of the waters. If two different Gods or forces were at work, some sort of transition statement between verses 2 and 3 would have been in order. But no such transition appears. The author freely uses "Spirit of God" and "God" interchangeably.

The Holy Spirit's involvement in creation ties Him in with the second person in the Trinity as well. In Colossians the apostle Paul referred to Christ as the creator of all things:

For He [God the Father] delivered us from the domain of darkness, and transferred us to the kingdom of His beloved Son, in whom we have redemption, the forgiveness of sins. And He is the image of the invisible God, the first-born of all creation. For by Him [the Son] all things were created, both in the heavens and on earth, visible and invisible . . . all things have been created by Him and for Him.

—*Colossians 1:13–16*

Being one of the premier religious leaders of his day, Paul was very familiar with the Old Testament. More than likely he had memorized the creation story as a child. As a Christian, Paul continued in his belief that the Old Testament was from God. Yet without any explanation he credited Christ with the work of creation. Paul had no problem accepting the idea of the Trinity. And he felt no need to explain it, either.

"Let Us Make Man"

Later in the creation story we find another reference to the Trinity:

Then God said, "Let Us make man in Our image, according to Our likeness."

—*Genesis 1:26*

Who was God talking to? Who was "Us"? Whoever He was referring to was clearly part of the creation process: "Let Us make man." The only other living beings at that point in history were animals and angels. There is no indication from Scripture that either animals or angels were part of the creation process.

In the next verse God clarified exactly whose image He was referring to:

And God created man in His own image, in the image of God He created him; male and female He created them.

—*Genesis 1:27*

Adam and Eve were not created in the image of animals or angels. They were created in the image of God. The "Us" in Genesis 1:26 must refer to God alone: God the Father, God the Son, and God the Spirit.

There are many other examples where the Holy Spirit and God are referred to interchangeably. One is found in the fifth chapter of Acts:

But a certain man named Ananias, with his wife Sapphira, sold a piece of property, and kept back some of the price for himself, with his wife's full knowledge, and bringing a portion of it, he laid it at the apostles' feet. But Peter said, "Ananias, why has Satan filled your heart to *lie to the Holy Spirit*, and to keep back some of the price of the land? . . . Why is it that you have conceived this deed in your heart? *You have not lied to men, but to God."*

—*Acts 5:1–4*, emphasis mine

Peter saw God and the Holy Spirit as equals. From his perspective, to lie to one was to lie to the other. Each deserved equal reverence and respect. Apparently, God thought so, too, for both Ananias and his wife, Sapphira, lost their lives as a result of their deceit.

The authors of both the Old and the New Testaments saw no problem with interchanging God and the Holy Spirit. To speak of one was to speak of the other. The actions and attributes of one were the actions and attributes of the other. They were seen as one in power, omniscience, wisdom, and even eternalness (see Heb. 9:14). No distinction is made because no distinction is needed. Now let's look at the second statement.

The Holy Spirit Lives Inside the Believer

As I said earlier, for a long time the deity of the Holy Spirit was nothing more to me than orthodox theology. That is, until I began to think about the fact that He indwells me.

There are several popular theories concerning the indwelling work of the Holy Spirit. What makes it confusing is that the Bible is used to support every one of them. Some say the Holy Spirit indwells the believer at the moment of salvation. Others teach that it happens sometime after salvation. A couple of groups believe the Holy Spirit comes and goes; some days you have Him, and some days you don't.

The confusion stems primarily from two sources. First is the coming of the Holy Spirit in the book of Acts. Many Christians see this as the normative pattern for every generation. In Acts we find the Holy Spirit coming to indwell men who had been believers for possibly two or three years. Some see this as strong evidence for believing that the Holy Spirit is not necessarily given at the moment a person is born again.

A second source of confusion originates with those who do not hold to the doctrine of eternal security (once saved, always saved). Christians who believe they can lose their salvation are forced to believe that the Holy Spirit comes and goes as a man's or woman's salvation comes and goes. Since I have written an entire book on this subject, I won't attempt to deal with this problem here. If that is an issue you are struggling with, however, I recommend *Eternal Security* (Nashville: Oliver-Nelson, 1990).

As to the problems created by the book of Acts, I have devoted an entire chapter to examining the peculiarities of that wonderful, but often misunderstood, book. For now I want to focus on the one thing we all agree on—however and whenever it happens—the Holy Spirit indwells the believer.

Various Descriptions

The authors of Scripture used several terms to describe the relationship between the believer and the Holy Spirit. Jesus Himself explained it differently on different occasions. To the apostles, He said, "Receive the Holy Spirit" (John 20:22). To the multitude who gathered with Him just before the Ascension, He said, "You shall receive power when the Holy Spirit has *come upon* you" (Acts 1:8, emphasis mine).

The apostle John refers to the Holy Spirit as being given *to* the believer (see 1 John 3:24; see also 1 Thess. 4:8). Peter talks about the Holy Spirit being *in* believers (see 1 Pet. 1:11). Paul says, "God has sent forth the Spirit of His Son into our hearts" (Gal. 4:6); in another place he speaks of the believer as the temple of the Holy Spirit (see 1 Cor. 3:16–17).

All of these terms lead us in the same direction. The Holy Spirit resides *in* the believer. The verb used most often to describe this unique relationship comes from the Greek word *oikeo*. In the New American Standard Bible it is translated "dwell," "indwell," and "live." In the New King James Version it is translated "dwell." *Oikeo* actually comes from the Greek word for house—*oikos*. It means "to live in," "reside," or "dwell."

Oikeo is used four times to describe the believer's relationship with the Holy Spirit (see Rom. 8:9, 11; 1 Cor. 3:16; 2 Tim. 1:14). The most descriptive of the four is found in Paul's first letter to the church in Corinth:

> Do you not know that you are a temple of God, and that the Spirit of God dwells in you?

One writer summarized Paul's thoughts beautifully when he wrote,

> Clearly, to Paul, to be indwelt by the Holy Spirit is to be inhabited by God. By equating the phrase "God's temple" with the phrase "a temple of the Holy Spirit," Paul is clear: The Holy Spirit is God.[2]

The significance of the term *oikeo* is that it speaks of *permanency*. The idea is that the Holy Spirit takes up residency in believers—forever. He doesn't just pass through. He makes us His home. He comes to stay.

Paul's reference to believers as temples underscores this point. Having grown up a devout Jew, Paul had a great deal of respect for the temple. To the nation of Israel, it represented the presence of God among His people.

When Christ was crucified, there was no longer any need for the temple. God no longer needed a building. He was free to take up residency in the heart of man. The barrier of sin had been removed. Man's relationship with God had been restored. To symbolize the change, God tore the veil of the temple from top to bottom (see Mark 15:38). (The veil was a thick drapery separating the Holy of Holies from the rest of the temple.) The fact that it was ripped from top to bottom signified that God, not man, had initiated the change.

By referring to believers as temples, Paul was announcing that God had changed His residency for good. He had left the temple in Jerusalem and, through the person of the Holy Spirit, had moved into the hearts of His people.

Sealed by the Spirit

Another role that the Holy Spirit plays in our lives is further evidence of the permanency of His relocation. The Bible says that He has been given to us as a *pledge:*

> In Him [Christ], you also, after listening to the message of truth, the gospel of your salvation—having also believed, you were sealed in Him with the Holy Spirit of promise, who is given as a *pledge* of our inheritance, with a view to the redemption of God's own possession, to the praise of His glory.
> —*Ephesians 1:13–14*, emphasis mine

When you became a Christian, you were sealed into Christ. The term *sealed* is used in various ways throughout the New Testament. In Matthew we read that Jesus' tomb was sealed (see Matt. 27:66). In Revelation we are told that Satan will be sealed in the abyss for one thousand years (see chap. 20). During the Tribulation, God will place a seal on 144,000 people from the tribes of Israel (see Rev. 7).

In every case the term *sealed* carried with it the ideas of protection and security. To seal something was to close it off from outside influences and interference. We use the term in a similar way today. We seal windows and doors to keep the wind out. We seal letters. We seal basements to keep water out. We even seal furniture to keep dust from getting into the wood.

In our culture we do not normally think of putting a seal on people. Consequently, it is difficult for us to grasp the significance of being sealed by God. Fortunately, Scripture gives us a helpful illustration.

During the Tribulation, God will place a seal on 144,000 Jews (see Rev. 7:4–8). The seal will apparently be a visible mark on the forehead. As the Great Tribulation progresses, it becomes evident that the members of this group bearing God's seal have been granted supernatural protection from the chaos surrounding them. At the end of the Tribulation, the entire group reappears intact to welcome the King (see Rev. 14:1–5).

This future event sheds light on the ramifications of God's seal on the believer. The primary benefit of the seal is protection. The seal will protect the 144,000 during the most dangerous period of human history. Nothing will be able to overcome the protecting power of that seal, not even the Antichrist himself.

Unlike the 144,000, our seal is not visible—to us, that is. Our seal is spiritual. Instead of receiving a mark on our foreheads, we were given the Holy Spirit as a pledge of God's intent to preserve us to the day of Christ's appearing:

> And do not grieve the Holy Spirit of God, by whom you were sealed for the day of redemption.
> —*Ephesians 4:30*

When God looks at you, He sees the Holy Spirit within you. The presence of the Holy Spirit is a spiritual reminder of God's promise to finish what He has begun in you. It is a sign to the spirit world that you belong to Someone else. And as long as you belong to the Father, the Holy Spirit will be there, living in you, signifying His ownership. When He moved in, He moved in to stay. He's not going anywhere!

So, Do Something!

For the two weeks prior to D day (the first day of class), I meditated on the two thoughts: *The Holy Spirit is God. The Holy Spirit lives in me—permanently.* I just knew that somewhere, hidden within the two ideas, was the answer I was looking for.

I remember thinking, *Well, if You are in there, do something!* I was convinced that if God—through the Spirit—indwelt me, I should have all kinds of new potential. I should be able to do anything He called me to do. So I certainly shouldn't fear teaching a couple of classes. Reading through Torrey's book, I ran across a passage that hit me right between the eyes. He described my dilemma perfectly:

> So it is clear that every regenerate man has the Holy Spirit. But in many a believer the Holy Spirit dwells away back in some hidden sanctuary of his person, away back of conscious experience. So just as it is one thing to have a guest in your house living in some remote corner of the house where you scarcely know that he is there, and quite another thing to have the guest taking entire possession of the house, just so it is one thing to have the Holy Spirit dwelling way back of consciousness in some hidden sanctuary of our being, and quite another thing to have the Holy Spirit taking entire possession of the house. In other words, it is one thing to have the Holy Spirit merely dwelling in us but we not conscious of His dwelling, and *quite* another thing to be filled or baptized, with the Holy Spirit. So we may put it with perfect accuracy in this way: Every regenerate person has the Holy Spirit, but not every regenerate person has what the Bible calls "the gift of the Holy Spirit," or "the baptism with the Holy Spirit," or "the Promise of the Father."[3]

Whatever you call it, I didn't have it. I had the Holy Spirit. But for some reason He wasn't making much difference. It was as if He was hibernating. Like Torrey said, it was as if He was dwelling "in some hidden sanctuary" in my being.

I was relieved to know that someone else understood my dilemma. But understanding it better didn't solve it. I wanted to know why nothing was changing. I wanted to know how to get the Holy Spirit out of the "hidden sanctuary" and into my daily activities. Specifically, I wanted Him to empower me to teach those men. That approaching crisis ultimately paved the way for the next step in my journey. I didn't know it then, but I was just hours away from discovering how to be filled with the Spirit.

Don't Touch That Dial!

I know what you are thinking: *Get on with it!* That is exactly how I felt. But remember, spiritual growth is a process. There is an order. Lessons must be learned before other lessons can be assimilated. I will not guarantee that reading the next few chapters of this book will result in your being filled by the Holy Spirit. I certainly hope it will. But more than likely this book will only bring you one step closer to the final reality of the Spirit-filled life.

I must have read twenty books on the subject before I recognized and experienced the filling of the Spirit. Each one played a part in what God was doing, some more than others. Much of what I read, I wasn't ready for at the time. Sometimes it was on my second or third trip through a book that God spoke.

I don't know where you are in the process, but God does. He is engineering your circumstances with a definite result in mind. Part of His plan is to bring you to the end of yourself, to a point of desperation where you get so sick of yourself and your inability to change that you throw up your hands in surrender. When that happens, you are closer than you have ever been to knowing the joy of the Spirit-filled life. So, relax. There is no rush. God is in control. After all, He wants this for you more than you want it for yourself.

NOTES

1. R. A. Torrey, *The Holy Spirit* (Old Tappan, N.J.: Revell, 1927).

2. Millard J. Erikson, *Christian Theology* (Grand Rapids, Mich.: Baker, 1986), 3:85.

3. Torrey, *The Holy Spirit*, p. 115. Torrey believed that the phrases "filled with the Spirit," "baptized by the Spirit," "the gift of the Spirit," "the Holy Spirit fell upon them," and "endued with power from on high" all refer to the same experience, an experience that generally occurs sometime after salvation (see p. 107).

I believe there is a definite distinction between being baptized by the Spirit and being filled with the Spirit. The baptism of the Spirit takes place once at salvation (see 1 Cor. 12:13). The filling of the Spirit is something that takes place in accordance with our willingness to surrender to the influence of the Spirit (see Eph. 5:18).

―――――――― **THINK ABOUT IT** ――――――――

Take a minute to meditate on the two major points of this chapter:
The Holy Spirit is God.
The Holy Spirit indwells me.

It wouldn't hurt to get a pen and write out a few implications of these two statements.

- How does the truth of these statements apply to you?
- What does it say for your potential?
- What do they imply about your character, your parenting skills, your marriage?
- Spend some time thinking about it, for herein lies the key to experiencing the Spirit-filled life.

CHAPTER 4

D Day

———————❦———————

It was four o'clock Friday afternoon. My first class was to begin the following Monday. I had done everything I knew to do. I had read, memorized, fasted, prayed, begged, bargained, pleaded, and bordered on threatening a few times. Nothing had changed. From my vantage point, stretched out on the floor in our den, I was just as far away from understanding the Spirit-filled life as I had ever been. But in reality, I was only moments away.

I had been praying for almost an hour. I was reading and meditating on two verses in 1 John:

> And this is the confidence which we have before Him, that, if we ask anything according to His will, He hears us. And if we know that He hears us in whatever we ask, we know that we have the requests which we have asked from Him.
> —1 John 5:14–15

I was at the end of my emotional rope. I glanced at my watch and then buried my face in my hands. "Lord," I prayed, "You promised that if I ask anything according to Your will, You will hear me. I know it's not Your will for me to be frustrated and overwhelmed with this feeling of inadequacy. I believe it's Your will for me to experience the power of the Holy Spirit. I have done everything I know to do. And nothing has worked. I know You don't want me to go in there unprepared on Monday. And I know

37

You don't want me to quit. So I'm just going to trust You because I don't know anything else to do."

Immediately, I was overwhelmed with an amazing sense of confidence and assurance. It was a feeling. But it was in such stark contrast with what I had been feeling for the past three months that I knew something had happened. My fear was gone. It had vanished completely.

I didn't see stars or hear a voice. I didn't speak in tongues. In fact, that was the point. I didn't *do* anything—except trust Him. Then it hit me. I had been consumed with a desire to *do* something, to somehow win the Holy Spirit. I had been trying to convince God with my sincerity. Furthermore, I had been seeking some kind of physical manifestation to confirm that He had done, or was doing, something. I wanted to see something.

As I sat there thinking all of this through, two verses ran through my mind: "For we walk by faith, not by sight" (2 Cor. 5:7), and "Blessed are they who did not see, and yet believed" (John 20:29). The Spirit-filled life is a life of faith. I had missed the obvious. I had been looking all over for something that was right in front of me. I didn't need to beg. God wanted it for me more than I wanted it for myself. All I needed to do was believe and move out in faith.

Monday Morning

I woke up early Monday morning. I couldn't wait for that first class to begin. As the men filed in, the devil whispered in my ear, "Charles, what do you think you can teach these men? You are the youngest one in the room!" I whispered back, "Maybe so, but I'm filled with the Spirit of truth, and He can handle anything these men throw at Him."

This first encounter with the Holy Spirit resulted primarily in a heightened sense of confidence. When feelings of insecurity and fear surfaced, I would remember that God—through the Holy Spirit—was living in me. He was adequate for anything that came my way. I would find myself praying throughout the day, "Holy Spirit, I can't, but You can. Fill me for the work You have called me to do." And He did. It was evident in the classroom and in the pulpit. I preached with greater authority and boldness. As a pastor and faculty member, I led with a passion. The ironic thing was that I was more aware than ever of my inadequacy. But it was no longer a handicap. The Holy Spirit more than compensated.

Back to Basics

The Christian life is a life of faith. We usually don't have much trouble accepting that fact in connection with our salvation. But when it comes to our daily routine, faith is sometimes conspicuously missing. We tend to take matters into our own hands and do the best we can. Simply put, we walk by sight. If I don't see it or feel it, it must not be true. If I don't *feel* God's presence, He must not be with me. If I don't *see* a manifestation of the Holy Spirit, He must not be around. In the weeks that followed my *enlightenment* I was riveted to any passage of Scripture that said anything about the Holy Spirit. During that time, I discovered several things that revolutionized my perspective concerning what it meant to be filled with the Holy Spirit.

The Waiting Is Over!

For years I believed that it was my responsibility to wait on the Holy Spirit to fill me. At some point I guess I grew tired of waiting and tried to win Him or talk Him into filling me. Thus, all the praying and begging and fasting. But as Billy Graham stated so perfectly, "This is the good news: we are no longer waiting for the Holy Spirit—He is waiting for us. We are no longer living in a time of promise, but in the days of fulfillment."[1]

Looking back, I think my confusion stemmed from two things. First, I had attended churches where that idea was taught. At the end of a service or camp meeting people would come forward and have a pastor or elder lay hands on them, and they would supposedly be filled with the Spirit. I say "supposedly" because there is no doubt that something happened. But upon close examination of their life-styles, I don't think what happened had anything to do with the Holy Spirit. More on that later.

Sometimes those folks would go through a lengthy ordeal before the Holy Spirit finally "fell." Others would return night after night, seeking the filling of the Spirit, before they received Him. The point is, for years the only people I heard talk about the Holy Spirit talked in terms of receiving Him (or it) after a period of waiting and crying out for Him to fill them.

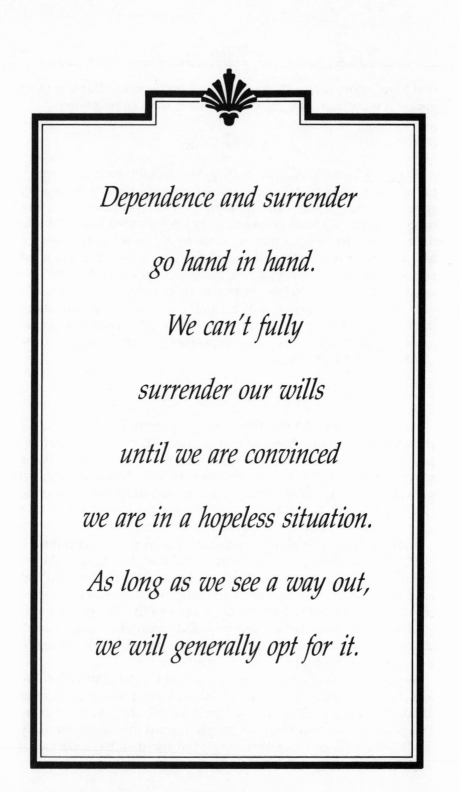

Dependence and surrender

go hand in hand.

We can't fully

surrender our wills

until we are convinced

we are in a hopeless situation.

As long as we see a way out,

we will generally opt for it.

The other thing that led me to believe I had to wait for the Holy Spirit to fill me was certain passages in the book of Acts. The big one was Acts 1:4. Jesus' disciples were clearly "believers." They would no doubt have gone to heaven had they died before the day of Pentecost. Yet, they were not baptized with the Spirit until Jesus finished His earthly ministry and departed to be with His Father. Jesus told them to *wait* in Jerusalem. So they returned to wait on the Holy Spirit.

In Acts 19 we read about another group of men who were believers yet had not been filled with the Holy Spirit (see Acts 19:2). After Paul laid his hands on them, however, we are told that the Holy Spirit "came on them, and they began speaking with tongues and prophesying" (Acts 19:6). Once again, there was a gap between the experience of salvation and being filled with the Spirit. The men were forced to wait. It was as if there was an appointed time for them to receive the Holy Spirit.

From those two passages in Acts I incorrectly assumed that every believer is forced to wait for that special moment when the Holy Spirit decides to grace him or her with His presence. But nowhere in the Bible is such an idea stated or even implied.

Lying there on my floor in Fruitland, North Carolina, I realized that I had made the Spirit-filled life much more complicated than it really is. Like every other aspect of the Christian life, the Spirit-filled life is a life of faith. I had been approaching it as if it were a formula. But the Spirit-filled life is not a formula; it is a relationship, a relationship with a person—the Holy Spirit.

A Shocking Discovery

As I mentioned earlier, my encounter with the Holy Spirit there on my floor in Fruitland left me with an unquenchable thirst to discover more. I began scanning the Scriptures for anything that had to do with the Holy Spirit. I realized how ignorant I was. At the same time, something had definitely happened to me, and I wanted an explanation.

My first discovery was probably my most shocking of all. The phrase "filled with the Spirit" appears only ten times in the entire New Testament: three times in Luke; six times in Acts; and once in Ephesians.[2] It isn't even mentioned in twenty-four of the twenty-seven books of the New Testament! How could that be? How could something of such consequence be so underemphasized?

Further study revealed some interesting facts about the filling of the Spirit—not the least of which was that there is a distinct difference between the use of the phrase "filled with the Spirit" in Luke and Acts and its use in the book of Ephesians.

For nine of the ten times the phrase "filled with the Holy Spirit" or "filled with the Spirit" is mentioned, the preposition *with* does not actually appear in the Greek. The English translators added it —and rightly so—because the form of the Greek noun *Spirit* expresses content and thus the addition of *with*.[3] The English language is not as precise as Greek, so we are forced to use several words to express what they could say in one.

The meaning of these nine verses is clear; the people in question were filled up with the Spirit. That is, the Holy Spirit came to dwell inside them. The classic example is found in Acts 2 when the disciples were filled with the Holy Spirit (see also Luke 1:41, 67). They entered the Upper Room without Him; they left the Upper Room full of Him.

Of the nine verses in question, three use the phrase "filled with the Spirit" in a descriptive way.[4] For example, Acts 4:8 records, "Then Peter, filled with the Holy Spirit, said to them. . . ." The author of Acts was simply stating that Peter was one of those who had been indwelt by the Holy Spirit. He was not commenting on the control or the influence that the Holy Spirit had in Peter's life at that moment. He was characterized as a man who had been filled with the Spirit or a Spirit-filled man (see Acts 13:9, 52).[5]

Trends in Acts

In studying the passages in Acts that dealt specifically with the filling of the Spirit, I noticed a couple of things they all had in common. First, in every instance the Holy Spirit initiated the filling. The recipient was always taken by surprise to some extent. Even those in the Upper Room did not know exactly when the filling of the Spirit would take place. It just happened.

Another good example of the same phenomenon is found in Acts 10:44 (see also Acts 19:1–7). Peter was preaching, and suddenly, with no warning, the Holy Spirit interrupted the sermon and fell on those listening. The word *filled* was not used, but Peter said it was just like what happened to him and the other apostles on the day of Pentecost (see Acts 10:47). In each instance the Holy Spirit initiated the process.

The second thing I noticed about the references to the filling of the Spirit in Acts was that they seemed to be permanent. There was no evidence after Pentecost of anyone's being unfilled in the sense of the Holy Spirit's departing. And there were no examples of anyone's being refilled *with* the Holy Spirit. On the contrary, Luke seemed to go out of his way to remind us that Peter and Paul were still filled after their initial filling.

Review

Let's put all of this information together before we go any further.

1. Jesus promised the coming of the Spirit. He said those who waited would be *baptized* with the Holy Spirit.
2. When He (the Spirit) finally came, Luke said they were all "filled with the Spirit." That is, the Spirit came into them.
3. Paul was filled with the Spirit for the first time (see Acts 9:17).
4. A group in Cornelius's house was filled with the Spirit for the first time (see Acts 10:44).
5. A group of John the Baptist's disciples received the Holy Spirit for the first time (see Acts 19:6).[6]

From all of that I concluded that the filling of the Spirit as described in Acts refers to the unique arrival of the Holy Spirit in the world after the resurrection of Jesus Christ as well as in the life of certain believers. Jesus promised such an arrival (see Acts 1:8). And the remainder of the book of Acts uses the term *filled* to describe that arrival.

Now you are probably wondering, "But what about when Paul commanded the Ephesian believers to be filled with the Spirit?" We are getting to that. But I want you to see that the book of Acts uses this phrase consistently to refer to the fulfillment of Christ's promise—the arrival of a Helper who would indwell the believer (see John 16:7). Now, on to Ephesians.

"But Be Filled with the Spirit"

During my search for the *secret* of the Spirit-filled life, I returned time and time again to Paul's familiar instruction to the believers in Ephesus:

> And do not get drunk with wine, for that is dissipation, but be
> filled with the Spirit.
>
> —*Ephesians 5:18*

This verse irritated me. I said, "OK, OK, but how? How do I do it? What do I do? Where do I begin?" My problem was not one of willingness. I just didn't know how to go about being filled. And unfortunately for all of us, Paul didn't include a step-by-step plan.

As I took a closer look at this verse, several things stood out, things that set it apart from other verses about being filled with the Spirit. That distinction revolutionized my understanding of the Spirit-filled life. It was through the truth of Ephesians 5:18 that I finally understood what happened to me that afternoon on my floor in Fruitland.

My confusion centered on Paul's example of being drunk with wine. I had always understood him to be saying, "Don't fill yourself up with wine and thus become drunk. But be filled up with the Holy Spirit instead." I thought the parallel ideas were *wine* and *Spirit*. Consequently, I set about trying to figure out how to get the Holy Spirit to fill me. I knew how a person would be filled with wine. But his illustration left me without a clue about how to be filled up with the Holy Spirit.

Aha!

Then I noticed an interesting thing about this verse. As you recall, I pointed out that in Acts there was no preposition preceding the word *Spirit*. Translators added the word *with* because the Greek form of the term *Spirit* necessitated it. *With* communicated the idea of content. Believers were filled up with the Spirit.

In Ephesian 5:18, however, the word *with* does appear in the Greek. Paul inserted a preposition before the word *Spirit*. Although the preposition is translated *with* in our English Bibles, this little preposition does not imply *with* in the sense of *content* (what the believer is to be filled up with). It carries the idea of *agent*— who is doing the filling. Paul was admonishing his audience to be filled *by* the Spirit rather than *with* the Spirit.

Imagine for a moment that someone asked you for a cup of water. You would serve as the agent (the cup filler), and the water would serve as the content. Paul referred to the Spirit as the filler; in other words, "Let the Spirit fill you." The obvious question would then be, "Fill me with what?" This is where the wine illustration is helpful.

The Filling of the Spirit in Acts versus Ephesians

Acts
- The apostles were instructed to wait.
- The Holy Spirit initiated the filling.
- The term *Spirit* is not preceded by a preposition; the noun form implies the idea of *content*.
- Filling is permanent.

Ephesians 5:18
- Believers are instructed to act.
- Believers are commanded to be filled.
- The term *Spirit* is preceded by a preposition that implies *agent*.
- The fact that it is a general command to a group of people implies that this type of filling is repeatable.

Paul used the term *fill* in tandem with *drunk*. To be drunk means more than to drink. It means more than to fill up. To be drunk is to be under the control of alcohol, to surrender one's body, mind, and spirit to its influence. *To be filled with the Spirit—in this particular case—is to voluntarily put oneself under the influence of the Holy Spirit.* J. Oswald Sanders explained it this way:

> From the contrasting commands, "Be not drunk with wine wherein is excess," and "Be filled with the Spirit," we would be justified in concluding that the person who is filled with the Spirit will be dominated and controlled by the Holy Spirit even as a drunkard is dominated and controlled by his intoxicating wine.[7]

It is important to understand the distinction between this key verse and what was happening in the book of Acts. Otherwise, like me, you may find yourself caught between Paul's command to do something and a phenomenon over which you have no control.

When Paul said to be filled with the Spirit, he was not commanding us to sit around passively and wait for something to be poured into us. The Holy Spirit has already been poured in. If you are a believer, you have already been filled *with* the Holy Spirit the way the men and women in Acts were filled. He has taken up permanent residence in your heart. You have all of Him you are ever going to get. The question is, How much of you does He have?

That is Paul's point in Ephesians 5:18. He was calling for total surrender to the gentle—yet firm—promptings of the Holy Spirit. To be filled in this fashion is similar to being filled with fear or sorrow. When we are filled with fear or sorrow, the emotion takes such preeminence in our lives that all other thoughts and feelings are pushed into the background.

A Trip I Shall Never Forget

In 1971 I flew to Seattle, Washington, to preach a revival for a friend. As we began our final approach, the captain informed us that they were having some trouble. The jet pulled back into a holding pattern, and we were informed that the lock light on the front landing gear had not come on. That meant the cockpit crew had no way of knowing whether the front landing gear had locked into position. After several minutes the captain informed us that we would circle the airport several more times to burn up excess fuel and then attempt an emergency landing.

I could see emergency vehicles lining up along the airstrip below. We all leaned over—with head down in lap—as the captain counted the seconds to touchdown.

If we could have looked into the hearts and minds of the people on that flight, we would have found they were filled with an emotion that took such preeminence in their lives that nothing even came in a close second. They were controlled by whatever filled their hearts in those anxious moments.

In the same way, we are to allow the Holy Spirit to have complete control over our hearts and minds. To be filled with Him is to allow His influence to invade every crack and crevice of our being—our thoughts, our motives, our relationships, and our dreams.

> In the heart of the believer who is filled with the Spirit, He reigns supreme over the will, the emotions, the intelligence, but with his full consent and cooperation. The word [filled]

carries the idea of being filled to the point of saturation, a fullness that leaves nothing to be desired. . . . So to be full of the Holy Spirit means the habitual experience of having the Holy Spirit in the free and unhindered exercise of all His attributes—knowledge, power, holiness, peace, joy—exercising His sway and dominion in every realm of life.[8]

Oh, yeah, back to my story. The captain counted the seconds. Everyone was dead silent. When the front landing gear touched down, it held.

Back in Fruitland

In the days that followed my personal revival I began to analyze what had happened. I wanted to share my new treasure with others. But I wanted to make sure that what I shared was in keeping with what the Bible teaches. As I thought back on the process God had brought me through—and as I continued to pore over the verses concerning the ministries of the Holy Spirit—things finally began coming together.

As I see it, God used that entire series of events to accomplish two things in my life. These two things are essential to understanding and entering into the wonderful Spirit-filled life. Simply put, God brought me to the place of *total dependence* and *total surrender*.

1. Total dependence

The Spirit-filled life begins once we are absolutely and thoroughly convinced that we can do nothing apart from the indwelling strength of the Holy Spirit. Notice I didn't say it begins when we *say* we are convinced. It begins when we *are* convinced. And *1-4-17* some of us are harder to convince than others. *This is my need*

The Spirit-filled (or Spirit-controlled) life begins with an overwhelming realization that we are absolutely helpless and hopeless apart from the empowerment of the Holy Spirit. Until that one simple truth grips us at the core of our being, we will never experience the full-blown power of the Holy Spirit. Why? Because we will always be out there doing things *for* God in our strength. And when we fail, we will promise to do better next time.

Without meaning to, many Christians live independently of the Holy Spirit every day. They never give Him a second thought. He is nothing more than a theological category. They have their assignments. You know, love your neighbor, don't steal, don't commit adultery, and so on. They go about their business committed to doing the best *they* can do.

As I have shared my experience through the years, I have found that a great number of people have similar stories to tell. Some call it brokenness. Some, utter desperation. When the process is complete, what's left is a man or woman who understands the need of God.

The mental, physical, and emotional valleys often hold the most fertile soil when it comes to spiritual growth. More people discover the wonderful Spirit-filled life in the valley than in any other place. God uses sickness, financial pressure, appetites, habits, children, work, whatever it takes. Because once He finally has our attention, He knows the best is yet to come.

God is an expert at engineering circumstances so that we find ourselves with nowhere to turn but to Him. He knows how to bring us to the point where we feel out of control. In His wisdom He knows that some of us must be pushed to the brink of disaster before we come to the place mentally, emotionally, and spiritually where we throw in the towel and entrust ourselves fully to the God who created us.

2. Total surrender

The second thing God accomplished through the teaching scenario was that He brought me to a point of total surrender. I didn't realize what was happening at the time. But by being placed in a position where I was obligated to do something that I felt totally unprepared to do, I was willing to do anything if He would only come through for me. He engineered my circumstances in such a way as to back me into a corner. It was do or die. Either He was going to do something, or I was dead! There was no way out. I was going to have to face those men whether I was ready or not.

I was desperate. And when we are desperate, we can't do a thing—but we are willing to do anything. And that is exactly where God wanted me. It's where God wants you as well.

Dependence and surrender go hand in hand. We can't fully surrender our wills until we are convinced we are in a hopeless situation. As long as we see a way out, we will generally opt for it.

In water safety courses a cardinal rule is never to swim out to a drowning man and try to help him as long as he is thrashing about. To do so is to commit suicide. As long as a drowning man thinks he can help himself, he is dangerous to anyone who tries to help him. His tendency is to grab the one trying to aid him and take them both down in the process. The correct procedure is to stay just far enough away so that he can't grab you. Then you wait. And when he finally gives up, you make your move. At that point the one drowning is pliable. He won't work against you. He will let you help.

The same principle holds true in our relationship with the Holy Spirit. Until we give up, we aren't really in a position to be helped. We will work against Him rather than with Him. Surrender to His will follows the surrender of our own. When we recognize that we can't make it, we are like a drowning man surrendering to the aid of his rescuer.

Easier Said . . .

The length of time it takes to catch on to this relationship depends on us—not God. The more willing we are to confess our inadequacy, the easier it is for us to fully surrender to His will for our lives. Let's face it. All of us have made overarching commitments from time to time. With the right combination of music and preaching we can be persuaded to promise God just about anything. That is not what I am talking about here. In fact, that is just the opposite of what I am saying.

This isn't about rededication. Rededication usually amounts to our telling God how much better *we* are going to *do* next time. Part of the reason these types of commitments are so short-lived is that they are not preceded by brokenness. They are not couched in the context of the realization that apart from Him, we can do absolutely nothing. Surrender and rededication are two completely different things. You can only rededicate yourself to do something that you are capable of doing to begin with. Surrender is the acknowledgment that you can't do something and that you need help.

During the Gulf War, we were given a fresh look at surrender. Do you remember the faces of the Iraqi soldiers who surrendered in the first few days of fighting? They didn't come out of their foxholes and trenches in the spirit of rededication. They didn't march out promising the Americans what they were and were not

going to do. They simply surrendered. Their raised hands signified their willingness to do whatever they were instructed to do.

In her classic work *The Christian's Secret of a Happy Life,* Hannah
Whitall Smith gives an excellent illustration of what it means to be
surrendered or, in her terminology, consecrated:

> I was once trying to explain to a physician who had charge of
> a large hospital the necessity and meaning of consecration,
> but he seemed unable to understand. At last I said to him,
> "Suppose in going your rounds among your patients, you
> should meet with one man who entreated you earnestly to
> take his case under your especial care in order to cure him,
> but who should at the same time refuse to tell you all his
> symptoms to take all your prescribed remedies, and should
> say to you, 'I am quite willing to follow your directions as to
> certain things, because they commend themselves to my mind
> as good, but in other matters I prefer judging for myself, and
> following my own directions.' What would you do in such a
> case?" I asked. "Do!" he replied with indignation—"Do! I
> would soon leave such a man as that to his own care. For, of
> course," he added, "I could do nothing for him unless he
> would put his whole case into my hands without any
> reserves, and would obey my directions implicitly." "It is nec-
> essary then," I said, "for doctors to be obeyed if they are to
> have any chance to cure their patient?" *"Implicitly obeyed!"*
> was his emphatic reply. "And that is consecration," I contin-
> ued. "God must have the whole case put into His hands with-
> out any reserves, and His directions must be implicitly fol-
> lowed."[9]

Laying a Foundation

Surrender is essential because the Spirit-filled life is a relationship. It is not a military mission where we are handed an assign-
ment and expected to carry it out. The Spirit-filled life is a moment-by-moment relationship characterized by dependency on
the Holy Spirit. And surrender is the foundation upon which that
unique relationship is built and maintained.

Like salvation, the Spirit-filled life is available to anyone. But
the way is narrow. And there are no shortcuts. Every husband
would enjoy a Spirit-filled marriage characterized by joy and
peace and love. But there is a price to pay, a price so high that

many work to imitate those things that characterize a genuine Spirit-controlled life.

In an attempt to have the best of both worlds (control and the benefits of a surrendered life), they try to produce the fruit of the Spirit through self-effort. The result is a cheap, short-lived imitation. After years of struggle, many Christians draw the conclusion that there is nothing to the Christian life: "I tried it, and it just didn't work for me."

Timing Is Everything

Timing is so important. And if you are like me, your timetable is a little different from God's. You cannot rush this lesson. It's not purely academic. It's not just a matter of understanding a few verses and praying a magic prayer. The whole thing hinges on where each of us is in our pilgrimage with Christ.

Some people will read this book and get so much out of it that they will go out and buy a dozen to give away as gifts. On the other hand, there will be those who won't make it past the first few chapters.

As you think about your life and experience as a Christian, where do you stand in all of this? Do you feel as if you've hit bottom and there's no place to look but up? Does the idea of total surrender scare you? Are you like the drowning man who is still doing his best to keep his head above water? *yes*

I'm not asking these questions because I can't think of a better way to end this chapter. Your answer—your position on this spiritual continuum—determines how meaningful and helpful the rest of this book will be for you.

The remarkable things God did publicly in my classroom in Fruitland, North Carolina, could not have taken place apart from what God did privately in my heart. I really didn't know what was going on at the time. I felt abandoned. But all the time God was moving me to a place of *total dependence*. From there it was an easy transition to becoming *totally surrendered*.

I thought I needed to do something or receive something. God knew better and gently brought me to the end of my self-effort. It was then that I saw the big picture. The work was done. I didn't need any more ability. I needed to move out in faith that He who had begun a good work in me would finish it through me as I went about my daily responsibilities.

The incident in Fruitland was not the last time I was in what appeared to be a hopeless situation. Several years later I found myself backed into another corner. There I learned another wonderful lesson about the Spirit-filled life. In the next chapter I'll share it with you in detail.

NOTES

1. Billy Graham, *The Holy Spirit* (Dallas: Word, 1988), p. 14.

2. There are six other references to men described as "full of the Holy Spirit." All appear in Luke and Acts. See note 4 for further information.

3. In Acts 13:52 Luke writes that "the disciples were continually filled with joy and with the Holy Spirit." *Joy* and *Spirit* are parallel concepts in this verse. Just as they were filled *with* joy, they were filled *with* the Holy Spirit. This substantiates the interpretation of *with* as content.

4. There are six references to men said to be "full of the Spirit" (Luke 4:1; 10:21; Acts 6:3, 5; 7:55; 11:24). The passages in Luke refer to Jesus as "full of the Holy Spirit." The context of Luke 4 follows the baptism of Jesus where the Holy Spirit descended on Him in bodily form. When Luke refers to Jesus as One who was full of the Holy Spirit, he is referring to the indwelling presence of the Holy Spirit. This definition fits with the other uses of this phrase in the New Testament.

5. Describing Peter and Paul as men filled with the Holy Spirit put a divine stamp of approval on the authority with which the men spoke. Paul, being a newcomer, especially needed something to authenticate his authority in the church. Paul was given equal authority with Peter, which substantiated Paul's apostleship.

6. The term *filled* is not used here, but the events surrounding the incident closely parallel what happened in Cornelius's home.

7. J. Oswald Sanders, *The Holy Spirit and His Gifts* (Grand Rapids, Mich.: Zondervan, 1940), p. 138.

8. Sanders, *The Holy Spirit and His Gifts*, p. 139.

9. Hannah Whitall Smith, *The Christian's Secret of a Happy Life* (Old Tappan, N.J.: Revell, 1989), pp. 47–48.

─────── **THINK ABOUT IT** ───────

- Have you ever found yourself begging, bargaining, and pleading with God for some spiritual change in your life?
- Better yet, have you ever worked hard in order to please God so that He'd give in to your request?
- Have there been times that you've felt it was your responsibility to wait on God to fill you with His Holy Spirit?
- Have you ever experienced the frustration of desiring to be filled with the Spirit but not knowing how to go about it?
- Have you come to the place in your life of total dependence and total surrender to God, thus making it possible for the Holy Spirit to maximize His work in your life?

CHAPTER 5

My Life as a Branch

❋

I emerged from my ordeal in Fruitland with a new sense of confidence and boldness. The changes that took place in me were most apparent in my public ministry. But there is more to life than ministry. And so God started getting me ready for my next big lesson.

We left North Carolina in 1959 and moved to Fairborn, Ohio. After pastoring there for four years, I accepted a call to the First Baptist Church of Miami. I thought I had died and gone to heaven —especially after those cold Ohio winters.

Things went well at the church. People were joining and being baptized. Everybody seemed to like me. My family adjusted quickly to the change. But early in the spring of 1964 I saw a trend in our worship services that disturbed me.

A group of church members made repeated trips down the aisle during the invitation. Each time they came they would confess the same sins. We would pray at the altar together, and I would send them back to their seats. But in a few weeks they would be right back down front with the same problems. The situation really bothered me. I remember thinking, *Am I not helping these folks? Is there something I'm not telling them?*

They Were Not Alone

Eventually, it occurred to me that I was struggling with some of the things they were struggling with. And I didn't have solutions. The irony was that I continued to sense the Holy Spirit's presence

54

in my preparation and public presentations. But He was conspicuously missing in my private life.

I believed that the Holy Spirit was to play an important role in
every facet of my life. But I couldn't make the connection. I didn't
know how to make it work for me.

For a long time I had a hunch something was missing in my life.
But I couldn't put my finger on it. I had a nagging suspicion that
there was more to the Christian life than I was experiencing. But I
didn't know where to turn for the answer.

For the most part I was doing all the right things and doing my
best to live a good life. But it was as if I was serving a distant
King. God was way out there somewhere. Watching. Taking notes
perhaps. There was no warmth or intimacy in my relationship
with Him.

What really got my attention, however, were several secret sins
in my life. Things that no one knew about. Nothing out of the
ordinary. But things I knew were displeasing to God. I did everything I knew to do to change. But I experienced no consistent
victory. I would retreat to that age-old excuse, "Well, Charles,
nobody is perfect." I knew in my heart that didn't cut it with God.
Then I would feel even more guilty. I would promise and pray
and at times even fast. But there was no change. I concluded that
either the Bible didn't have a message adequate for my personal
life or I was missing something. Looking back, I can see that God
was setting me up for another wonderful lesson.

The Fruit of the What?

At the same time I was wrestling with all this, I was preaching
through the book of Galatians on Sunday nights. It was going
well. Our people were taking notes and inviting their neighbors.
You could feel the excitement in our services as we made our way
verse by verse through the book.

There was only one problem. As I looked ahead to chapter 5, I
realized that in a few weeks I would arrive at the passage that
described the fruit of the Spirit. *How can I preach on the fruit of the
Spirit when I don't see much in my own life?* I thought. To compound
the problem, there were those verses just before it that discussed
walking by the Spirit—one more thing I knew nothing about.

Once again my back was against the wall. It would be a little
strange to skip the fifth chapter. And my conscience wouldn't let

The vine is Christ,

I am the branch.

The Holy Spirit is the sap

that runs from the vine

into the branch.

The branch lives, grows,

and bears fruit

not by struggles and effort

but simply by abiding.

me get up there and pretend to know something I didn't. So I started praying urgently: "Lord, please open my eyes to the truth of what Paul is saying in these verses."

Granted, my motivation was somewhat selfish—I didn't want to look like a fool. But at the same time I knew that I desperately (there's that word again) needed a change in my life. And I felt sure that the truth I needed was there in the fifth chapter of Galatians. If the Holy Spirit could produce patience, gentleness, and self-control, I wanted in on all that.

Just in Time

One Saturday afternoon, June 6 to be exact, I was headed out our back door toward my study in the backyard. On the dining room table beside the back door was a book my wife had purchased weeks earlier to read during a train trip. She had mentioned to me on several occasions that I should read it. But for some reason I had not even picked it up to look at it.

Without thinking, I picked the book up and headed out to study. It was two weeks before I was to begin Galatians 5. I remember how discouraged I was. Here is my personal journal entry for that day:

DIARY June 6, 1964

For months I have had one experience after the other where my heart yearned for a deeper walk with God. There have been moments of victory, but more defeats. My private communion with Jesus has been inconsistent.

There are spurts of inspiration which soon dwindle into insignificance. I have prayed, begged, pleaded, striven, worked, done everything in my power to receive victory in my personal devotions. Satan has defeated me continually.

There is something I do not have which I must have. My present experience with Christ is not real, it is only words. My heart is aching to the breaking point. Oh God please I beg you give me victory tonight. You have said in your Word, "How much more shall the Heavenly Father give the Holy Spirit to them that ask Him."

I do not feel I can pray or preach publicly again till I get victory. I need continuous victory, consistent victory. I beg of you to search my heart, lay it bare, reveal to me my every sin.

Reveal thyself to me tonight. I believe the human heart has no
desire which you cannot satisfy. Oh God out of my heart let
the rivers of living water flow.

At some point in the afternoon I opened my wife's little book
and began to read. The title of the book is *They Found the Secret,* by
V. Raymond Edman.[1] The work is composed of twenty short bio-
graphical sketches of great men of God. The author's goal was to
chronicle the time in each man's life when he entered into what he
called *the exchanged life.*

God used the first chapter in that book to revolutionize my life.
It was on Hudson Taylor. After the first paragraph, I was hooked.
Here was a man who knew exactly what I was going through.
Writing to his mother, he described my situation perfectly:

> My own position becomes continually more and more respon-
> sible, and my need greater of special grace to fill it; but I have
> continually to mourn that I follow at such a distance and learn
> so slowly to imitate my precious Master. I cannot tell you how
> I am buffeted sometimes by temptation. I never knew how
> bad a heart I had. Yet I do know that I love God and love His
> work, and desire to serve Him only in all things.[2]

God used a man named John McCarthy to show Taylor the way
into the Spirit-filled life. John, a missionary himself, heard of his
struggles and wrote a letter that transformed Taylor's life. As I
read McCarthy's letter and the comments that followed, it was
like a light switch was turned on in my heart. It was so clear, so
simple. I don't know how I could have missed it.

The central theme of Taylor's testimony is *abiding.* The Christian
life is a life of abiding in Christ.

> How does the branch bear fruit? Not by incessant effort for
> sunshine and air; not by vain struggles for those vivifying
> influences which give beauty to the blossom, and verdure to
> the leaf: it simply abides in the vine, in silent and undisturbed
> union, and blossoms and fruit appear as of spontaneous
> growth.

> How, then, shall a Christian bear fruit? By efforts and strug-
> gles to obtain that which is freely given; by meditations on
> watchfulness, on prayer, on action, on temptation, and on
> dangers? No: there must be a full concentration of the

thoughts and affections on Christ; a complete surrender of the whole being to Him; a constant looking to Him for grace. Christians in whom these dispositions are once firmly fixed go on calmly as the infant borne in the arms of its mother.[3]

It dawned on me that I had been like a branch straining to produce fruit on its own. No wonder there was so little fruit in my life. Branches were not designed to produce fruit—they were designed to have fruit produced through them!

I had been going about the whole thing backward. In Galatians, Paul contrasts the *deeds* of the flesh with the *fruit* of the Spirit. My approach had been to try to do *deeds* of the Spirit. How foolish!

Awakening

When I finished the section on Hudson Taylor, I dropped to my knees there on that cold concrete floor and began to cry. I was so happy. I kept thinking, *That's it. It's the vine that does the work. The fruit is a product of the sap that runs from the vine into the branch.* I couldn't get over the fact that the Holy Spirit was willing and able to produce through me the very fruit I had been trying so hard to produce on my own.

I was on my knees for almost three hours just crying and thanking God for opening my eyes to this wonderful truth. When I got up, I was a new man. My whole perspective on the Christian life was different. The verse that kept running through my mind was one I had preached on just a few weeks earlier:

> I have been crucified with Christ; and it is no longer I who live, but Christ lives in me; and the life which I now live in the flesh I live by faith in the Son of God, who loved me, and delivered Himself up for me.
>
> —*Galatians 2:20*

The part I clung to for the next several weeks was, "It is no longer I who live, but Christ lives in me." It was no longer I who was expected to produce patience, self-control, and love in my life. That was a job for the Holy Spirit. It was no longer I who was expected to produce joy in the midst of stress. That, too, was the Holy Spirit's responsibility. It was no longer I who was expected to produce anything in the way of character. It was Christ, working through the Holy Spirit, producing character in me. What a relief! A huge burden was lifted off my shoulders that afternoon. And I walked out of my study a free man.

A New Man

I went into the house and told Anna that something wonderful had happened to me. When she asked me what, I didn't know what to tell her. I fumbled around for a few minutes, doing my best to explain it. Then I had an idea. I went over to the bookshelf in our den, pulled out an old Bible, and opened it to Galatians 2:20. "This is it," I said. "It's no longer I, but Christ through me."

My only concern at the time was losing my new treasure. Mountaintop experiences were nothing new to me; however, they always faded in time. Somehow I knew this was different. But I wanted to make sure. I read and reread the section on Hudson Taylor in Edman's little book. I went to bed each night meditating on any verse I could find that dealt with abiding or the Holy Spirit.

A portion of John McCarthy's letter to Hudson Taylor ministered to me in a special way:

> Abiding, not striving nor struggling; looking off unto Him; trusting Him for present power; trusting Him to subdue all inward corruption; resting in the love of an almighty Savior.[4]

My initial fears were unfounded. A profound change took place in my life. Whereas my experience in Fruitland affected my ministry, what happened in my study that Saturday afternoon touched every facet of my life.

I knew it was for real when I overheard my wife explaining to a friend on the phone the change that had taken place in my life. She said, "Something wonderful has happened to my husband. It's like I'm living with a different man." Another close friend of ours was overheard saying, "I don't know what it is, but something has sure happened to our pastor."

Two weeks later I made the following entry in my journal:

June 23, 1964

These past two weeks have been two of the greatest spiritually. The night I made the above entry [June 6] I began to abide in Christ. The miraculous and incomparable truth of John 15:1–8 became a living reality in my heart.

For seven years I have searched for the truth, the secret of the victorious life. Now I have found it—abiding in Christ. The vine is Christ, I am the branch. The Holy Spirit is the sap that runs from the vine into the branch. The branch lives, grows, bears fruit not by struggles and effort but simply by abiding.

There has been a peace, a tranquility, a calmness, a serenity about my life that outweighs anything I have known. By faith I have accepted the relationship of abiding. The sap that runs in the vine flows through the branch.

I am abiding in Christ and His Spirit is filling my heart, the fruit of the Spirit, love, joy, peace, long-suffering, kindness, goodness, meekness, faith, self-control, Christ has begun to live it through me.

Christ has become more real to me as I understand Him to be within. The Word of God has become more precious to me. Scriptures such as Romans 7 and 8 have suddenly become alive and Paul's statement in Galatians: "I am crucified with Christ, nevertheless I live, yet not I, but Christ lives in me: and the life I now live, I live by the faith of the Son of God."

To abide by faith is simply to live in Christ—from Him every need is supplied. How I wish I had learned this years ago.

Lord Jesus I come this morning abiding in thee; asking for the forgiveness of my every sin and to ask that the fruit of the Spirit today may be made manifest in my life.

Father make me continually aware that if I live in the Spirit this does not mean that life will be easy, but life far easier, and at least with peace and tranquility in the soul.

In the midst of confusion and strife make me like a rock. Enable me to stand firm. May the Spirit of Jesus be revealed without question through my life.

Thy Word says, "Love never faileth." Let that be the principle by which I live. Teach me to be able to love those that love me and those that do not. Help me not to court the favor of anyone but Jesus.

Lord Jesus that I might be like the Apostle Paul—to count all things but loss for the knowledge of Jesus Christ. Lord I want to know you. I love you and want your Spirit to fill me and to overflow. Let nothing be so important as loving you, spending time with you.

May the patience and willingness to wait upon the Father be as real in my life as yours.

Oh Lord I pray to be emptied of all that I am and to be filled with Jesus overflowing daily with Thy precious love and truth. May every person sense something in my life they have never sensed before—love for Jesus and man, a firmness of spiritual conviction, a heart that is compassionate for the needs of man.

Lord let me be diligent in the seeking of the will, and when I have found it live by it in faith.

Thank you for the statement of Chambers I read Sunday night, "The main job of the Christian is intercessory prayer."

Oh Lord I have so many to pray for. As I abide today in the Lord may I continually be in prayer for those who need my prayers.

Lord Jesus may I today speak only in love, and only of my Lord, only in truth, only for the good of that one whose name I call. May my speech always magnify Christ Jesus.

Lord make my life a stepping stone to thee for others who are longing for you.

Lord Jesus, live through me your precious life today.

In the following weeks I continued to gain great insight and encouragement from Jesus' illustration of the vine and branch.

The True Vine

The disciples must have known from the tone of Jesus' voice that something big was about to happen. He repeatedly alluded to His departure (see John 14:2–3, 25, 28). Up until that time they had drawn their strength and security from His presence. The thought of carrying on without Him must have been depressing. After all, even when He was there, they were prone to being sidetracked.

Jesus knew their fears. He knew how dependent on Him they were for direction and perspective. So as He moved toward His final hours, He explained the way things would work after He was gone:

I am the true vine, and My Father is the vinedresser. Every branch in Me that does not bear fruit, He takes away; and every branch that bears fruit, He prunes it, that it may bear more fruit. . . . Abide in Me, and I in you. As the branch cannot bear fruit of itself, unless it abides in the vine, so neither can you, unless you abide in Me. I am the vine, you are the branches; he who abides in Me, and I in him, he bears much fruit; for apart from Me you can do nothing.

—*John 15:1–5*

Much Fruit

I don't fully understand a great deal about this passage. But two things are clear. First, Christ expected His followers then and now to bear fruit. Notice He did not expect them to *produce* fruit, just *bear* it. And not just *some* fruit but *much* fruit. The amount of fruit we bear correlates with how apparent it is to others that we are believers (see John 15:8). Our faith is known to others through the good deeds that overflow from our character (see Matt. 5:16), or the fruit we bear.

You know as well as I do that for others to be impressed with our life-styles or good deeds, they must be consistent. Unbelievers are very sensitive to our inconsistencies. Oftentimes they look for them. So if we are to bear the kind of fruit Jesus is talking about—the kind that draws others to our way of believing—there must be a regular harvest.

Mission Impossible

The second thing that is clear from these verses is that what Jesus calls us to do is impossible. It's not merely difficult. It's not simply a struggle. It's not just hard. IT'S IMPOSSIBLE! "For apart from Me you can do *nothing.*" Not a *little.* Not a *few things.* NOTHING.

This should come as good news. If you are like I was for so long, you may wonder whether something is wrong with you, whether everybody else knows something you don't. That's not the case at all. You struggle like you do because you are attempting the impossible. No one can live the Christian life apart from Christ—at least not with the consistency necessary to accomplish what Jesus has called us to accomplish.

In essence, He was saying to His followers, "Men, if you think you are dependent on Me now, wait until I'm gone!" He knew that their tendency would be to do exactly what we do. After He was gone, they would conduct themselves as soldiers who had been given orders. They would strike out to fulfill their mission of righteousness.

He wanted them to understand that though He was not going to be with them physically, He still expected them to depend on Him. And the same holds true for us today.

To put it in more practical terms, if you do not learn to abide in Christ, you will never have a marriage characterized by love, joy, and peace. You will never have the self-control necessary to consistently overcome temptation. And you will always be an emotional hostage of your circumstances. Why? Because apart from abiding in Christ, you can do nothing.

The Life of Christ

Jesus makes a clear delineation between the vine and the branch. The two are not the same. *He* is the vine; *we* are the branches. The two are joined but not one. The common denominator in nature is the sap. The sap is the life of the vine and its branches. Cut off the flow of sap to the branch, and it slowly withers and dies.

As the branch draws its life from the vine, so we draw life from Christ. *To abide in Christ is to draw upon His life.* His life is made available through the presence of the Holy Spirit in our lives. The abiding presence of the Holy Spirit is the life of Christ in us. That is why Paul could use these phrases interchangeably in his letter to the Romans:

> However, you are not in the flesh but in the Spirit, if indeed the *Spirit of God dwells in you.* But if anyone does not have the Spirit of Christ, he does not belong to Him. *And if Christ is in you,* though the body is dead because of sin, yet the spirit is alive because of righteousness.
> —*Romans 8:9–10*, emphasis mine

Jesus Christ dwells in us through the person of the Holy Spirit. To have the Spirit is to have the life of Christ within. So Paul was accurate when he wrote,

When Christ, *who is our life*, is revealed, then you also will be
revealed with Him in glory.
—*Colossians 3:4*, emphasis mine

Jack Taylor, in his wonderful little book *After the Spirit Comes*,
declares, "It may be said then, without being irreverent, that the
Holy Spirit is for us the presence of Jesus Christ, the spiritual
presence of Jesus Himself. . . . We are indwelt of the Spirit of
God who is the living Essence of Jesus in us."[5]

Christ *is* our life. When the Holy Spirit takes up residency in us,
He brings with Him an inexhaustible source of life. After all, He is
life. While conversing with the woman at the well, Jesus described
it as a "well of water springing up to eternal life" (John 4:14).
Peter described it as becoming "partakers of the divine nature" (2
Pet. 1:4).

Bearers, Not Producers

The practical outworking of all this is twofold: (1) personal victory over sin and (2) Spirit-energized service. *God never intended for
His children to live defeated lives.* Did you get that? God never,
never, never intended for His children—that includes you—to live
a life characterized by defeat. He doesn't expect you to live with
defeat in your thought life, your emotions, your attitudes, your
self-control, or your faith. He paid much too high a price to allow
you into His family just to watch you fail in your attempts to
function as a full-blown family member.

God's plan of salvation includes a provision for saving you
from yourself. And the key player in that part of His plan is—you
guessed it—the Holy Spirit. The Holy Spirit is God's answer to the
problem of righteous living. He is the abiding presence of Christ's
life in you. That is why Paul could say with confidence, "It is no
longer I who live, but Christ lives in me" (Gal. 2:20). He understood that upon receiving the Holy Spirit, he was endowed with a
source of power and strength that could bring his character into
line with God's righteous standard. Paul knew, as we must come
to know, that he never had to say, "Well, I'd like to change, but
that's just the way I am."

As a Spirit-indwelt child of God, Paul understood his potential
for change. He understood that change was contingent not upon
him but upon the new life that flowed through him.

The Change Agent

The life of Christ in you has the potential to produce all kinds of change in your life. "Wait," you say, "I've tried to change, and I can't." Exactly! You are not equipped to produce change—only bear it. Your new life produces change. You are simply the vehicle through which it is expressed, as a branch is the vehicle through which the fruit-producing life of the vine is expressed. You are a bearer, not a producer. Branches are totally dependent on the vine for fruit. And we are totally dependent on the Holy Spirit.

The Holy Spirit is a change agent. Change is what He is all about. He took a man who made his living destroying churches and changed him into the greatest church planter of all time! He took a group of uneducated fishermen and changed them into world-class evangelists and pastors. Through the years He has indwelt men and women with every imaginable habit, reputation, and persuasion and changed them into people of excellence. And He will do the same for you.

I know. Because when I was thirty-five years of age, in my third pastorate, after I thought I knew all there was to know about how to live the Christian life, He changed me. Some things changed overnight. Other areas changed over a period of time. And the work continues. But what a wonderful work it is! I am simply the recipient of the life-producing—change-rendering—work of the Holy Spirit. He produces; I bear:

> For it is God who is at work in you [and me], both to will and to work for His good pleasure.
>
> —*Philippians 2:13*

Who is at work? God—through the Holy Spirit.

Radical change is possible. We have everything we need to become all He wants us to become (see 2 Pet. 1:3). By abiding in Him and Him in us, we have the potential to produce a consistent harvest of fruit, the kind that makes even the most skeptical unbeliever sit up and take notice.

Our part is simply to plug into the new life that indwells us. We are to draw upon His life in us. How? By faith. But we will get to that in the next chapter.

Finding the Right Label

Through the years, I have met dozens of believers who have a testimony similar to mine. Like me, they entered into the Spirit-filled life years after their salvation. They, too, went through a period of struggle and defeat, which eventually led them to the point of desperation. In their own way, each of them threw up the white flag of surrender. Their yieldedness and brokenness cleared the way for the Holy Spirit to take control.

There is a tendency on the part of some to label this experience. Some call it the second blessing. Others call it the baptism of the Holy Spirit or the second baptism of the Holy Spirit. I have heard it called other things as well. Since the Bible doesn't label or title this experience, we shouldn't, either. Doing so only confuses things.

My observation has been that labeling this blessed experience creates two categories of Christians—the haves and the have-nots, those who have had the experience and those who have not. The Bible does not teach that a crisis experience is necessary for entering into the Spirit-filled life. It is a common experience—but not a necessary one.

I have seen genuine Spirit-controlled believers alienated from certain Christian circles because they did not have a testimony that fit a particular pattern. As we will see in a later chapter, the sign of a Spirit-filled believer is fruit, not a particular experience. Some point to Paul's experience described in Romans 7 as the struggle of a Christian just before entering into the Spirit-filled life. This may be the case. But nowhere does Paul say that his experience is a pattern for all believers.

God leads different people in different ways: some through crisis, others through watching and learning from someone else's crisis. I share my story in the hopes that you can learn from it—not repeat it.

NOTES

1. V. Raymond Edman, *They Found the Secret* (Grand Rapids, Mich.: Zondervan, 1960).
2. Edman, *They Found the Secret*, p. 2.
3. Edman, *They Found the Secret*, p. 6.
4. Edman, *They Found the Secret*, p. 2.

5. Jack R. Taylor, *After the Spirit Comes* (Nashville: Broadman Press, 1974), pp. 10, 14.

─────────── **THINK ABOUT IT** ───────────

Before you go any further, take a few minutes to meditate on these statements:

- Christ is my life.
- The Holy Spirit is the presence of Christ in me.
- I am a bearer, not a producer, of fruit.
- He is the vine; I am the branch.
- To abide in Christ is to allow the Holy Spirit to produce His fruit through me.
- I can change because Christ lives in me.
- Christ desires to live His life through me.
- Nothing comes against me that the new life within me cannot handle.
- The life of Christ can produce the character of Christ through me.
- Christ is my life.

PART TWO

Looking Within

The ministries of the Holy Spirit in the believer

And do not get drunk with wine, for that is dissipation, but be filled with the Spirit.

—*Ephesians 5:18*

CHAPTER 6

The Faith Factor

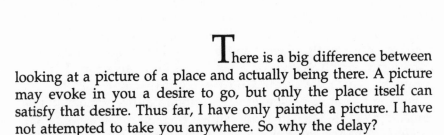

There is a big difference between looking at a picture of a place and actually being there. A picture may evoke in you a desire to go, but only the place itself can satisfy that desire. Thus far, I have only painted a picture. I have not attempted to take you anywhere. So why the delay?

Much like a physical journey, our spiritual pilgrimage is undertaken first by way of acknowledgment, then by application. Before you make plans to go somewhere, you must first believe that such a place really exists and that you can get there.

In our pursuit of the Spirit-filled life we begin by accepting that there is such a life; that we can experience it; and that the Spirit who indwells us has the power and desire to bring about great change in our character and perspective.

We begin by accepting what is true as true. Only then *can* we act upon it. Only then *will* we act upon it. Remember, we are transformed in the truest sense by the renewing of our minds, not our wills (see Rom. 12:1–2). Jesus said that freedom comes through *knowing* the truth, before doing anything (see John 8:32). The Spirit-filled life is a life of faith. Faith, as opposed to hope, always has truth as its object. Faith does not create truth. What is true is true, whether we ever accept it or not. The truth that serves as the object and foundation of the Spirit-filled life is (1) the Holy Spirit indwells you, (2) He is the life of Christ in you, and (3) He is willing and able to produce the character of Christ through you. These, and possibly more, are the objects of your faith. Believe them. Cling to them. They are true. And as they become part of your thinking, you will be transformed.

In some ways, this book has thus far been a brochure advertising a place I am convinced you ought to visit. I hope that my experiences have whet your appetite. If you are convinced that this life I have described is what you have been looking for, and if you sense a need in your life, read on. Beginning here, I will attempt to lead you beyond the picture and into the reality of the Spirit-filled life.

Essential Truth

As a child, I had no problem understanding and accepting the concept of salvation by faith. There was nothing I could do to save myself so I simply trusted Christ's death on the cross as the payment for my sin. By placing my trust in that fact, or truth, I was born again. Faith is the way we enter into salvation. It is the means by which we accept God's free gift (see Eph. 2:8–9).

For some strange reason, after entering into this wonderful relationship by faith, I began conducting it by works. It was as if I said to God, "Thanks for the gift. I'll take it from here." I wrongly assumed that it was *my* responsibility to produce righteousness, that God had left it up to me to change myself and become a better person.

How absurd! If I could produce righteousness on my own, why did Christ need to die for me? The truth is, on my own I can't produce one ounce of righteousness, neither before nor after salvation. *As believers, our potential for righteous living is in direct proportion to our willingness to allow the Holy Spirit to produce His fruit through us.* Before June 6, 1964, I thought my potential for holy living was contingent upon my self-effort. So when I failed, what did I do? I promised to try harder next time around. I was convinced that I had a dedication problem. So I was continually rededicating.

The Audition

If you think about it, that whole approach doesn't make any sense at all. Imagine a woman who has no musical ability whatsoever auditioning for the lead singing part in a musical. By no musical ability, I mean she is completely tone-deaf. After the audition, the director calls her over and says, "I'm sorry, but you really aren't qualified for this part. Music isn't your strong suit. Perhaps you—"

"Oh, please," begs the woman as she drops to her knees. "I'll work so hard. I'll practice every day. I'll be so dedicated. I know I can do it. Have mercy. It means so much to me. I know I don't deserve the part, but please let me have it anyway."

Obviously, the would-be soloist isn't getting the message. Allowing her to have the part will not change the fact that she can't sing. Whether she gets the part or not, somebody else will have to do the singing if the musical is to be a success.

The same holds true in relation to our righteousness. We failed the righteousness audition:

> There is none righteous, not even one.
> —*Romans 3:10*

> For *all* have sinned and fall short of the glory of God.
> —*Romans 3:23*, emphasis mine

God, however, because of His amazing love, gave us the part anyway. He did so by applying the righteousness of Christ to our account:

> He made Him who knew no sin to be sin on our behalf, that we might become the righteousness of God in Him.
> —*2 Corinthians 5:21*

By putting our sin on Christ and placing Christ's righteous standing on us, God allowed us entry into His family, a family where only the righteous are allowed. Keep in mind, it's not our righteousness. It's Christ's. Notice the last two words in the verse quoted above: *in Him.* Our righteousness stems from the fact that we are in Christ.

God's motive was His unconditional love. It was not because He thought it would in any way increase our potential for living righteous lives. He knew better. Simply letting us into His family did nothing to reverse our inability to produce righteousness. Unfortunately, most of us expend a great deal of energy acting as if it had. What results is the frustration of knowing we have adopted a standard for our lives that we cannot maintain. So we lean, with reservations, toward adopting as our motto *Nobody's perfect—be-*

If pressure or temptation

automatically pushes you

into the reaction mode,

you are destined for failure

most of the time.

Why? It's a sure sign

that you are trying to produce

righteousness on your own.

sides, God understands. Our problem? We have a tendency to leave faith at the front door.

Trying to produce righteousness ourselves is like trying to grow apples on a grapevine. The two just aren't compatible. They weren't made for each other. In the same way, our unredeemed, selfish, sinful flesh is not tooled to produce good fruit. Far from it. It is programmed to do bad deeds (see Gal. 5:19). And it does an excellent job, I might add.

When we take on the responsibility of producing the fruit of the Spirit ourselves, we are attempting to improve our flesh. And I've got some news for you. In my forty-seven years as a Christian, my flesh has not improved one bit. There has been absolutely NO progress.

The Faith Factor

"So," you ask, "what about all this new potential I have? How does all this potential power that now indwells me interface with my behavior? What brings together my inadequacy with His adequacy? How do I get His power involved with my weakness?"

Before I answer, let me ask you a question. What allowed you to hook up with God to begin with? What was the means by which you—a sinner—entered into a relationship with a holy God? What brought the two of you together? Was it dedication on your part? Was it a result of your unceasing effort? Of course not. You entered in by faith. And nothing has changed.

> Are you so foolish? Having begun by the Spirit, are you now being perfected by the flesh?
> —*Galatians 3:3*

> As you therefore have received Christ Jesus the Lord, so walk in Him, having been firmly rooted and now being built up in Him and established in your *faith,* just as you were instructed.
> —*Colossians 2:6–7, emphasis mine*

> And the life which I now live in the flesh I live by *faith* in the Son of God.
> —*Galatians 2:20, emphasis mine*

These verses attest to the fact that we are not the first generation of Christians who have tried to take matters into our own hands. The early church had the same problem. It's part of fallen human nature to want to maintain control, to do things ourselves. But when it comes to righteousness—whether for salvation or for living—we must allow God to do the work. Producing righteousness falls outside our job description.

The Spirit-filled life is a life of faith. It started by faith, and it runs on faith. It is faith from start to finish.

> *Then* we believed that Jesus was our Savior from the guilt of sin, and according to our faith it was unto us; *now* we must believe that He is our Savior from the power of sin, and according to our faith it shall be unto us. *Then* we trusted Him for forgiveness, and it became ours; *now* we must trust Him for righteousness, and it shall become ours also. *Then* we took Him as a Savior in the future from the penalties of our sins; *now* we must take Him as a Savior in the present from the bondage of our sins. *Then* He lifted us out of the pit; *now* He is to seat us in heavenly places with Himself.[1]

The Bible never makes a distinction between the faith that *saved* us from the penalty of sin once and for all and the faith that *saves* us from the power of sin daily. It is all the same.

Faith Defined

Faith is *believing that God will do as He has promised.* Faith is not a power. It's not something we are supposed to drum up inside ourselves. Faith is trusting that God will honor His promises. That is all there is to it.

Our part in the faith process is fairly simple. We are to go about our lives—making decisions, handling crises, raising our families, and so on—as if God is really going to do what He said He would do. That is what it means to walk by faith.

A Big Lesson

One of the best examples of how this works is also one of the most familiar stories in the Old Testament—the story of David and Goliath. The armies of Israel were lined up on one side of the valley, and the Philistines were on the other side. Every day Goliath would walk down into the valley and taunt the armies of Israel.

Then young David arrived on the scene with a fresh outlook on the situation. Notice what he said when he heard Goliath's threats:

Who is this uncircumcised Philistine, that he should taunt the armies of the living God?

—*1 Samuel 17:26*

David didn't see Goliath as merely the enemy of Israel. He was coming against the armies of God! He was God's enemy. And David knew that God could take Goliath out of the picture with no problem. So David acted on his faith.

There were hundreds—maybe even thousands—of trained Israelite soldiers who were much more qualified to do battle with Goliath. But their response to his threats was paralyzing fear. Stress. Frustration. Get the point?

David, on the other hand, didn't seem to be upset at all. Why? Because it was God's battle, not his. Apart from the Lord, he knew he didn't stand a chance. But with the help of the Lord, he was confident that everything would turn out all right.

Do you see the contrast? Neither party had the ability to do battle with the giant. But while one party focused on its inability and panicked, the other party, David, focused on God's provision. The only difference was focus, or what each was trusting in.

So what did David do? *Exactly what he knew how to do—while trusting God to do the rest.* That is what living by faith boils down to, living as if God is really faithful to keep His word. David gathered a few stones . . . walked down into the valley . . . carried on a short but rather heated exchange with Goliath . . . loaded and fired. Those actions were not out of the ordinary for David. But once that stone left the sling, God stepped in to do what only He could do. And Goliath went down.

Giving God the Green Light

Faith is the Holy Spirit's signal to go into action. David activated his faith before he activated his will. Before he began his walk into the valley, he exercised his faith in the Lord. Remember his dialogue with King Saul just before the big battle?

And David said to Saul, "Let no man's heart fail on account of him; your servant will go and fight with this Philistine. . . .
Your servant was tending his father's sheep. When a lion or a

bear came and took a lamb from the flock, I went out after him and attacked him, and rescued it from his mouth. . . . *The Lord who delivered me from the paw of the lion and from the paw of the bear, He will deliver me from the hand of this Philistine.''*
—1 Samuel 17:32–37, emphasis mine

David walked into the valley in response to what he believed God would do. *His activity flowed from his faith.* He did what he knew to do while trusting God to keep His word. David didn't react to his circumstances. He responded with faith in the promises of God.

Different Valleys, Different Giants

When you are under pressure, are you a reactor or a responder? When you are face-to-face with the giant of lust or jealousy— when your emotions are redlined—do you find yourself thinking, *Oh, God, I know what I should do. I know what I ought to do. I know I should just walk away. But I don't know if I can do it?* If pressure or temptation automatically pushes you into the reaction mode, you are destined for failure most of the time. Why? It's a sure sign that you are trying to produce righteousness on your own.

A responder activates his faith before he activates his will. He believes before he behaves. Granted, David had the luxury of several hours to prepare mentally and spiritually for his battle. Often we have milliseconds!

Your wife casually mentions that she forgot to pick up the cleaning (for the third day in a row) and wonders if you could get it on the way to work tomorrow. Instantly, you are overcome with a desire to remind her of how little you ask her to do and how busy your schedule is.

You are in the middle of your third attempt to explain to your husband the importance of spending time with the kids. Without so much as a nod, he reaches for the remote control and pushes "on." You want to scream.

You are making your way down concourse A—determined not to even look toward the newsstands. You make it to your gate. As you sit down to wait for the plane, you notice a men's magazine lying face down in the seat next to you. Without thinking, you reach down and pick it up—and that old familiar battle flares up all over again. Everything in you screams, "Open it up!"

Every Moment Counts

You may be tempted to argue that there is no time to exercise faith before exercising will. Not in the real world anyway. Things happen too fast. We are usually taken off guard. There is no way to get a jump on temptation and rejection and jealousy. More times than not, we are taken by surprise.

But I beg to differ. We *can* get a jump on it; we *can* make the first move. Let me ask you a question. How many days a week, on the average, are you tempted? How many days a week are you forced to deal with some inordinate emotion that has the potential of doing serious damage to your reputation and relationships if expressed? For me, it averages out to seven days a week. And I imagine the same is true for you. We know it's coming. Therefore, the wisest thing to do is to begin every day by exercising our faith against the anticipated onslaughts.

We don't need to wait until we are in the thick of the battle to claim the promises of God. By that time it's too late. Certainly, there is time to express faith in the Holy Spirit when you see things building. But even better, go ahead and exercise your faith before the struggle begins. And when it does, you will think, *I've already dealt with this.*

Remember, David claimed victory long before the battle began. And we have the opportunity to do the same. Isn't it true that we fight the same giants every day? We just can't time our battles the way David did. But God knows. They never catch Him off guard.

The Holy Spirit dwells in you and is ready to go to work producing the character of Christ through you. All He needs is your faith. His green light is your willingness to say, "Holy Spirit, I cannot handle this. I'm not even going to try. Respond through me. Give me Your perspective on all of this. I trust You."

At that point you do what you know to do and trust Him to fill in the gaps. That is the essence of the wonderful Spirit-filled life. It is a life of taking God at His word and acting on it.

Begin Now!

Why not begin right now? Think for a moment. What giants are you more than likely going to face in the next few hours? What emotions will you battle? If today is like most days, what temptations will you face? Begin claiming victory right now. Activate your faith. Pray,

> Lord, I claim victory right now over the giant of _fears and doubt._ I recognize that this giant is coming against the Christ in me. Just as You defeated this giant when You walked on this earth, You can defeat it through me now, for You are my life. I trust You to produce peace and self-control through me. I cannot handle what is to come. But You can. Respond through me. When the pressure comes, remind me that the battle is Yours.
> Amen.

If you will begin every day with a declaration of victory over the specific giants in your life, you will experience victory. Begin tomorrow morning on your knees. Think through the temptations you will face, the pressure you will feel, and the rejection you are likely to encounter. Item by item, thank God for the victory. Remind Him that at the cross Christ paid the price not only for your sin but for your victory.

By doing so, you activate your faith before activating your will to resist on your own. When the temptation or pressure does come, tell the Holy Spirit, "Christ has already dealt with this, and I have already claimed His power, so handle it through me. I am simply a branch. Produce Your good fruit through me!"

NOTE

1. Hannah Whitall Smith, *The Christian's Secret of a Happy Life* (Old Tappan, N.J.: Revell, 1989), p. 52.

─────── **THINK ABOUT IT** ───────

- First and foremost, have you by faith accepted Christ's death on the cross as the total payment for your sin debt? *yes*
- Are there times when you realize that you are trying to produce righteousness on your own? Have you come to grips with the fact that this is impossible apart from the work of the Holy Spirit? *yes*
- Are you willing to allow the Holy Spirit to produce His fruit through you? *yes*
- Are you able to accept the fact that the Spirit-filled life is a life of faith—from start to finish? *yes*
- In difficult situations, are you able to do what you know to do and trust God with the outcome? Can you imagine yourself maintaining peace in a David-Goliath–type situation? *not there yet*
- Would you be willing to commit to begin every day with a declaration of victory over the specific giants in your life? *yes*

CHAPTER 7

Keeping in Step

❧

When our kids were growing up, Anna and I felt it was important for them to have some responsibility around the house. As is the case in most families, it started with small things, such as keeping their rooms clean and taking their dishes to the sink. As they grew older, the size and significance of their chores increased.

I will never forget the first time I asked Andy to help me with the yard work. He was so excited. I was a little surprised. Boys usually hate yard work. I know I always did. But Andy was really looking forward to getting out and working in the yard—or so it seemed.

Things went great at first. I started out by showing him how to weed. We both got down on our hands and knees and began working our way down the side of the house. We talked about all kinds of things as we worked.

After about an hour, he seemed to have the hang of it, so I said, "I tell you what. You keep weeding until you get down to the corner of the house. I'll get the lawn mower and start cutting the grass."

I got up and went around to the backyard to get the mower out of our tool shed. I had been in there about two minutes when I heard something behind me. I turned around, and there was Andy. "Did you already finish?" I asked.

"Yes, sir," he said.

Well, I knew he hadn't finished. "Let's go take a look."

"Wait," he said. "What are you doing in here?"

"I'm getting the lawn mower ready."

"Can I help?" he asked.

Just as I was about to tell him to get back to his weeding, it hit me. Andy wasn't excited about doing yard work. He was excited about being with me. Until that time, all of his and Becky's chores were things they did alone. It wasn't pulling the weeds he disliked; it was working alone. Needless to say, we didn't get a lot of yard work done that day. But we sure spent some valuable time together.

The Spirit-filled life is a life of working in harmony with the Holy Spirit. It is not a life of struggling alone to please a distant King. There are no solo chores. There are no marching orders. The Spirit-filled life is a relationship wherein two work as one. Immediately following the arrival of the Spirit, this unique relationship takes center stage in the New Testament's description of the ministry of the Holy Spirit. In this chapter we will trace that transition.

A Quick Review

If you recall, I said that the phrases "filled with the Holy Spirit" and "Spirit filled" in every case but one (see Eph. 5:18) refer to the initial entry of the Holy Spirit into a person's life. Jesus promised the coming of the Holy Spirit. When He arrived, Luke records that the people in the Upper Room were "filled with the Holy Spirit." The Holy Spirit came to indwell them.

After the book of Acts, the filling of the Holy Spirit is not mentioned again except for the one instance in Paul's letter to the Ephesians. There, however, his grammar and word order indicate that he has something in mind other than the indwelling ministry of the Holy Spirit. As pointed out, he is talking about surrendering to the influence of the Spirit.

Now all of this raises two questions. First, why aren't there any more references to the filling of the Spirit in the New Testament? Surely in application-oriented books such as Romans and James, there should be some mention of the believer's responsibility to be filled with the Spirit! But there isn't. After the book of Acts, the whole concept of being filled with the Spirit drops out of sight except for once in Ephesians.

In light of that, the second question that begs to be asked is, What does the remainder of the New Testament have to say about

The Holy Spirit

is constantly tuned in to both

our emotional state and our

surrounding circumstances.

He is always sensitive to both.

He leads at the perfect pace.

He always takes our weaknesses

and strengths

into consideration.

the believer's relationship with the Holy Spirit? If being filled with the Holy Spirit is not emphasized, what is?

These are two very important questions. Much confusion has stemmed from people's refusal to deal with the implications of the biblical data or their ignorance of that data. But there is no cause for confusion.

A Time of Transition

When the Holy Spirit arrived on the day of Pentecost, there was tremendous excitement. Keep in mind, the focus of that excitement was His arrival and the manifestations of His presence through those He had come to indwell. The first manifestations were not *character* oriented. They were *sign* oriented. The Bible doesn't say that after being filled with the Holy Spirit, those in the Upper Room went out with great patience, kindness, gentleness, and so on. It says they immediately began talking in other tongues. In that way, the unbelievers in the city knew that something supernatural had taken place.

Initially, it appeared that He came to indwell only those gathered in the Upper Room (see Acts 2:3–4). Soon, however, other believers were filled with the Holy Spirit (see Acts 4:31; 9:17). Everybody was not filled with the Holy Spirit at the same time. It happened in stages. Some have described it as a wave that slowly swept over the Christian community. During that time, some had Him, and some didn't. That is why the author of Acts described some people as full of the Holy Spirit (see Acts 7:55). He wasn't talking about their yielding to the Spirit. How would he know that? He was talking about the fact that the Holy Spirit had definitely come to dwell in them.

At some point, not too long after the day of Pentecost, the Holy Spirit came to indwell *all* believers. Two things lead us to this conclusion.

1. There are no other recorded instances of individuals being filled with or receiving the Holy Spirit—apart from salvation—after Acts 19.

Paul encountered some believers who had never heard of the Holy Spirit (see Acts 19:2). He asked them, "Did you receive the Holy Spirit when you believed?" Why did he ask them that? Because apparently by that time the Holy Spirit was filling people when they believed. The waiting was over!

When the fellows informed Paul that they didn't know anything about the Holy Spirit, Paul was a little confused. The men were clearly an exception to what had become the rule by that time. He asked, "Into what then were you baptized?" It was his way of saying, "How in the world could you *not* know there was a Holy Spirit?"

The men had come to faith under the teaching of John the Baptist. After John was taken off the scene, those faithful men continued preaching his message: *The Messiah is coming!* Don't you know they were amazed to hear all that had transpired in their absence?

The book of Acts continues for nine more chapters. But there are no other recorded instances of people being filled with the Spirit. Within a few years following the day of Pentecost, the Holy Spirit had swept through the world, filling those who had put their faith in Christ.

2. The New Testament authors specifically state that all believers are indwelt by the Holy Spirit.

In an open letter to the church in Corinth, Paul wrote,

> For by one Spirit we were all baptized into one body, whether Jews or Greeks, whether slaves or free, and we were all made to drink of one Spirit.
> *—1 Corinthians 12:13*

Paul felt free to use the term *all* because he believed every believer had by that time been indwelt or filled by the Holy Spirit. He used two figures of speech to describe the filling of the Spirit. We have all been *baptized* into the body by the Spirit, and we have all been made to *drink* of the Spirit.

In an open letter to Christians everywhere, the apostle John wrote,

> By this we know that we abide in Him and He in us, because He has given us of His Spirit.
> *—1 John 4:13*

Like Paul, John believed that believers everywhere were filled with the Spirit. The presence of the Holy Spirit is a source of assurance. We know we belong to Christ because His Spirit dwells in us. Without Him, there is no assurance.

Shifting the Focus

As the filling of the Holy Spirit became more and more something that occurred at salvation, the focus shifted away from His coming to His ministry in the believer. Undoubtedly, some were asking, "Now that we have Him, what do we do with Him?" or "Now that He's in us, what can we expect?"

Paul began discussing the believer's relationship with the Holy Spirit in terms of a *walk*. We are not sure why he departed from the filling terminology. Perhaps he thought it would be confusing to use the same word picture to describe two different concepts— indwelling and influencing. We can only speculate. The point is, other than Ephesians 5:18, Paul never used the filling model again to describe the believer's ongoing relationship with the Holy Spirit. He spoke instead of walking by the Spirit:

> But I say, *walk* by the Spirit, and you will not carry out the desire of the flesh.
> —*Galatians 5:16*, emphasis mine

Two verses later he described what he meant by the term *walk:*

> But if you are led by the Spirit, you are not under the Law.
> —*Galatians 5:18*

To walk by the Spirit is to be led by the Holy Spirit. We are to take our cues from Him. By sending the Holy Spirit to indwell us, God provided each of us with a personal guide, a moral compass, Someone to show us the way.

Paul did not say we are *directed* by the Holy Spirit. That would have presented an inaccurate picture altogether. The Holy Spirit is not out there somewhere directing us like a police officer directs traffic. We are not to envision Him as a controller in a tower telling jets where to land. These examples do not take into consideration the personal aspect of being led by the Spirit.

Have you ever been in an unfamiliar building and stopped someone to ask for directions? Have you noticed how comforting it is when the person says, "Follow me, and I'll show you where you need to go"? There is all the difference in the world between that and someone saying, "OK, what you do is, take these stairs to the third floor, turn left at the second door, go down the hall to the water fountain . . ."

That is the difference between being led and being directed. The Holy Spirit is a leader. He is our guide. He is always with us. He is constantly tuned in to both our emotional state and our surrounding circumstances. He is always sensitive to both. He leads at the perfect pace. He always takes our weaknesses and strengths into consideration.

Being led by someone assumes a continuing relationship. It implies fellowship. It brings to mind cooperation, sensitivity, and common goals. When someone is following another, there must be trust, even to the point of dependency. All of these describe the believer's relationship with the Holy Spirit as the person allows Him to be the guide. *To walk by the Spirit is to live with moment-by-moment dependency on and sensitivity to the initial promptings of the Holy Spirit.*

The Path of Righteousness

I learned a long time ago that one sure way to get a crowd is to announce you are going to speak on the topic "How to Find the Will of God." People want three easy steps to know God's will for their lives—His personal will, that is. On the other hand, announce that your topic will be "God's Plan for Holy Living," and you will be lucky if anybody shows.

As we will see a little later, the Holy Spirit does aid the believer in discovering God's personal will. But His primary role as a leader and guide is to lead the believer into holiness. God's ultimate will for our lives is Christlikeness (see Rom. 8:29), or Christlike character and behavior. Therefore, we should not be too surprised to discover that the Holy Spirit's primary goal as a guide is to lead us into Christlikeness. J. I. Packer writes,

> Twice Paul speaks of being "led" by the Spirit (Romans 8:14; Galatians 5:18). Both times the reference is to resisting one's own sinful impulses as the flip side of one's practice of righteousness. . . . *Leads* is rightly taken to mean "guides," but the guidance in view here is not a revealing to the mind of divine directives hitherto unknown; it is, rather, an impelling of our wills to pursue and practice and hold fast that sanctity whose terms we know already.[1]

The Holy Spirit's primary goal is to lead us down the path of righteousness. Take a close look at what's being contrasted in this verse:

> But I say, walk by the Spirit, and you will not carry out the desire of the flesh.
>
> —*Galatians 5:16*

The immediate result of walking by the Spirit is not discovering which job to take, which person to marry, or which car to buy. The immediate result is that you will not carry out the desires of the flesh. To do one is not to do the other. Paul does more than command us not to fulfill the desires of the flesh. The command is to live in dependency on and sensitivity to the promptings of the Holy Spirit. Saying no to the desires of the flesh will be the natural outcome of walking in the Spirit.

A few verses later we find another reference to walking in the Spirit. This time, however, Paul uses a different and more descriptive Greek word for *walk:* "If we live by the Spirit, let us also walk by the Spirit" (Gal. 5:25). This word means to "be in line with" or "agree with." In the New International Version this verse reads, "Since we live by the Spirit, let us keep in step with the Spirit." The idea here is to walk in such a way as to avoid the moral land mines buried all around us.

A New Perspective

This is such a fresh approach. It's such a positive approach. Instead of being told what *not* to do, we are given positive direction that will result in avoiding those things we have no business involving ourselves in.

Let's face it. Our tendency is to think about all the things we are not allowed to do. Consequently, they become our focus. What we focus on we drift toward. No wonder we don't make any progress. The Spirit-filled life is not a life of DON'TS, it is a life of DO'S. Do walk in the Spirit, and you will avoid fulfilling your sinful desires.

The Mechanics

Walking in the Spirit is not an automatic thing. We have a part in the process. Our part, however, is made possible by what happened at the cross.

When Christ died on the cross, He changed our relationship to sin. Before our salvation, we were slaves to sin (see Rom. 6:20). It was as if Satan had a big collar around our necks with a leash on it. Whenever he pulled our leash, we followed. We might have fought back at times to show our independence, but eventually, he had his way. Practically speaking, we were slaves to certain of our natural desires.

When we trusted Christ as our Savior, we were placed into Christ. At that point in time we were set free from slavery to sin (see Rom. 6:22). The leash was cut. We no longer had to give in to the temptations of Satan or the desires of our sinful flesh. But nobody told us! So when a temptation came along, what did we do? What we had always done—we gave in. But we felt guilty because the Holy Spirit was living in us. And He was grieved.

To walk in the Spirit, you must come to grips with the fact that you are free from sin. Otherwise, you will assume that the tug of flesh is a tug you cannot resist. Your inclination will be to follow your flesh. After all, that's the way you've always done it. And besides, nobody's perfect.

You cannot follow two masters. You will follow either the lead of the Spirit or the desires of the flesh. But you can't have it both ways. I believe many Christians follow their flesh because they really don't believe they have any choice. They have lost the same battles so many times that they have given up. The least little temptation sends them scurrying after their flesh.

Satan can call to you. He can stir up your natural appetites. He can do anything he wants—from the sidelines. But he can't touch you. His power over you is broken. You are a free agent:

> Even so consider yourselves to be dead to sin, but alive to God in Christ Jesus. Therefore do not let sin reign in your mortal body that you should obey its lusts . . . for sin shall not be master over you.
>
> —*Romans 6:11–14*

You may feel the way you have always felt. You may desire the things you have always desired. But the fact is, you are free. Begin now renewing your mind to this transformational truth, for you will never walk in the Spirit until you are convinced of your freedom.

Mind Over Flesh

There is an important relationship between our thinking and our ability to follow the Spirit. Paul described it this way:

> For those who are [walking] according to the flesh set their *minds* on the things of the flesh, but those who are [walking] according to the Spirit, the things of the Spirit. For the *mind* set on the flesh is death, but the *mind* set on the Spirit is life and peace.
> —*Romans 8:5–6*, emphasis mine

Where we set our minds determines who we follow and what we do. To walk in the Spirit, we must set our minds on the things of the Spirit. By that, I don't mean we are to walk around in some sort of hypnotic state. Far from it. In fact, there is nothing mystical about setting our minds on the Spirit.

Paul's point is that we are to set our minds on the things pertaining to the Spirit—not on the Spirit Himself. The same holds true for the mind set on the flesh. It's not thoughts about the flesh itself that lead us astray. It's thoughts about the *things* pertaining to the flesh that get us into trouble.

Jesus referred to the Holy Spirit as the Spirit of truth (see John 16:13). One of the Holy Spirit's primary roles as a leader is to lead us into truth. Therefore, *the mind set on the Spirit is a mind filled with and focused on truth.*

The Battle Before the Battle

Every sinful act is committed twice: once in our heads and once in our behavior. To win the behavior battle, we must first win the battle that takes place in our minds.

For years I was defeated in this area. Part of the reason was that I focused almost exclusively on not *doing* wrong things. My idea of walking in the Spirit was allowing the Holy Spirit to direct my actions. I was preoccupied with good behavior. But no matter how committed I was, at best I was inconsistent.

Not too long after my life-changing encounter with the Holy

Spirit, I saw what my problem was. I wasn't taking part in the battle before the battle. Walking in the Spirit requires a mind-set, a preoccupation with truth. The battle begins not with the temptation to do something but with the temptation to dwell on anything that conflicts with what is true. This is the battle before the battle.

Once I became aware of this, a number of verses took on new significance:

> Therefore, gird your *minds* for action, keep sober in spirit.
> —*1 Peter 1:13*, emphasis mine

> Set your *mind* on the things above, not on the things that are on earth.
> —*Colossians 3:2*, emphasis mine

> And do not be conformed to this world, but be transformed by the renewing of your *mind.*
> —*Romans 12:2*, emphasis mine

> Finally, brethren, whatever is true, whatever is honorable, whatever is right, whatever is pure, whatever is lovely, whatever is of good repute, if there is any excellence and if anything worthy of praise, let your *mind* dwell on these things.
> —*Philippians 4:8*, emphasis mine

No wonder there is so much emphasis on the mind. As the mind goes, so goes the body. When we refuse to get involved in the battle before the battle, there is no hope for change at the behavior level. By then it's too late.

Walking in the Spirit requires that we become hypersensitive to any thought that conflicts with truth. Anything that clashes with what is true is not of the Spirit. Anything that is not of the Spirit only gets in the way of our ability to follow the lead of the Spirit. Therefore, to walk in the Spirit, we must get serious about guarding our minds.

Speculations

Like so many people, I wasn't always careful with what I allowed myself to think about. When I got serious about setting my mind on the things of the Spirit, I realized just how polluted my mind really was. God used one verse in particular to help me get on, and stay on, track in this area:

> We are destroying speculations and every lofty thing raised
> up against the knowledge of God, and we are taking every
> thought captive to the obedience of Christ.
>   —*2 Corinthians 10:5*

To speculate about something is to develop a mental scenario
about it. It is to daydream or fantasize about it. Speculations begin
with thoughts like,

- I wonder what would happen if . . .
- I wonder what it would be like if . . .
- If I had only . . .
- If she hadn't . . .

The ability to imagine is a gift from God. The world's great
inventions were created first in someone's mind. They began as
speculations, dreams, ideas. Everything is constructed mentally
before it becomes a physical reality. The fact that God spoke the
world into being is evidence that our universe was at one time just
a thought in the mind of the Creator.

But like almost all of God's gifts to man, the ability to imagine
has been corrupted by sin. Our ability to speculate is often the
very thing that interrupts our fellowship with the Holy Spirit.
*There is no legitimate place in the mind of the believer for ideas, notions,
dreams, or fantasies that have as part of all their content things that are
contrary to the truth of God.* To entertain such thoughts for even a
moment is to set our minds on the flesh and therefore walk after
the flesh.

To imagine yourself being happy and fulfilled in a relationship
with another man's wife is to dwell on a lie. To envision yourself
telling someone off and winning the respect of others in doing so
is to deceive yourself. To rehearse in your mind imaginary conversations in which you emotionally slam-dunk another person is to
meditate on sin. To mentally devise a scheme where you are benefited at the expense of someone else is to walk after the flesh.
These are speculations.

A New Standard

Look again at the standard by which we are to judge our
thoughts.[2]

- Is it true?
- Is it honorable?
- Is it right?
- Is it pure?
- Is it admirable?
- Is it excellent?
- Is it praiseworthy?

These are stiff criteria. They may seem somewhat unrealistic. But Paul was no hermit. On the contrary, one trip through the book of Acts is enough to convince anyone that he lived right on the cutting edge—and sometimes beyond! No doubt his experience in the real world moved him to lay out such strict mental parameters. He knew how important it is to stay in touch with the Holy Spirit. I believe he saw it as a matter of survival.

Note the aggressive language he uses in talking about this whole issue: "And we are taking every thought captive to the obedience of Christ" (2 Cor. 10:5). This is spiritual warfare at its most fundamental level. To win the battle here is to eliminate dozens of potential battles later on. If nothing else, this statement assures us that we do have control over what we think. We are not victims. The power of sin has been broken.

When any deceitful, lustful, self-destructive thought pops into our minds, Paul says, "Destroy it!" Recognize it for what it is; call it a lie; refuse to think about it; and reset your mind on what is true. And do it immediately!

Red Alert!

Once you set this as your standard, you will be amazed at how quickly the Holy Spirit will alert you to those mental intruders. The Spirit of truth is divinely sensitive to anything that even hints of deception. He knows that to allow even one thought to slip through undetected is to run the risk of breaking fellowship.

If you are like me, you will be shocked at how many times a day you are tempted to take hold of one of these deceitful speculations and dwell on it. I am convinced that most Christians aren't aware of what they are doing. It becomes habit.

As long as we don't follow through with what we are thinking, we usually don't consider our thoughts much of a problem. That is the trap. Without knowing it, we have begun walking in the flesh—and we aren't even aware that anything is different. But remember, "those who are [walking] according to the flesh set their minds on the things of the flesh" (Rom. 8:5). Our mind-set is the chief indicator as to who or what we are allowing to lead us.

Immediate Progress

Nothing I have done has produced more immediate change in my life than destroying speculations and taking every thought captive. I was amazed. The difference was instantly recognizable. Victory became a way of life rather than the exception.

I noticed, too, that most battles are easier to win at that level than at the behavior level. There are certain sins that once we allow the thought to take hold, it's all over. It seems as if there is no going back. When we allow the struggle to become one of, "I know I shouldn't, but . . . ," the success ratio is embarrassing. When I began dealing with the initial thoughts at the door of my mind, it was a different story. Where there had been defeat, I began seeing victory.

The Sword of the Spirit

One afternoon as I was in the middle of taking some intruding thought captive, it occurred to me why Paul called the Word of God the sword of the Spirit (see Eph. 6:17). Viewing the Bible as a sword was not a new concept. But up until that time I had never given much thought to why it was associated with the Holy Spirit. Then I realized that the Word of God is the weapon the Holy Spirit uses to expose and destroy the lies confronting the children of God.

I had always enjoyed memorizing Scripture. Usually, I focused on verses that encouraged me or promised something. But when I saw the connection between the Word of God and my responsibility to take every thought captive, I changed my focus. I began filling my mind with the specific truths that corresponded with the lies I was most tempted to believe.

For example, my flesh takes a certain amount of pleasure in daydreaming about how to get back at people who have wronged me. So I memorized 1 Peter 3:9:

> Do not repay evil with evil or insult with insult, but with blessing, because to this you were called so that you may inherit a blessing (NIV).

When thoughts of revenge enter my mind, I confront that lie with the sword of the Spirit. The lie is that revenge is beneficial to the one who carries it out. The truth is, however, that blessing comes to those who refuse to take revenge.

Another issue I wrestle with sometimes is the question of why God allows good people to suffer. I can't think of anything that has more potential for putting a dent in my faith. Suffering brings into question the faithfulness of God. This verse always puts it back into proper perspective:

> Therefore, let those also who suffer according to the will of God entrust their souls to a faithful Creator in doing what is right.
>
> *—1 Peter 4:19*

If walking in the Spirit is a matter of walking in truth, then memorizing Scripture and meditating on it are the best things you can do to facilitate that walk. The more familiar you are with truth, the easier it will be to recognize error. Scripture is the primary source of truth. It is the Holy Spirit's weapon of choice.

In closing, let me take some pressure off by reminding you that we are not responsible for the thoughts that pop into our heads. We have no control over what drifts through our minds. Evil thoughts are not sin. Sin is grabbing hold of those thoughts and dwelling on them (see Matt. 5:28).

To walk in the Spirit, you must get involved in the battle before the battle—the battle for your attention. That is the only way you can avoid being controlled by your fleshly desires. The focus of your attention determines your direction. Therefore, to walk in the Spirit, you must set your mind on the things of the Spirit.

The Holy Spirit is committed and equipped to guide you. He will guide you according to truth. But He will not override your will and force you to follow. You have a part to play. And it begins with your mind.

It is essential that you remain surrendered because walking by the Spirit involves following. You can't follow and lead at the same time. Somewhere along the way there is going to be a conflict. Somebody is going to lose out. Most of the time it is the Holy

Spirit. As powerful as He is, He never forces Himself on anyone. He simply stands aside and allows us to hang ourselves.

To walk by the Spirit is to live with moment-by-moment dependency on and sensitivity to the initial promptings of the Holy Spirit. It is a life-style. It is my hope that you will begin today.

NOTES

1. J. I. Packer, *Keep in Step with the Spirit* (Old Tappan, N.J.: Revell, 1984), p. 118.
2. Philippians 4:8.

─────────── **THINK ABOUT IT** ───────────

- Make a list of the things you tend to speculate about, your recurring daydreams or fantasies, or some areas in which you tend to struggle.
- Use a study Bible or concordance, or consult a friend who is very familiar with Scripture, and locate verses that deal specifically with those areas in which you struggle.
- Begin memorizing your list. Maybe develop a system of memorization that works well for you. For me, having my verse on a card on the dash of my car is a great opportunity to memorize—during traffic, while stopped at red lights, and so on.
- Practice them aloud. An accountability partner is an excellent way to make sure you will be faithful to your memory plan.
- Ask the Holy Spirit to increase your sensitivity to thoughts that are not in harmony with what is true.

CHAPTER 8

What Does It Look Like?

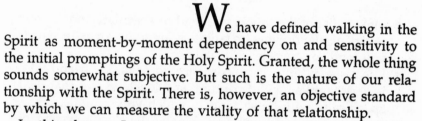

We have defined walking in the Spirit as moment-by-moment dependency on and sensitivity to the initial promptings of the Holy Spirit. Granted, the whole thing sounds somewhat subjective. But such is the nature of our relationship with the Spirit. There is, however, an objective standard by which we can measure the vitality of that relationship.

In this chapter I want to answer the question: What does a person look and act like when he or she is walking in the Spirit? or How do we know when we are and when we aren't walking in the Spirit?

To begin with, recall the vine and branch illustration. What is the compelling evidence that a branch is actually abiding in the vine? Simply being connected doesn't prove they are sharing the same life source. The only objective evidence is the presence or absence of fruit. The same holds true for the believer.

The Signature of the Spirit

Fruit is a public testimony to a believer's sensitivity to and dependency on the Holy Spirit. It is the telling sign. Fruit sets the abiders apart from the producers. It is not simply *one* mark of a Spirit-filled life; it is the *preeminent* mark. When we see fruit in a life, we know without a doubt that the Holy Spirit has custody over that particular child of God. The person is more than His possession; the person is under His influence.

The closer you get to believers who are truly walking in the

98

Spirit, the better they look. There is nothing plastic about them. You don't get the impression that they are hiding something. They radiate integrity. You get the impression you could trust them with your most intimate secret. You may even find yourself opening up to them in a way that is uncharacteristic for you.

Intimidation is not their game. They don't rely on personality and trumped-up enthusiasm to win you over. They seem to be at peace with who they are. And they seem almost anxious to accept you for who you are as well. For that reason, you may feel drawn to them. They are the people you find yourself wanting to be like, not because of a particular skill or talent, but because of the depth of their character.

We are not talking about perfection. In fact, you will hear more apologies from the lips of those who walk by the Spirit than any other group of people. Their sensitivity to the Spirit provides them with an uncanny ability to know when they have offended or hurt someone. Their internal security allows them to respond quickly once they realize their sin or error in judgment. They are not afraid to admit their faults. They have reconciled themselves to the fact that they are sinners. However, they are aware that they have within them the power to rise above their fleshly appetites and desires.

Spirit-filled believers make their biggest impression during troubled times. Then it becomes most apparent that the source of their abiding character is something that lies deep within them. When all the crutches and props are kicked away and they are still standing, no one can argue that their uniqueness was simply a by-product of their environment. They have their down times. They don't win every battle. Doubt and temptation take them out of the race from time to time. But their recovery time is remarkably short. They don't stay down. And once they are back, it's as if they actually benefited from the experience. Specifically, their lives will be characterized by the following nine virtues:[1]

- Love
- Joy
- Peace
- Patience
- Kindness
- Goodness
- Faithfulness

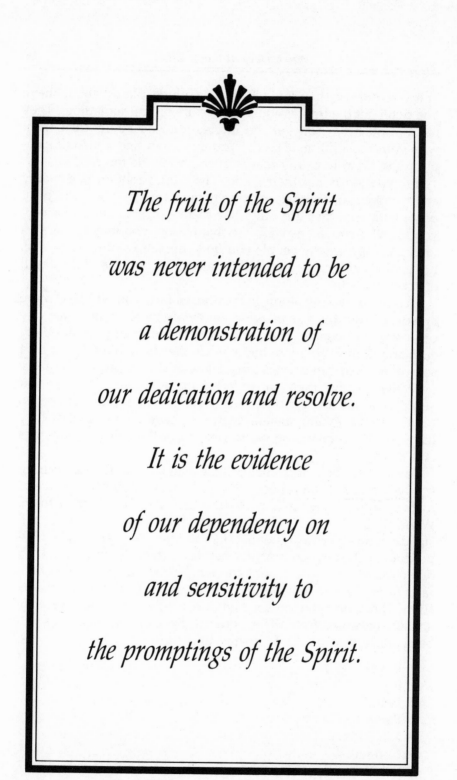

The fruit of the Spirit

was never intended to be

a demonstration of

our dedication and resolve.

It is the evidence

of our dependency on

and sensitivity to

the promptings of the Spirit.

- Gentleness
- Self-control

I have elected not to give a blow-by-blow description and definition of each quality. In some ways an elaboration would be helpful to our discussion. But it also creates a problem. Let me explain. In preparing to write this chapter, I read several chapters in other books that gave expanded definitions of each quality. When I read what each author had to say about kindness, for instance, I quickly became preoccupied with being more kind. I began thinking of all the unkind things I had done and said recently. Then I prayed and asked God to make me a kinder person. I found myself launching out on a mission of kindness.

When I read their descriptions of gentleness, the same thing happened. I realized how abrupt I am. I was reminded of how insensitive to people's feelings I can be. I caught myself telling God how much gentler I was going to be. Do you see the problem?

- "I need to act more loving."
- "I need to be more patient."
- "I need to exercise more self-control."
- "I'm going to become a more faithful person."
- "I . . . I . . . I . . . I . . . I . . ."

I believe there is a reason Paul listed these virtues and moved on. They aren't given to us as goals to pursue. Why? Because you and I cannot produce fruit. Remember? That's not our responsibility. The Holy Spirit is the producer. We are merely the bearers. The fruit of the Spirit was never intended to be a demonstration of our dedication and resolve. It is the evidence of our dependency on and sensitivity to the promptings of the Spirit.

Buckle Up!

I can't think of a perfect illustration, but here's one that gets close. When I get in my car, I instinctively put on my seat belt. I don't think about it. I just do it. But that has not always been the case. There was a time when I rarely wore it. I would go through the routine of, "I know I ought to wear it . . . but . . ." Sometimes I would, and sometimes I wouldn't. What changed me? Was it a matter of commitment and discipline? Did I suddenly enjoy putting on a seat belt? Was it the seat belt law? No. What changed me had nothing to do with seat belts specifically. It had to do with safety.

Years ago the Department of Transportation along with the major car manufacturers began a national safety campaign. Before long we were all convinced that *Seat Belts Save Lives!* Now, to be honest, I'm not all that interested in seat belts, but I am interested in living! The more safety conscious I became, the more instinctively I began wearing my seat belt. Now I don't feel comfortable without it.

I am still not dedicated to seat belts. I never even think about them. I don't think I could describe what my buckle apparatus looks like. Yet it's a part of my life. Why? Because I am dedicated to safety. And seat belts save lives.

The fruit of the Spirit is a by-product of being tuned in to the Spirit of God. The more Spirit conscious we become, the more fruit we will bear. Walking in the Spirit is not about focusing on fruit. It's about sensitivity to the Spirit. Fruit is not to be the center of our attention. We are not to begin the day with a commitment to bear fruit. Our commitment must be to walk in the Spirit. The result of that decision will be the fruit of the Spirit.

A Wonderful Discovery

It is not uncommon for the fruit of the Spirit to take us by surprise. I have seen this happen many times in the lives of new believers especially. Bret is a good example. Everybody knew Bret. He grew up in our church. During his junior year of high school, he got involved with some rebellious friends. By the time he graduated, he had developed some real problems. His parents were devastated. But no one could get close to him. He was a church kid. He already knew everything. After several years of intense rebellion Bret finally came to the end of himself.

Bret reentered our fellowship through the youth department. He felt comfortable around the teenagers, and he believed that what he had been through might be helpful to others. In a short time we saw a remarkable transformation. His anger and frustration were replaced with peace and joy. His intimidating demeanor disappeared, and he became one of the kindest gentlemen you could imagine. He took on a group of junior-high boys as a ministry project and demonstrated supernatural patience. When asked about his old friends, he said, "I'm not even tempted by all of that. My desire for that life-style is gone."

If you ask Bret what he believes brought about the dramatic changes in his life, one answer you will not hear is, "My commitment." I have been close enough to the situation to know that he never focused on change. He didn't set out to master the qualities listed in Galatians 5. When you ask Bret what made the difference, he replies, "I just gave it all to God. I told Him that I couldn't do it and that He would have to do it through me. I just stay focused on Him."

The fruit took Bret by surprise. That's what happens when we get our focus off ourselves and onto the Spirit. Abiding frees Him to do what only He can do. The results are uncharacteristic character, effortless change, and fruit that remains (see John 15:16).

For weeks after my ordeal in Miami, I would catch myself doing and not doing things that were completely out of the ordinary. In what would normally be very stressful situations, I would have peace. Instead of reacting defensively when confronted, I was gentle. As for temptations that would normally take me down for the count, I handled them with self-control. I found it much easier to admit I was wrong. I lost my fear of being unprepared. And the strange thing is, none of that was the result of my determination to change. It just happened. I caught myself being kinder, gentler, and more sensitive.

That is the nature of fruit. It takes us by surprise. We don't produce it; we discover it. As you begin walking in the Spirit, you will walk away from a heated conversation and think, *Wow, I didn't lose my temper.* You will finish a round with your kids and realize you didn't raise your voice. You will be asked to go somewhere you have no business going, and you will hear yourself saying, "No thank you." Eventually you will overhear someone saying something to the effect of, "I don't know what's gotten into him, but he's really different." And you will realize that the person is right. But not because you set out to change. It will happen only when you surrender to the initial promptings of the Holy Spirit. Remember, fruit is not something you produce; it's something that takes you by surprise as the Holy Spirit produces it through you.

Counterfeiters Beware!

The mark of Spirit-filled men and women is the fruit they bear. Fruit is *the* standard by which our walk with God can be measured. The Bible is crystal clear at this point. Yet it never ceases to amaze me how prone believers are to substitute other measuring devices or standards. R. C. Sproul spells it out perfectly:

> It is no accident that the fruit of the Spirit is not elevated in our ranks as the highest test of righteousness. There abides so much flesh in us that we prefer another standard. The fruit test is too high; we cannot attain it. So within our Christian subcultures we prefer to elevate some lesser test by which we can measure ourselves with more success. We can compete with each other with greater facility if we mix some flesh together with Spirit. How hard it is to be measured by our love![2]

The two most popular substitutes for fruit are (1) spiritual gifts and (2) natural talent. We will look at spiritual gifts in detail later. But suffice it to say, spiritual gifts were never intended to be a measure of our spirituality. As we will see, they play a very important role, but nowhere in Scripture are they depicted as a spiritual measuring tool. Even the most fleshly believers have gifts. God gifted every believer. There is no merit in having a gift. And in the flesh, there is no merit in exercising your gift.

It's not hard to figure out why gifts and talents are so readily substituted for fruit. It's easier to exercise a gift than to walk in the Spirit. Not only that, certain gifts and talents have a high entertainment value. When exploited in the right way, gifts and talents can be real crowd pleasers. They can be very profitable as well. You can organize conferences and revivals with gifts. You can administer fund-raisers with gifts. Gifts are a great help when it comes to writing books and preparing emotionally charged sermons. But none of these things are indications that a man or woman is under the control of the Holy Spirit. Jesus had a great deal to say about men and women who substituted gifts for fruit:

> Beware of the false prophets, who come to you in sheep's clothing, but inwardly are ravenous wolves. . . . So then, you will know them by their fruits. Not everyone who says to Me, "Lord, Lord," will enter the kingdom of heaven; but he who does the will of My Father who is in heaven. Many will say to Me on that day, "Lord, Lord, did we not prophesy in

Your name, and in Your name cast out demons, and in Your name perform many miracles?" And then I will declare to them, "I never knew you; depart from Me, you who practice lawlessness."

—*Matthew 7:15–23*

Jesus was warning the people of His day to be on the lookout for gifted leaders who would take advantage of them and lead them astray. They would be men who looked good on the outside but were corrupt on the inside. They would *perform* well. They would know all the right things to say. They would have no problem drawing a crowd. But, He said, there is a way to find out what's really going on. Look for fruit. That was His way of saying there will be a marked contrast between their public performances and their character.

Look again at the specific things the men would be doing—in the name of Jesus. They weren't merely good orators. They would be doing some amazing things. The false prophets would be prophesying. They would be known for their ability to cast out evil spirits. And they would come onto the scene performing miracles. Notice, all very glitzy—spectacular—types of things. Crowd pleasers. People would look at their gifts and think, *These must be men of God.* But Jesus said, "Don't be impressed. Instead, check their fruit. And if you come up empty, move on."

Giftedness does not determine greatness in God's book. Jesus said, "You will know them by their fruits." Not by how *anointed* they may appear to be. Not by the miracles they perform. Not by the revelation knowledge they claim to have. You will recognize God's hand of blessing on men and women by the fruit they bear. *A man who claims to be doing miracles by the power of the Spirit but who exhibits no fruit of the Spirit in his life is either lying or confused.* That's what Jesus said.

To put it bluntly, great preachers are not necessarily great Christians. The same goes for famous gospel singers and best-selling Christian writers. If you want to know what kind of Christian I am, interview my family and staff. That is the real indicator. It is a whole lot easier for me to preach a great sermon on patience than to be patient. Preaching comes natural for me; it's something I'm gifted to do. In the same spirit, R. C. Sproul writes, "It is easier for me to write a book about peace than to practice peace."[3]

Our flesh is performance oriented. Consequently, we will always be tempted to substitute performance for fruit. To do so is to deceive ourselves. Things that come natural for us can easily be mistaken by us and others for spiritual maturity.

- A woman with the gift of teaching jumps at an opportunity to teach a women's class, and everybody marvels at her "commitment."
- A father who loves sports—and happens to have a son on the team—volunteers to coach the church softball team, and he is automatically heralded as a leader in the church.
- A gifted organizer who is tired of sitting at home all day volunteers to work in the church office. She does such a good job that the pastor calls her up to the platform during a morning worship service and claims that she is a "gift from the Lord."
- A gifted speaker gives his testimony in church, and before long, he is being invited to speak in churches all over the city. Soon the word is out, "He's really anointed."

It happens all the time, doesn't it? It's no wonder we have so much division in our churches. As long as talent and giftedness are the primary considerations in choosing our leaders, we are asking for trouble. Think about it. Have you ever heard of a church having problems because it didn't have enough talented and gifted people? I haven't. The church problems I hear about involve people with lots of talent but very little fruit. Many churches are suffering from a fruit shortage. This will continue to be the case until fruit—not talent or giftedness—becomes the number one criterion for leadership. Remember, "you will know them by their fruits." He may be a great communicator. She may be a marvelous soloist. Her books may have changed your life. But are they kind? Do they exercise self-control? Do they love those around them? Are they patient? Don't be fooled. And don't fool yourself. Resist the urge to hold up the measuring stick of performance.

A Distinguishing Characteristic

One of the things I learned early in marriage is that the areas in which Anna and I are different provide the best opportunities for demonstrations of unconditional love. For example, we both love barbecue. So when I say, "Let's grab some barbecue sandwiches for dinner," she doesn't know if I'm saying that because I want barbecue or because I know she enjoys it. But suppose I hated barbecue and she loved it. Then when I suggest barbecue, she knows I'm doing it for her. Differences provide opportunities for expressing unconditional love. When my suggestions are contrary to what she knows I really want, she knows I have her best interests in mind.

This same principle holds true in distinguishing Spirit-filled believers from "nice people." After all, lost people can demonstrate patience or kindness. Just about everybody exercises self-control at some level. So just because a person is patient doesn't mean he or she is walking in the Spirit. The same goes for the other eight qualities. In fact, I have met some nonbelievers who demonstrate more "fruit type" character than many Christians I know.

The thing that sets the fruit of the Spirit apart from its counterpart is that the fruit of the Spirit is not environmentally sensitive. It's one thing to have peace and joy when everything is going your way. It's another thing altogether to maintain your peace and joy when the bottom falls out. It's one thing to love your children; it's another thing to love your enemy.

What is often passed off as fruit of the Spirit is nothing more than the fruit of desirable circumstances or mutually beneficial relationships. This counterfeit fruit has its root system deeply embedded in the surrounding environment. Consequently, when the environment changes, the fruit withers and dies—and it is usually a quick death.

That explains why "wonderful Christian people" can turn into such ogres. It explains why "godly men" up and leave their wives and children. It explains why "model Christian women" sometimes go off the deep end emotionally or morally. As long as a person's character is tied into their surroundings, the character is fragile at best. It is as subject to change as the weather. Those people really are not in control of their lives. They are slaves to their environment. The problem is, nobody knows until the winds of change begin to beat upon their door.

Most people don't ever change. Their surroundings change. The gratification they receive from relationships changes. What appears to be change is simply a reaction to what is going on around them. People whose character is tied into their surroundings will invariably respond in accordance to their environment. They are very consistent.

The peace and joy experienced by an unregenerate man is the fruit of peaceful circumstances. Once the circumstances change, that same man may exhibit a violent temper. The affection shown by a man or woman who is head over heels in love may be only the fruit of infatuation. But once the infatuation wanes, his or her expressions of love may become less frequent. The self-control demonstrated by an employee who doesn't like his boss may be the fruit of wise company politics. But on the day his boss hands him his pink slip—and there are no more perks for being kind—we may see a different side to this otherwise congenial fellow.

Just as unconditional love shines brightest in the midst of our differences, so the fruit of the Spirit demonstrates its divine source when circumstances and relationships take a turn for the worse. The reason is, the fruit of the Spirit is just that: *fruit produced by the Spirit.* It is not fragile. It is not subject to change. Its root is deeply embedded in the person of Christ. When we abide in Him and allow Him to live His life through us, the result is character that endures the chaos of life.

The fruit of the Spirit is

- love—for those who do not love in return.
- joy—in the midst of painful circumstances.
- peace—when something you were counting on doesn't come through.
- patience—when things aren't going fast enough for you.
- kindness—toward those who treat you unkindly.
- goodness—toward those who have been intentionally insensitive to you.
- faithfulness—when friends have proved unfaithful.
- gentleness—toward those who have handled you roughly.
- self-control—in the midst of intense temptation.

The Perfect Example

It is not unusual for men to react a little negatively to all of this. At first glance the whole picture tends to look a little wimpy, somewhat unrealistic in light of the environment in which many are forced to work. As one man put it, "I spend ten to twelve hours a day fighting alligators. If I start acting gentle and kind, they will have me for dinner!" I heard another fellow say, "The people I work with don't understand kindness."

Take courage. The Holy Spirit has never produced a wimp or a failure. Just the opposite is true. Hundreds of believers attribute their success to the changes that took place in their lives once they surrendered to the promptings of the Holy Spirit. Think about it this way. Would the following characteristics increase or decrease your productivity at work?

- Hateful
- Depressive
- Stressed
- Impatient
- Rude
- Insensitive
- Back stabbing
- Rough
- Controlled by passions

Let me ask it a different way. If you had the opportunity to choose nine qualities that would characterize the people you worked with and for, would any of the nine listed here appear on your list? I doubt it.

The virtues embodied in the fruit of the Spirit are all relational in nature. The presence of these characteristics makes a person more attractive, pleasant to be around, and a joy to work with and for. They make for better customer relations, better marriages, better parent-child relations, better everything. You cannot lose by walking in the Spirit.

The best picture of what a Spirit-filled man looks like is Christ. His life was characterized by love, joy, peace, patience, and so on in the midst of a world characterized by just the opposite of those things. He was certainly no wimp. He stood up to His detractors when it was appropriate. But He knew when to keep silent as well. He had the courage and wit to take on the intellectuals of His day on their turf according to their terms. He spoke with authority. People, especially children, were attracted to Him. Even sinners loved to be with Him. He was a very secure man. There was nothing pretentious or intimidating about Him. He didn't need those props. And at the end of His life He tackled the toughest account of all—death. And He won!

This same Jesus, who lived such a remarkable life, has sent His Spirit to dwell in you. His goal is to reproduce Himself through you—the courage, the self-control, the love, everything. Notice what He said to His disciples:

> Peace I leave with you; *My* peace I give to you; not as the world gives, do I give to you. Let not your heart be troubled, nor let it be fearful.
> —*John 14:27*, emphasis mine

His peace is available to you and me. His peace doesn't disappear when the roof caves in. His is the kind of peace that withstands being abandoned by a close friend in a dark hour. His is the kind of peace that survives a mock trial based on trumped-up charges that result in the death penalty. His peace is of such quality that it endures death, even death on a cross.

His peace is not like the world's peace, which shifts with the changing winds of circumstance. Oh, no. His peace is the peace that remains, the peace that finds its source in the unchanging nature of God. The Spirit-filled life is not a passive life. It's not about rolling over and playing dead. It's about reigning in life through Christ Jesus our Lord (see Rom. 5:17).

A Quick Recovery

Spirit-filled men and women are not isolated from what's going on around them. And they are not without their faults. They experience hurt and disappointment like everybody else. They have their daily bouts with temptation.

What sets them apart from the rest of the world is their response. When circumstances wreak havoc with the peace of Spirit-filled people, there will be some downtime. But they won't stay down. They refocus their attention on the big picture, acknowledge the truth that their peace is from the Lord, and then move on. They don't allow disappointment and sorrow to control them. They don't deny or run from those things. But they don't dwell on them, either. They reset their minds on the things above. They know that "the mind set on the things of the Spirit is life and peace" (Rom. 8:6).

When Spirit-filled believers are treated unjustly, they feel the outrage and frustration that accompany such acts. There may even be a period of time in which thoughts of revenge cloud their thinking. But before long, they regain perspective. They refocus on the truth. They remind themselves that "all things . . . work together for good" (Rom. 8:28), and that as believers, they are not to repay evil for evil (see 1 Pet. 3:9). Again, they don't deny the pain; they just look at it differently. They choose not to become bitter. They forgive and move on. Their recovery time is short.

Spirit-filled Christians are not perfect. They still have the flesh to contend with. They can be as unkind and insensitive as anybody else. Again, it's their response that sets them apart. When they realize their sin, they are quick to apologize. Reconciliation is a high priority for them. Believers who are walking in the Spirit do not have a difficult time admitting they are wrong. Their internal security allows them the freedom to be transparent.

In the next chapter we will discuss the relationship between the power of God and the fruit of the Spirit. Before we get to that, however, I thought it would be good for you to take an inventory. Now don't make the same mistake I made. Remember, God never intended for fruit to become our focus. It is simply an objective measure of our dependency on and sensitivity to the Spirit.

NOTES

1. See Galatians 5:22–23.

2. R. C. Sproul, *The Mystery of the Holy Spirit* (Wheaton, Ill.: Tyndale, 1990), p. 165.

3. Sproul, *The Mystery of the Holy Spirit*, p. 166.

─────────── **THINK ABOUT IT** ───────────

- Would you say your life is characterized by the following qualities?

Love	Patience	Faithfulness
Joy	Kindness	Gentleness
Peace	Goodness	Self-control

- What would your best friend say? How about your spouse?
- Is your character environmentally sensitive? Do you lose your peace and joy when circumstances shift? How long before you get them back?
- How easy is it for you to apologize? Is it something you put off? Or do you find it difficult to move on to something else until you take care of it?
- Do the people you admire in the Christian community have lives characterized by the fruit of the Spirit? How about the ones you support financially?
- Which of the nine qualities listed would you most like to see the Holy Spirit produce in your life? Would you be willing to begin praying to that end?

CHAPTER 9

The Power of the Produce

———————————⚜———————————

Nobody enjoys power-hungry people. For the power hungry, everything and everybody are means to ends. They are driven by a desire to control their environment and everybody in it. They don't do well with authority. They can't be trusted. And they usually hurt the people closest to them.

As you read the preceding paragraph, did anyone come to mind? Your boss? Your father? A character in a movie? A business executive? It is easy to sit back and shake our heads disapprovingly at the power-hungry people of the world. But I believe they have a counterpart in the church. I'm not talking about power-hungry pastors and elders. I'm referring to believers who are obsessed with the desire to harness the power of the Holy Spirit.

On the surface, that may not sound like such a bad thing. After all, didn't Jesus send the Holy Spirit to empower believers? Shouldn't we learn how to activate His power within us? Wouldn't we be poor stewards to allow all of that power to lie dormant within us? Wouldn't we be better off if we could tap into the inexhaustible power of God?

Questions such as these have a tendency to make us discontent. They make us think we are missing something; that God has made more available to us than we are taking advantage of. If you are not careful, these questions will send you searching for the wrong thing—in the wrong places.

In my experience I have found that people who talk repeatedly about activating or tapping into the power of the Holy Spirit talk very little about personal holiness. Their emphasis is usually spectacular spiritual things such as healing, miracles, or tongues. There is something conspicuously self-centered about it. The Holy Spirit is treated like an errand boy rather than holy God.

CAUTION: Stay clear of any teacher, preacher, or anyone else who encourages you to do something, read something, or say something to harness the power of the Holy Spirit. The Holy Spirit's power cannot be harnessed. His power cannot be used to accomplish anything other than the Father's will. He is not a candy dispenser. He is not a vending machine. He is not a genie waiting for someone to rub His lamp the right way. He is holy God.

People who are always looking for a way to direct or control the power of the Holy Spirit are confused. *The Holy Spirit was sent to control us!* He is not available to do our bidding. He is looking for surrendered believers to do His. Notice what Jesus said,

> But you shall receive power when the Holy Spirit has come upon you; and you shall be My witnesses both in Jerusalem, and in all Judea and Samaria, and even to the remotest part of the earth.
>
> *—Acts 1:8*

The power of the Holy Spirit was given for a very specific purpose—to enable us to be effective witnesses for Jesus Christ. The way some people talk about the power of the Holy Spirit you would think it was given to make life easier for us. If I read my Bible correctly, life got worse for those who received the power on that day. Most, if not all, of them were murdered or executed! If I am evaluating my experience correctly, it would be a much easier life if I didn't have to be a witness.

The Holy Spirit manifests His power in whatever way He deems necessary to enable believers to be effective witnesses for Christ. I have found Him to be very flexible in form but never in focus. He is out to accomplish one thing and one thing only. That being the case, those who are persuaded of His cause can expect to see the power of the Holy Spirit manifested through their lives. And those who are not will not. We cannot force His hand—not with faith, not with prayer, not with anything. He is God. We would do well to stop trying to harness His power and, instead, focus on allowing it to harness us.

Keeping the Main Thing the Main Thing

The power of the Holy Spirit is manifested in a believer's life through two channels—the gifts of the Spirit and the fruit of the Spirit. We will discuss spiritual gifts in the next chapter. In this chapter I want to look closely at the often-overlooked relationship between the power of God and the fruit of the Spirit.

One reason this relationship is overlooked involves the confusion surrounding the Holy Spirit's power. When we think about power, we are prone to think about the blind being healed, the Resurrection, the Second Coming, and so on. Our minds are catapulted into the realm of spectacle and miracles. Consequently, many are caught up in seeking these things.

But the purpose behind the Holy Spirit's power being made available to mankind was not a spectacle. Neither was it the performing of miracles for miracles' sake. His power was given for the express purpose of enabling believers to be more effective witnesses. If that means healing someone, He can handle that. If that means enabling someone to clearly present the gospel, He can do that as well. But neither is any more or less a demonstration of His power.

We must not allow ourselves to get caught up in pursuing the more spectacular demonstrations of the Holy Spirit's power. To do so is dangerous. Jesus warned the people of His day against the same thing. They became enamored with His ability to do the unusual. Finally, they just came right out and asked Him how they could get in on the action.

> They said therefore to Him, "What shall we do, that we may work the works of God?"

In His answer, Jesus pointed them away from the spectacular and back to the main thing.

> Jesus answered and said to them, "This is the work of God, that you believe in Him whom He has sent."

That didn't satisfy them. They wanted to see more miracles. They had lost sight of the purpose behind the things Jesus was doing. So they tried to con Him into performing another wonder.

The Holy Spirit's power
cannot be harnessed.
His power cannot be used
to accomplish anything
other than the Father's will.
He is not a candy dispenser.
He is not a vending machine.
He is not a genie waiting
for someone to rub His lamp
the right way.
He is holy God.

They said therefore to Him, "What then do You do for a sign, that we may see, and believe You? What work do You perform? Our fathers ate the manna in the wilderness; as it is written, 'He gave them bread out of heaven to eat.' "
—*John 6:28–31*

Like so many today, they were sidetracked by the unusual. But Jesus refused to use His power—God's power—to satisfy man's vain curiosity. Jesus pointed them back once again to the real issue —who He was, why He came, and how to enter into eternal life (see John 6:32–35).

Jesus would not allow Himself to be reduced to a circus act. And He will not allow such a thing to happen today. Men and women who claim to be doing miracles in the power of the Holy Spirit, but who are doing it in such a way as to draw attention to the miracle rather than to Christ, are deceivers. Jesus wouldn't have a part of it then, and He will have no part of it now.

Power, Fruit, and Witnesses

From all that was said in the last chapter, one might mistakenly assume that the purpose of the fruit of the Spirit is merely to make us good people. That is certainly a nice by-product. But there is more to it than that. The fruit of the Spirit is one of two channels through which God releases His power in and through the believer. Whenever and wherever fruit is being produced, God's power is manifested. This power, as expressed through the fruit of the Spirit, enables us to be His witnesses in three ways:

1. It attracts nonbelievers to the body of Christ.
2. It provides the relational qualities necessary to enable members of the body to work together in harmony.
3. It protects believers from the destructive consequences of sin.

An Attractive Invitation

Nothing makes the kingdom of God more attractive to unbelievers than believers whose lives are characterized by the fruit of the Spirit. On the other hand, nothing is a greater stumbling block for non-Christians than believers whose lives are characterized by the deeds of the flesh, especially fleshly Christians who are always talking about Jesus. Jesus said it this way:

> Let your light shine before men in such a way that they may see your good works, and glorify your Father who is in heaven.
> —*Matthew 5:16*

The fruit of the Spirit is the most effective evangelistic tool we have. Nothing is more powerful than a life characterized by love, joy, peace, patience, kindness, goodness, faithfulness, gentleness, and self-control. The most powerful sermon in the world can't match the power of a fruit-filled life. Why? Because unbelievers are not nearly as impressed with what we believe and preach as they are with how we act, especially under pressure. If you don't think they are paying attention, just let out a string of profanity and watch their reactions. If it had been one of them, nothing would be said. But YOU! YOU are supposed to be a Christian! And Christians don't talk that way. At least unbelievers don't think so.

Our light is not primarily in the words we say. It is in the life we live. A life filled with the fruit of the Spirit *is* the most powerful sermon anyone can preach. It is a sermon that leaves critics dumbfounded. Peter says it "silences" them:

> Submit yourselves for the Lord's sake to every human institution, whether to a king as the one in authority, or to governors as sent by him for the punishment of evildoers and the praise of those who do right. For such is the will of God that *by doing right you may silence the ignorance of foolish men.*
> —*1 Peter 2:13–15,* emphasis mine

In a world such as ours, a Spirit-filled life is an anomaly. It doesn't make sense. It forces people to ask the all-important question, "Why?"

- "Why won't you go with us?"
- "Why don't you fool around?"
- "Why didn't you get back at him?"
- "Why are you so faithful to her?"
- "Why don't you sue them?"
- "Why aren't you mad?"

The life characterized by the fruit of the Spirit cannot help being noticed. It stands out like a candle in a dark room. It draws attention. It makes some people uncomfortable. It makes others downright mad. But it will consistently capture the curiosity of a few. There will always be a handful who say, "There's something different about you. What is it?"

That's the power of the Holy Spirit in action—producing fruit—drawing men and women. In Jesus' farewell speech, He drew an interesting parallel between the power associated with the Holy Spirit and the unsaved (see Acts 1:8).

As I mentioned earlier, the power of the Holy Spirit was directly associated with that group's commissioning as witnesses. In other words, they would receive the power they needed to be effective witnesses. Whatever it took to convince people, they would have the power to pull it off.

Today, our world desperately needs to see men and women whose lives transcend the norm. The world needs to see husbands and wives who really love each other. The world needs to see Christian businessmen and businesswomen who put honesty before profit and integrity ahead of a paycheck. This generation needs to see teenagers and college students who haven't just said, "No!" to drugs but who have said, "Yes!" to a life of purity. Our world needs to see some fruit. Real fruit. The kind that remains.

If that is what the world needs to see, the Holy Spirit will bring it about by producing it through us. That is the promise of Acts 1:8. To allow the Holy Spirit to produce fruit in our lives is to serve as a channel of His power. In that way we become His witnesses because He knows the influence of a life that bears fruit. Whereas the gifts of the Spirit are for building up the body (see Eph. 4:12), the fruit of the Spirit is the fragrance that invites nonbelievers to become members of the body.

Working Together

There is a second way in which the fruit of the Spirit serves as a channel for the Holy Spirit's power. The fruit of the Spirit provides the relational qualities necessary to enable members of the body to work together successfully. As I mentioned earlier, the fruit of the Spirit is relationship oriented. The body of Christ is one big bundle of relationships. It is made up of all sorts of people who are expected to work together to accomplish the purposes of God. For this to take place, there must be fruit.

In this sense, the fruit of the Spirit functions like oil in an engine. Without oil, an engine can run only a short while. Eventually, the friction between the parts causes them to destroy each other. And the engine comes to a grinding halt! Sound familiar?

When believers who are not walking in the Spirit come together to carry on the work of the church, it is just like running an engine with no oil. They have all the right parts (gifts) but no lubrication. There is going to be friction. Eventually, there will be a breakdown. We call them church splits.

On the other hand, when a group of Spirit-filled believers get together, there is a supernatural dynamic. The whole is significantly greater than the sum of its parts. Things happen that have no human explanation. You can walk into their midst and feel the excitement and anticipation. It is the power of God. And it is being released as a result of their willingness to allow Him to produce His fruit in their lives. You see, our God loves to draw attention to fruit-bearing believers. Why? Because when men see our fruit, they glorify our Father in heaven!

Divine Protection

There is a third way in which the fruit of the Spirit serves as a channel for the Holy Spirit's power. The fruit of the Spirit protects us from the destructive forces of sin. We discussed this in detail in the last chapter. I bring it up again only to emphasize the relationship between the power of God and the fruit of the Spirit.

When you and I allow the Holy Spirit to produce in us the rare virtues of faithfulness and self-control, we allow Him to provide us with a powerful defense system. Of the nine qualities Paul lists, these two are the ones I need the most when temptation comes knocking. Consequently, I have a tendency to try to produce them on my own.

Consistent victory in my life is never the result of my trying to become more self-controlled. Think about it. How can *self* be more *self-controlled*? Can a wild animal tame itself? Would a puppy ever give itself a bath? Of course not. These things run contrary to natural instinct. In the same way, self is never going to deprive self of something desirable.

Victory comes when I focus not on becoming more self-controlled but on the things of the Spirit. It is then, and only then, that self-control and faithfulness are produced in my life. It is then that I experience the power necessary to overcome temptation.

1-4-19

Moving into Position

The Holy Spirit wants to make you an effective witness for Christ. He is more than willing to manifest His power through you to do so. But first, two things must be true: (1) you must be willing to be used as a witness, and (2) you must be bearing fruit.

The Holy Spirit works through our fruit. He must have something to work with. Once these two elements are in place, watch out. You will be surprised and amazed by His power. You will catch yourself saying things you never dreamed you would say. You will find yourself talking to people you would ordinarily be afraid to talk to. You will walk through open doors that previously would have been very frightening for you.

Each will be a demonstration of the power of the Holy Spirit. He is ready. He is creative. He knows what is needed. He is simply waiting on us to make ourselves available.

——————— **THINK ABOUT IT** ———————

- On a scale of one to ten, how would you rate your witness for Jesus Christ?
- Do you tend to focus on the more spectacular demonstrations of the Holy Spirit's power or on what Jesus considered the main thing—*Who He is*?
- Are you "miraculously" experiencing the power necessary to overcome temptation by focusing on the things of the Spirit?
- Is your life helping to provide the "oil," thus enabling members of the body of Christ to work together successfully?
- Are you willing to be used as a witness?
- Are you bearing fruit through the Holy Spirit?

CHAPTER 10

The Giver of Gifts

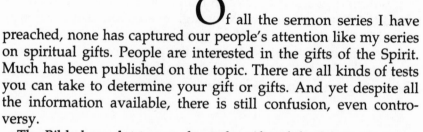

Of all the sermon series I have preached, none has captured our people's attention like my series on spiritual gifts. People are interested in the gifts of the Spirit. Much has been published on the topic. There are all kinds of tests you can take to determine your gift or gifts. And yet despite all the information available, there is still confusion, even controversy.

The Bible has a lot to say about the gifts of the Spirit. And part of me would like to take you through a careful analysis of each and every verse. Instead, I have chosen to limit our discussion to the significance of spiritual gifts in relation to the Spirit-filled life. I believe much of the confusion over the gifts stems from an attempt to understand them apart from the Spirit-filled life.

An Unexpected Reminder

Not too long ago I was photographing in a beautiful canyon. I was walking along the creek bed looking for a place to sit down when the next thing I knew, I was lying on my side with my arm twisted underneath me. Like any conscientious photographer, the first thing I looked for was my camera. Amazingly enough, it was still in my right hand. Not a scratch on it. Slowly, I rolled over to check the damage to my left arm. My arm and shoulder were fine. But my wrist was broken in two places.

I laid my camera down and got up slowly. I began looking for a place to regroup. My eyes spotted a big flat rock a few yards away. I made my way over and sat down. Before long my buddy caught up with me. I told him what happened—or what I could remember.

"How did you keep from dropping your camera?" he asked.

"I'm not sure," I replied. "When I went down, I probably instinctively held it up and stuck out my left arm to break my fall."

After a couple of X rays my doctor confirmed my suspicions. I had used my left arm to break the fall. If I hadn't, I could have really been hurt.

The whole situation reminded me of how dependent each member of the physical body is on the other members. My wrist took the shock of the fall. My legs picked me back up. My eyes located a place to sit down. My feet took my injured wrist (and ego) to safety. And my other hand and arm nursed my injury as we made our way out of the canyon.

Now let's use our imagination for a moment. Imagine that my arms, legs, hands, and wrists all had personalities of their own. As I started falling, my left arm shouted to my right arm, "Hey, you better get ready to absorb some extra weight!"

The right arm responded, "Are you kidding? He's falling toward you, not me! Besides, it's foot's fault. If he had been watching where he was going, none of this would have happened."

About that time my nose joined in the conversation, "Somebody do something! This is going to be serious."

"Don't yell at me," replied left arm. "I didn't do anything. And I'm not . . ."

By that time I'm face down on the rocks with a lot more to worry about than a broken wrist. If the members of our physical bodies acted independently of one another, we would be in a terrible mess!

One Body

The Spirit-filled life is a life of interdependency. We are to remain dependent *on* the Holy Spirit. But we are to live *interdependently* with other believers. Just as the members of a physical body work interdependently with one another to accomplish the will of the brain, so the members of Christ's body are to work together to accomplish His will. The apostle Paul declared,

> For even as the body is one and yet has many members, and
> all the members of the body, though they are many, are one

body, so also is Christ. For by one Spirit we were all baptized
into one body, whether Jews or Greeks, whether slaves or free,
and we were all made to drink of one Spirit. For the body is
not one member, but many. . . . Now you are Christ's body,
and individually members of it.
                              —*1 Corinthians 12:12–27*

Let's take a fresh look at this familiar analogy.

Everybody Is Somebody in the Body

You are a part of a living organism called the body of Christ—or
the church. You are not the entire organism; you are only one part.
In spiritual as well as biological terms, your survival hinges on the
health and well-being of the other members of the organism. Con-
versely, their health and well-being rest on yours. You are not an
independent operator.

If any member of your physical body began functioning independently of the others or stopped functioning at all, you would
take immediate action to correct the problem. You wouldn't dream
of saying, "Well, it's just my lung. After all, I do have two." Or
"I've got nine other good fingers. I'll just work around this broken
one." The members of your physical body are so interdependent
that they make it a priority to care for one another. Back to Paul's
illustration.

> And the eye cannot say to the hand, "I have no need of you";
> or again the head to the feet, "I have no need of you."
>   —*1 Corinthians 12:21*

What is true for the physical body is true for the body of Christ
as well. I cannot say of *any* member, "I don't need you. I don't
need to restore my relationship with you. I can do just fine without you. I can go my way, and it will have no impact on me
whatsoever." To do so is to deceive myself.

Referring to the actual body of Christ, Paul said,

> There should be no division in the body, but that the members
> should have the same care for one another. And if one mem-
> ber suffers, all the members suffer with it; if one member is

honored, all the members rejoice with it. Now you are Christ's
body, and individually members of it.
                                    —*1 Corinthians 12:25–27*

Did you get that? There should be *NO* division in the body. On
the contrary, we should make a priority of caring for one another.
Why? Because when one member suffers, we all suffer—just like a
physical body.

What would happen to a physical body if ailing members went
uncared for? First of all, the functioning members would be forced
to carry the load of the dysfunctional members. Eventually, the
disproportionate work load would cause undue wear and tear on
the good members, and they would begin to break down. An
early grave would be unavoidable. Sound familiar? It ought to.

Take a close look at the condition of the church in America. I see
scores of dysfunctional members of the body either going unat-
tended or refusing attention. I see healthy members doing their
best to pick up the slack left by the dysfunctional members and
working themselves to death in the process. And I see death in
congregations all across our land. Instead of *no* division, many
churches are characterized by division.

Every week, and I mean *every* week, I get a phone call or a letter
from a pastor whose church is either going through or headed
toward a split. I have heard one war story after another. And it
always goes back to the same fundamental problem—dysfunctional members of the body.

My wife and I were driving back from North Carolina not too
long ago on a Sunday morning. As we were passing through one
small town, I couldn't get over how many churches there were.
They were everywhere. And each one had a handful of cars in the
parking lot. I commented to my wife, "Imagine the impact they
could have if they would join together in an organized effort to
reach this city." We passed through several other small towns that
morning, and every one of them was full of churches. Now don't
get me wrong. I am all for people having the freedom to worship
in an atmosphere that is comfortable for them. But I have been
around long enough to know that many of those churches are as
dead as they can be. I can look at the parking lots and tell.

Think about it. Why would a town of five to ten thousand people need five or six Baptist churches? I can tell you why. Because
many of the people in those churches can't get along with one

another. So they compete. Competition between churches—within a denomination or between them—must truly grieve our Lord Jesus Christ! Imagine the members of a physical body competing with one another, one leg trying to outwalk the other, fingers trying to outtype one another, feet trying to outperform hands. A body in that condition would not be able to accomplish even the simplest tasks.

Headquarters

"So," you say, "what's the problem? And what does any of this have to do with the Spirit-filled life or gifts?" Hang on, we're getting there.

If a physical body has a member that acts independently (or not at all), the problem usually stems from that body part's inability to receive the proper signal from the brain. There are a variety of causes. But generally, the solution involves reestablishing proper contact.

Dysfunctional members in the body of Christ suffer from a similar ailment. The difference is that instead of being *unable* to receive the proper signal from the brain, they are *unwilling* to follow through with the order. It's not a problem of ability as much as it is availability.

The Head of the body is Christ (see Eph. 5:23). He functions as mission control for the church. We are to take our cues from Him corporately as well as individually. He has a plan and purpose for His church just as He has a personal will for your life. In fact, the two overlap. *As a member of His body, what you do or refuse to do as an individual affects the whole body.* Your participation counts. God's will for your life includes (1) discovering your niche in the body and (2) fulfilling your corresponding responsibility.

We resist this kind of accountability. Most of us would rather free-lance our way through the Christian life. Being accountable to Christ is one thing. Having to answer to the whole body of Christ is something else.

Regardless of how far you advance in your personal holiness, you will always need other believers. Not because you are weak. Not because God isn't sufficient for you. On the contrary, God planned it that way. It is by His design. Walking in the Spirit is not a solo mission. It is not an excuse for you to become detached and isolated from other Christians. A believer who pulls away from the pack to do his or her own "spiritual" thing cannot be walking in the Spirit.

You cannot walk in the Spirit apart from functioning in the body of Christ. You can't. It won't work. It has never worked. It wasn't designed to work that way. Spirit-controlled Christians do not function as Lone Rangers. They don't buy into the "me and God are a majority" bit. Instead, they actively pursue relationships with other believers. They look for ways to be involved. They don't sit back and let others do the work. Spirit-filled men and women jump at the opportunity to carry their fair share of the load.

Dividing Up the Work Load

A person's role in the body of Christ is determined by his or her spiritual gift(s). A spiritual gift is a special ability. One writer defined it as "an ability to function effectively and significantly in a particular service as a member of Christ's body, the church."[1] Billy Graham compares spiritual gifts to tools.[2] Each member of the body of Christ has been given at least one of these tools to use in building the body.

There is much discussion about the differences between a spiritual gift and natural talent and ability. The Bible, however, is silent on this subject, so I will be, too. One thing I do know is that both spiritual gifts and talent are from the Lord.

Through the distribution and networking of spiritual gifts, God has created a system ensuring (1) that every believer has a significant role in the body of Christ and (2) that believers work together to accomplish His overall purpose.

The Holy Spirit distributes gifts according to His will. And His will is in accordance with the Father's plan for the church.

> Now there are varieties of gifts, but the same Spirit. . . . But to each one is given the manifestation of the Spirit for the common good. For to one is given the word of wisdom through the Spirit, and to another the word of knowledge according to the same Spirit. . . . But one and the same Spirit works all these things, distributing to each one individually just as He wills.
>
> —*1 Corinthians 12:4–11*

Three truths from these verses need to be emphasized.

1. Spiritual gifts are manifestations of the Spirit (see 1 Cor. 12:7).

When a believer exercises his or her gift, it is an exhibition of the Spirit's power through that person. It is not simply a matter of a person doing something he or she is good at. Spiritual gifts are manifestions of the Holy Spirit. This is readily acknowledged when the more spectacular gifts are exercised. For example, we are quick to give the credit to God when someone is miraculously healed. But when someone with the gift of mercy exercises that gift, we say things like, "Isn't she sweet?" or "He is such a good listener." The gift of mercy or giving or administration is no less a manifestation of the Holy Spirit than the gift of healing or the effecting of miracles (See 1 Cor. 12:10).

Now, I want you to think about something. If walking in the Spirit involves sensitivity to the promptings of the Holy Spirit, and if the Spirit manifests Himself through the gifts, is it possible for someone to walk in the Spirit without exercising his or her gift? Absolutely not. The Holy Spirit will reveal Himself in a special way through you, through the exercise of your gift. To refuse to use your gift is to say no to the Holy Spirit.

2. Spiritual gifts are for the common good of the body (See 1 Cor. 12:7).

The primary purpose of spiritual gifts is the building up of the body—not the personal gratification of the individual member. Your nose is worthless apart from its service to the body. And the same holds true of any particular spiritual gift. Its worth is determined by its usefulness and availability to the body.

This should come as no surprise in light of Paul's body illustration. But I am continually amazed at the elitist attitude some believers develop. It's as if they get too spiritual for their own good. This tendency often characterizes those who think they have discovered a *deeper* truth of some kind. They feel as if they are a cut above the average Christian. So they pull back from the body. They say things like, "You know, pastor, I just don't get much from the service here anymore." Notice the *I* orientation. *I* am not benefiting from being here.

The more spiritual men and women are, the more involved they will be with the body of Christ. Why? Because as they give free reign to the Holy Spirit, He will continually lead them to exercise their spiritual gifts for the common good of the body. And that necessitates involvement.

Then there are the people who are against organized religion or who say they worship alone at home. Christians who subscribe to that philosophy are not filled with the Spirit. They can't be. They aren't exercising their gifts for the common good as the Holy Spirit is constantly urging them to do. They have said no to the Spirit.

Don't get me wrong. I know many believers have been burned by organized religion. But whether they like it or not (or know it or not—which they usually don't), they are part of an organized body. A body in which each member has a significant part. A body that cannot function as well without them as it can with them. To experience the power of the Holy Spirit in their lives to His fullest extent, they must get themselves in a position where the Spirit is free to express Himself through them for the common good of other believers. Men and women who are being led by the Spirit will be led to exercise their spiritual gifts within the body of Christ. Those who walk after the flesh will generally make excuses.

When we speak of building up the body, we are not talking necessarily about building a bigger body. The gifts were given to aid in developing a healthy body as well. Spiritual gifts are God's way of administering His grace to others. When we exercise our gifts, we function as the hands and feet of Christ. We are more than representatives. Our gifts allow us to become channels through which the very life and ministry of Christ flow.[3] When we exercise our gifts for the common good, we manifest the person of Christ on the earth.

For example, when a man loses his wife, it's comforting for him to know that he will see her again someday. But that is not nearly as comforting as having friends around to hold him and listen and pray. When believers with the gift of mercy gather around him to listen, when another with the gift of administration takes care of all the funeral arrangements, when a neighbor with the gift of hospitality invites him to spend several nights with his family, when these things happen, it is as if Christ Himself reaches down to take care of one of His own. Through the exercise of these gifts, believers dispense a healthy portion of God's grace to this wounded soul.

When a man or woman with the gift of giving pays another

believer's electric bill, it is God's grace. When a pastor gifted as an exhorter stands to deliver a message, it is God's grace to the people. When a believer with the gift of service gives his or her time to meet a need, it is God's grace in action. In these instances, Christ is at work through His body. It is more than a matter of people being *nice*. It is Christ manifest on earth.

This principle reminds me of the painter who slipped and fell while working on a roof. Just as he rolled over the edge, he shouted, "God, help me!" Almost immediately, his overalls caught on a nail, and he found himself hanging just below the gutter. Reaching up to pull himself back onto the roof, he said, "Never mind, God, this nail caught me."

Like the painter, many believers miss what God is doing. What they see as purely human is, in fact, a divine act. When we serve others through the use of our gifts, we are channels through which the grace and power of God are manifested. When you hear about believers in need, don't just pray. Become part of the answer. Exercise your gift. After all, isn't it a bit strange to pray for someone who has a financial need when you have the resources to meet it? Do you think God is going to create money and drop it out of the sky? Of course not. His plan to meet the needs of His people is *His people*. That is why He has gifted us. When one hand gets a splinter, what does your other hand do? Pray? Of course not. It goes to work to remedy the problem. And when you use your gift to remedy the problem of another believer, you become the hand of Christ.

I'm afraid the modern church has lost sight of this principle. Instead of organizing to meet the needs of the body, we hire pastors and expect them to do it. When a pastor's performance demonstrates a deficiency in one or more gifts, he or she gets traded in on a new model. The new model usually has the gifts the old one didn't have but, of course, lacks the strengths of the old one. When those weaknesses surface, the search continues.

God did not give pastors to the church to meet the needs of the body. Pastors were given to train the other body members to meet one another's needs:

> He gave some as apostles, and some as prophets, and some as evangelists, and some as pastors and teachers, for the equipping of the saints for the work of service, to the building up of the body of Christ.
>
> —*Ephesians 4:11–12*

A local body that does not understand these verses does not deserve to have a pastor. Why? Because until the people do, they will expect him to serve as if he has all the gifts. It's a no-win situation. Consequently, men and women are dropping out of the ministry in epidemic proportions.

The gifts listed in Ephesians 4 are what I call the *equipping gifts*. Their purpose in the body is to equip the other members to carry on the ministry—not to do the ministry themselves.

Several years ago we hired an evangelist as part of our staff. There is no doubt about it. This young man definitely has the gift of evangelism. Wherever he goes, he shares the gospel in a powerful, yet nonoffensive way. But his greatest contribution to our church is not the people he personally leads to Christ. His primary responsibility is to train our people in the art of personal evangelism. As a result of his nonassuming, behind-the-scenes work, hundreds of people have come to faith in Christ. Not as the result of a high-powered week of revival. But through our people who have been trained and have applied what they have learned. Such is the power of the gifts at work.

Think about this. If spiritual gifts are God's primary means of administering grace to His people, what does that say about believers who refuse to exercise their gifts for the good of the body? Four things come to mind:

1. They are robbing the body of Christ.
2. They are forcing other members of the body to carry their load.
3. They are dead weight on the body, dysfunctional limbs.
4. They are out of touch with the Spirit of God.

That is not a very encouraging report. Once again we are reminded that no one is a spiritual island. Our spiritual progress, as well as the progress of the whole church, hinges on our willingness to work together.

What about you? Are you plugged in? Are you using your gift for the common good of the body? Are you encouraging other members of your family to use their gifts? Or do you get in the way?

I know you are busy. Busyness has become the rule rather than the exception. Sunday may be the only time your family is able to do things together. If you travel during the week, you may need Sunday afternoon to prepare for the upcoming week. Your weekend trips to the lake may take you out of the leadership loop at your local church. PTA, Rotary Club, and Little League may make it impossible for you to attend the midweek service at your church or serve on any committees. But if I could be so bold, none of these activities excuse you from your responsibility to the body of Christ. You have an important role, a role only you can fill. Your God-given gift may serve you well in your secular pursuits, but those must be secondary to your involvement in God's work. It is God's will for you and your family to exercise your gifts for the common good of His people. If the church you attend does not provide you with flexible enough opportunities to do so, find another one. But whatever you do, exercise that gift! Peter exhorted the believers of his day in a similar fashion when he wrote,

> As each one has received a special gift, employ it in serving one another, as good stewards of the manifold grace of God. Whoever speaks, let him speak, as it were, the utterances of God; whoever serves, let him do so as by the strength which God supplies; so that in all things God may be glorified through Jesus Christ, to whom belongs the glory and dominion forever and ever. Amen.
>
> —1 Peter 4:10–11

Again, we see the emphasis on the importance of using our gifts to serve others, not ourselves. Peter was so convinced that God ministers directly through our gifts, he went so far as to say that the person who has a speaking gift should speak as if he were actually speaking for God. The one with a serving gift will be serving with the strength of God.

This latter illustration explains a phenomenon I have seen in churches all over the country. When people serve within the context of their spiritual gifts, they seem to do so effortlessly. There is little stress. And they don't tire easily. In fact, they emerge from their service with such excitement that they are generally ready for more. On the other hand, assign that same job description to someone who isn't gifted for it, and it becomes dreadfully stressful. Within a short time the person experiences burnout.

Mary Gellerstadt is a perfect example of what I'm talking about. Mary served on our church staff for several years. Her gifts are in the area of administration and organization. No matter how much responsibility I gave her, she was able to handle it. She seemed to thrive on it. Thinking about her responsibility stressed *me* out! I never saw her get in a hurry. To my knowledge, she never missed a deadline. As long as she was administering and organizing, she was in her element. She looked forward to tackling new responsibilities that called upon her to exercise her gifts.

Then there's me. I spell *stress* A-D-M-I-N-I-S-T-R-A-T-I-O-N. The very thought of it makes me tired. Nothing drains me of my energy more quickly. I dread the aspects of my responsibilities that call on me to administer. Those are the times I'm tempted to call in sick. Unfortunately, in my position there's no one to call!

On the other hand, I can't understand why anyone would be afraid to get up in front of a large group and speak. What an opportunity! I can't wait for Sunday mornings to roll around. Sometimes I am so excited on Saturday nights I can't sleep. Nothing motivates me like preaching the Word. I feel almost no stress preaching. And I'm just as motivated at the end of our services as I was at the beginning.

When we minister to others through our gifts, we are tapping in to the inexhaustible energy and motivation of God. When we exercise our gifts, the Holy Spirit flows through us like at no other time. We are doing what we have been called and equipped to do. We experience an extra measure of energy and joy.

Serving outside our gifts is a different story altogether. I believe this is the primary reason so many Christians get burned out on church work. Instead of finding a slot where they can use their gifts, they sign up for whatever opening there is at the time. They do their best as long as they can take it, then they quit.

I know a man who attends a Sunday school class where members take turns teaching the lesson. To put it mildly, he does not enjoy teaching. He loves the Lord and loves his class, but teaching is not his thing. He dreads the Sundays he is assigned to teach. In his words, "I would rather cut a truckload of wood."

Some misinformed soul may hear a comment like that and be tempted to say, "Well, I guess he isn't very committed!" But nothing could be further from the truth. It's not a question of commitment. It's a question of giftedness. This same man serves on the long-range planning committee for his church. When his church decided to build a new building, it was suggested that the pastor and several members of their committee visit other churches and look at their buildings. This fellow immediately volunteered to fly the group in his private plane—at his expense. From what I know

of this man I would welcome his participation on all our committees. But I wouldn't ask him to teach!

3. Spiritual gifts are distributed as the Holy Spirit wills (see 1 Cor. 12:11).

The last point I want to make in regard to Paul's comments on
spiritual gifts is that the Holy Spirit decides who gets which gifts.
There is much discussion these days about *getting* certain gifts. But
we would do well to leave the administering of the gifts to the
Holy Spirit. The apostle Paul said,

> But one and the same Spirit works all these things, distribut-
> ing to each one individually *just as He wills.*
> —*1 Corinthians 12:11*, emphasis mine

And a few verses later, he added,

> But now God has placed the members, each one of them, in
> the body, *just as He desired.*
> —*1 Corinthians 12:18*, emphasis mine

God has the big picture. He knows exactly how much of what is
needed in the church. From His perspective, things can be kept in
perfect order and balance.

Yet many Christians seek gifts, different gifts. It becomes an
Easter egg hunt; they're always trying to find a new one.

I heard a young lady say one time, "I have nine!"

I leaned over to the man she was talking to and said, "Nine
what?"

He said, "She has nine of the gifts. She has asked for twelve.
Whenever God gives her a new one, she lets me know."

I wanted to say, "Excuse me, young lady, how much of the fruit
of the Spirit do you exemplify consistently?" But that would have
been uncalled for. Besides, she was probably a victim of incorrect
teaching.

One reason so many people get caught up in seeking new gifts
is that it seems as if the apostle Paul encourages believers to do so:

> But earnestly desire the greater gifts.
> —*1 Corinthians 12:31*

Therefore, my brethren, desire earnestly to prophesy, and do not forbid to speak in tongues.
　　　　　　　　　　　　　—1 Corinthians 14:39

Let's assume for the moment that these verses do refer to the acquisition of new gifts. That is, Paul is encouraging believers to ask God for new and different gifts. If that is the case, we have caught Paul talking out of both sides of his mouth. Let me show you why.

He says that no single gift is given to every believer:

All are not apostles, are they? All are not prophets, are they? All are not teachers, are they? All are not workers of miracles, are they?
　　　　　　　　　　　　　—1 Corinthians 12:29

In this list he specifically mentions the gift of prophecy. Then he turns right around and says, "Therefore, my brethren, desire earnestly to prophesy" (1 Cor. 14:39). Now, if everybody can't have the gift of prophecy, why would he encourage everybody to ask for it?

The confusion stems from a misunderstanding of what Paul means by the phrase "desire earnestly." The assumption is that he means, "Ask God for" or "Pray for" or "Work for." But that is not what he means at all. He has already said in three places that the Holy Spirit decides who gets what gift. Why would he encourage believers to pray for different gifts from the ones God has chosen for them? To do so is to express a lack of faith in God's judgment.

The phrase "earnestly desire" comes from one Greek word. Interestingly enough, it appears again in the middle of the same section. But this time it is translated differently in our English Bibles. See if you can find it:

Love is patient, love is kind, and is not jealous; love does not brag and is not arrogant.
　　　　　　　　　　　　　—1 Corinthians 13:4

Did you see it? Believe it or not, the same word translated "earnestly desire" in chapters 12 and 14 is translated "jealous" in chapter 13. What's the connection?

This same word appears three other times in Paul's writings and in every case carries the idea of jealousy in a positive sense of admiration (see 2 Cor. 11:2; Gal. 4:17, 18). So why would Paul choose this term to describe what our attitude should be toward gifts?

Paul does instruct believers to "pray earnestly" about things (see Col. 4:12; 1 Thess. 3:10). But he uses completely different Greek terms. He doesn't mean for believers to pray about receiving new gifts. What does he mean?

Paul is instructing the believers in Corinth to place a high value on spiritual gifts. "Hold them in high regard," he says, "especially the greater gifts." He implies that believers should hold the gift of prophecy in such high esteem as to envy (not covet) those with that particular gift—for that is the greatest gift next to apostleship. When it comes to pursuing something, however, he says, "Pursue love" (1 Cor. 14:1). We can't ever get enough of that. And suddenly we have gone full circle! For Paul defines love as a life characterized by the fruit of the Spirit (see 1 Cor. 13). To sum up Paul's entire argument, "You can have all the gifts in the world, but if your life isn't characterized by the fruit of the Spirit, they don't mean a thing!" Gifts are very important. But apart from the fruit of the Spirit, they are worthless.

If Christians spent as much time pursuing the fruit of the Spirit as they did the gifts of the Spirit, the body of Christ would be much better off. Would you rather work for a boss who was constantly pursuing new gifts or one who was always pursuing new fruit? Would you rather have a spouse who was focused on exercising a gift or one who was focused on allowing the Holy Spirit to produce His fruit in his or her life?

It's the presence of fruit, not gifts, that demonstrates a believer's dependency on the Holy Spirit. Everybody gets a gift. *Possessing* a gift says nothing about a believer's compliance with the promptings of the Spirit. *Exercising* a gift is no proof, either. I have exercised my gift for selfish reasons plenty of times. As the apostle Paul says, the focus of our pursuit should be love.

Discovering Our Gifts

Probably the most common question asked in connection with gifts is, "How do I find out which ones I have?" When people ask me that question, I always respond, "What do you enjoy most about serving the Lord?" Notice, I don't ask, "*How* are you serving the Lord?" I am interested in what they *enjoy* doing.

You will enjoy exercising your gift. You will look forward to the responsibilities you are given that call on you to use your gift. On the other hand, you will not be as motivated for tasks that are outside your giftedness.

Several good gift tests are available.[4] But probably the best way to discover your gift is to serve in a variety of ministry situations. When you find the one that suits your gift, you will know it.

A delightful woman volunteers at a church in Mississippi. She organizes a large youth conference every spring involving several churches from her area. She is a master organizer. The thing people can't get over is that she does it all as a volunteer. And this is no small task. She secures the place, the speakers, and the musician. She organizes a committee to handle registration. And she puts together all the promotional material. She does it all. Hundreds of teenagers have been blessed as a result of her hard work and dedication.

Andy was talking to her one afternoon after a session, and he asked her how she got started working with teenagers. She said she knew God wanted her to get busy serving Him, but she didn't think she had anything to offer.

"I tried working in the nursery, but I dreaded that. Then I thought about teaching, but the idea of it scared me. Then I heard they needed some help putting together meals for our summer youth camp. I thought, *Hey, I can do that.* Before I knew it, I was in charge—and loving it."

The youth minister in Brenda's church recognized that she had skills in the area of organization and administration. His gifts were more in the area of counseling and discipleship. So he turned much of the administrative aspects of the ministry over to her. She had found her niche. She didn't know much at the time about spiritual gifts. She just knew she had found something she couldn't get enough of.

While serving as a volunteer assistant to the youth minister, she began thinking about organizing a youth conference. Fortunately, her church recognized her gifts and encouraged her in her pursuit. The following spring they had their first conference. Last spring they celebrated their eighth anniversary.

Most people discover their gifts like Brenda did. They just get out there and get busy. If you decide to approach it this way, remember that it may take a while. Don't be afraid to change positions every so often. You're not quitting. You're searching for a place to settle in for the long haul.

The second piece of advice I would give you in search of your gift is this: concentrate on bearing fruit, and eventually, you will discover your gift. The Holy Spirit wants you to know what your gift is. Follow His lead, and you won't miss it.

Don't forget. You are a unique blend of talents, skills, and gifts; you are an indispensable member of the body of Christ. You can do what only you can do. So don't cheat the rest of us. Get out there and get busy! For this, too, is a part of the wonderful Spirit-filled life.

NOTES

1. William McRae, *Dynamics of Spiritual Gifts* (Grand Rapids, Mich.: Zondervan, 1976), p. 18.

2. Billy Graham, *The Holy Spirit* (Dallas: Word, 1988), p. 134.

3. This is not to say, as some have said, that we become little Jesuses. Becoming a channel of His life and ministry is a far cry from becoming Him. Second, the fact that no one has all the gifts argues against this view as well. We are no more little Jesuses than an arm is a little person.

4. For an excellent description of all the gifts and some helpful hints for discovering your gift, see *Dynamics of Spiritual Gifts* by William McRae.

——————— THINK ABOUT IT ———————

- Do you tend to be a spiritual Lone Ranger? If so, begin today praying that God will give you a desire to be interdependent with the body of Christ.
- Have you identified the areas in which the Holy Spirit has specially gifted you?
- How can you plug in and get your gifts functioning in a way that maximizes your contribution to the body of Christ?

CHAPTER 11

Doing God's Work
God's Way

W_{hy} do so many men and women who are in the ministry fall by the wayside? I know the presenting circumstances. Some leave because of moral failure. Others just get burned out. But what is the root of all that? Don't you wonder how people serving the living God could become so discouraged or distracted that they would throw in the towel and walk away? In most cases it doesn't make any sense. Sure, there are pressures. But anybody with responsibility is going to face some pressure.

I believe there is a common denominator. Many of God's servants don't do God's work God's way. Consequently, they are doomed to failure from the outset of their ministries.

This is not a twentieth-century problem. It began with Adam and will continue until Jesus returns. There will always be a tendency on our parts to do God's work our way. But to do so is foolish and counterproductive.

Not by Might . . .

Zerubbabel was a man called by God to do an important job, namely, finish rebuilding the temple in Jerusalem. A group of Israelites, including Zerubbabel, had been released from captivity in Babylon and allowed to return home to accomplish the monumental task. They ran into some opposition, however, and abandoned the project. For fifteen years no work was done. Then God spoke specifically through the prophet Zechariah to Zerubbabel and gave him the responsibility of completing the work.

God knew that Zerubbabel and his team, like their predecessors, would face opposition. To prepare them for what lay ahead, He sent specific instructions to Zerubbabel through the prophet.

> So the angel who was speaking with me answered and said to me, "Do you not know what these are?" And I said, "No, my lord." Then he answered and said to me, "This is the word of the LORD to Zerubbabel saying, 'Not by might nor by power, but by My Spirit,' says the LORD of hosts. 'What are you, O great mountain? Before Zerubbabel you will become a plain; and he will bring forth the top stone with shouts of "Grace, grace to it!" ' "
>
> *—Zechariah 4:5–7*

That was God's way of saying to Zerubbabel, "The work *can* be completed. There are no immovable obstacles. And when it's finished, there will be a big celebration."

The Lord's Work

Very few, if any, of us will be commissioned like Zerubbabel. There was no way for him to miss what God had for him to do. It was easy for him to identify God's work. It is not always that easy for us. Consequently, we think of God's work as what the preacher does or maybe church work in general: singing in the choir, teaching Sunday school, serving on a committee, and so on. But that is not all that's involved in the Lord's work. Paul wrote,

> Whatever you do, do your work heartily, as for the Lord rather than for men; knowing that from the Lord you will receive the reward of the inheritance. It is the Lord Christ whom you serve.
>
> *—Colossians 3:23–24*

Paul defined the Lord's work as "whatever you do." Because we are servants of God, everything we do is considered part of that service. God makes no distinction between what is religious and what is secular. We are to consider Him our employer regardless of our place of employment. Just as our earthly employers pay us a wage, Paul said God will as well. Paul went so far as to say that our eternal reward is in some way tied to our performance on our jobs.

Isn't it true that we all need the Holy Spirit to help us fulfill our vocational responsibilities? Every time we pray for someone who is about to have surgery, what do we pray? "Lord, guide the hands of the surgeon." When a woman loses a job, how do we pray? "Lord, provide her with the job of Your choice, where she can be used to glorify You." A salesman who has the opportunity to open a large account will likely request prayer for wisdom. When Christians do an exceptional job in their line of work, there is always an opportunity for them to share the glory with God.

The marketplace is prime territory for doing God's work. He has put us where we are for a purpose. Our specific job descriptions are part of God's overall plan for our lives. God's work is done wherever God's children are found.

All of us who know the Lord—homemakers, bankers, mechanics, assembly line workers, construction workers—are involved in God's work. We are all a part of what He is doing. It takes just as much dependency on the Holy Spirit to do any of these jobs well as it does to preach a sermon or sing in the choir. In some cases it takes more. Many of God's children are forced to work in environments that are completely hostile to the things of the Lord. To be light in that kind of darkness takes a great deal of faith and endurance.

Secular and Spiritual

I'm afraid the devil has fooled many of us into believing that there are spiritual versus secular components in our lives. Any division we may perceive between *God's work* and *our jobs* is a false one. When you were saved by grace, God saved all of you. Once the Holy Spirit came to live inside you, you became a spiritual being. Every facet of your physical life is an expression of the spiritual. You are not two people. The Spirit-filled life reaches into every area of life, including your occupation. In fact, except for your home, your job will be the place where the Holy Spirit is needed the most.

One reason so many Christians are not happy in their careers is that they don't view their occupations as God's work. They see them as jobs. They love teaching Sunday school. They love working with young people. They wish they were in the ministry full

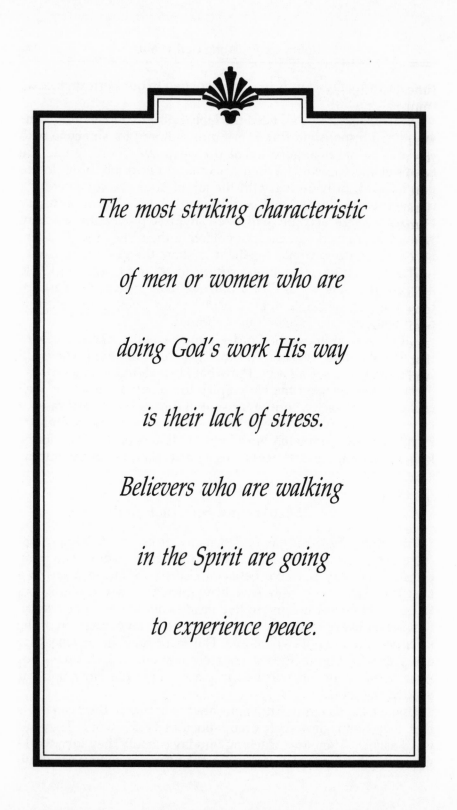

The most striking characteristic

of men or women who are

doing God's work His way

is their lack of stress.

Believers who are walking

in the Spirit are going

to experience peace.

time. But they hate their jobs. Each fails to see that their primary ministry *is* their job.

We don't need more full-time Christian workers in the church. We need more full-time Christian workers in the marketplace with the people who need to hear the truth. Please don't use church work as an excuse to escape from the ministry God has chosen for you. Some people you rub shoulders with every day will never darken the door of a church. You are their only link with the truth. Humanly speaking, you are their only hope. And that is why God put you there. Typing reports, filing records, selling widgets—it's all God's work. Your attitude and excellence on the job are the bridge to someone's heart.

The Holy Spirit is sufficient for you no matter what you are forced to put up with. The quicker the principles of this book begin to make their way into your thinking and perspective, the faster you will see a change in your attitude toward work. I know that because the Holy Spirit knows where you need help the most. And He has a remarkable way of showing up there first.

Two Options

There are two ways to approach God's work. The angel described the first way to Zerubbabel like this: "Not by might nor by power." In other words, the success of this job does not hinge on the things one would consider essential to get the job done. For Zerubbabel, approaching his task by might and power would have meant procuring enough workers and materials for the job. He would also need sufficient military power to protect his workers. The angel was letting him know up front that there was more to the job than arranging for workers and protection. God wouldn't get any glory if that was all it took. Zerubbabel would get the glory. That was the wrong approach.

The first way to do God's work is to do it in the flesh. To work in the flesh is to approach a task with the attitude that God has left us with a job to do and He expects us to get in there and get it done. Doing God's work in the flesh boils down to depending on influence, personality, gifts, natural resources, education, and experience.

Past success and the thrill of the challenge become the driving forces in a project undertaken in the flesh. The assumption is, "I can handle it." And so the man or woman laboring in the flesh sets about gathering the necessary tools, strategies, and manpower to get the job done. Planning and problem solving are approached by pooling the wisdom of the experts. Human understanding and determination reign supreme. And success is measured in terms of numbers, dollars, and profit margins.

I'm not picking on business professionals. Most churches are run the very same way. If men and women know nothing about walking in the Spirit, they are going to approach all of life from the standpoint of the flesh. As long as a church committee is chaired by someone who is walking in the flesh, the decisions of that committee are going to be fleshly decisions. Again, there is no secular versus spiritual dichotomy. What men and women are in one place is what they will be everywhere else. I don't mean they will act the same way. But they will have the same orientation. They will be either in the flesh or in the Spirit.

But What About . . .

"But wait," you say, "I know some folks who operate in the flesh, and they are very successful." By whose standard? I have been around long enough to see the rise and fall of dozens of men and women who were considered successful by the world. They are like flashes in the pan. Or as the psalmist says, "They are like chaff which the wind drives away" (Ps. 1:4).

From singers to businessmen to pastors—those who walk or work in the flesh will have lives characterized by the deeds of the flesh. And a life-style full of that stuff will eventually take its toll. Not overnight. But eventually. No one violates the principles of God and lives to rejoice about it. Be careful about praising those who walk and work in the flesh. Take a long, hard look at all the areas of their lives—not just their businesses or their ministries. It's easy to look good in one area. Only the Spirit-filled life has the balance necessary to be successful on all fronts.

God can't bless the man who is doing His work his way. Working in the flesh borders on idolatry. The self-talk goes like this: "I can do it. I'm sufficient for the task. I've got what it takes. No one can stop me. I'm better than the rest. I'm a cut above." Without realizing it, a person working in the flesh drifts into self-worship. Now, for the unsaved person, we shouldn't expect anything different. *He* is all he's got. *She* is all she's got. We shouldn't be critical. But the believer has no excuse.

When we come to Christ for salvation, we come with an attitude of humility: "Lord, apart from You I don't have a chance." We know that apart from Him, we are nothing. We soon learn that we can't live the Christian life apart from walking in union with the Spirit as well. So to think for a minute we can do His work in our strength is ludicrous. But we are all guilty of trying at some time or another.

A Different Approach

If ever a group of men had the ability, talent, experience, and motivation to carry out their assigned task, it had to be the disciples. Think about what they had seen! Talk about on-the-job training—not to mention their Trainer! And yet, with all that going for them, Jesus knew they weren't ready.

Experience, talent, motivation, willingness, training, clear directives—they had it all. But those things weren't enough. They needed the Holy Spirit. Why? Because God wanted His work done His way.

The second way to approach God's work is to carry it out under the direction of and in the power of the Holy Spirit. In the words of the angel, " 'Not by might nor by power, but *by My Spirit*,' says the LORD of hosts" (emphasis mine). When God's work is done God's way, it will bear the unmistakable mark of the Holy Spirit. There will be something unexplainable about it. People will know that what has happened can never be repeated by simply bringing the same components together. The whole is divinely greater than the sum of the parts. People will be moved by the spirit of the thing rather than the thing itself.

God's ultimate goal for man necessitates that His work be done in the Spirit. He is out to alter the heart of man, to bring about a renewal from the inside out. That cannot be done apart from the influence of the Holy Spirit. Only the Spirit of God can transform the spirit of man. Work done in the flesh goes no deeper than the emotions. It may look very impressive on the surface, but no one is changed by it. Stirred up, yes. Transformed, no.

That is why we should never judge the potency of a ministry by the excitement or crowds it generates. The mark of the Holy Spirit is not excitement or crowds. When the Holy Spirit has been a part of something, you will always find fruit, character, restored relationships, and men and women whose lives radiate the love of Christ.

Wrong Approaches

Here are three things that often get passed off as *God's way.*

1. Praying about it

Doing God's work God's way does not mean simply praying about it. Prayer is essential, but it is not necessarily evidence that one is relying on the Holy Spirit. It may be just the opposite. I've heard a lot of prayers that were nothing more than an attempt to get God to help someone accomplish something in the flesh. That is one reason God gets so much attention at the beginning of a project and so little credit at the end. When we work in the flesh, we forget to express our appreciation. Prayer becomes a formality. It's just something we do.

2. Desperation

God's way is not working ourselves to death and then throwing up our hands and saying, "I give up. Please take over. I can't do it anymore." That's desperation. And usually it's a desperate cry for God to get us out of a mess that we have created (or complicated) by attempting His work our way.

3. The "let go and let God" approach

To be honest, I'm not really sure what people mean when they say this. But it makes me uncomfortable. God has chosen to do His work through men and women. He has gifted each of us for a specific task. We are His means to His ends. To let go and let God implies that we have no part at all. The Scripture clearly illustrates that man has a very important role in fulfilling God's will on the earth.

His Way

In my study of the Scripture I have discovered five characteristics of all the men and women who have done God's work God's way. You will know you are doing God's work His way when these five things are true.

1. They were convinced that if God didn't come through, their project was doomed to failure.

The greatest achievements recorded in Scripture were accomplished through men and women who were convinced of their dependency on God. Read their prayers. God loves to hear His children confess their dependency on Him. The psalmist writes,

> Be gracious, O God, for man has trampled upon me;
> Fighting all day long he oppresses me.
> My foes have trampled upon me all day long,
> For they are many who fight proudly against me.
> When I am afraid,
> I will put my trust in Thee.
> In God, whose word I praise,
> In God I have put my trust;
> I shall not be afraid.
> What can mere man do to me?
> —*Psalm 56:1–4*

The people who do God's work His way don't wait until their efforts fail before they begin trusting Him. They *begin* their projects as dependent people. And in most cases, they maintain their dependent spirit to the end. On occasions when they do begin trusting in their own strength, God always lets them fall flat on their faces.

A self-sufficient spirit is not evidence of self-sufficiency. It is evidence of stupidity! There are no self-sufficient people. None of us have control over our entry into this world, the next breath we take while we are here, or our hour of departure. We are dependent in every sense of the word.

I begin every morning with a confession of my dependency on Christ. Before my feet hit the floor I let Him know what He already knows—I can't make a right move without Him. From my position as pastor to my role as husband and father, I need Him. The only way to ensure that I am fulfilling the responsibilities He has given me—His way—is to approach them from the standpoint of complete dependency.

2. They saw God as their only source for everything they needed.

To do God's work God's way, we must view Him as the ultimate source of all we need. Again, the psalmist writes,

He who dwells in the shelter of the Most High
Will abide in the shadow of the Almighty.
I will say to the LORD, "My refuge and my fortress,
My God, in whom I trust!"
For it is He who delivers you from the snare of the
    trapper,
And from the deadly pestilence.
He will cover you with His pinions,
And under His wings you may seek refuge;
His faithfulness is a shield and bulwark.
You will not be afraid of the terror by night,
Or of the arrow that flies by day. . . .
No evil will befall you,
Nor will any plague come near your tent.
For He will give His angels charge concerning
you,
To guard you in all your ways.
                       —*Psalm 91:1–11*

God will use various people and resources to provide for us. But HE is the source. Remembering that is the key to staying dependent. We have a tendency to confuse the gift with the giver. It is easy to get our eyes focused on the provision rather than the provider. When that happens, our loyalty and trust shift as well. We begin seeking things and people rather than God. Without realizing it, we become idolaters.

God is the source of everything you need. Your children, job, spouse, and friends are only tools He uses to meet the needs in your life. He, however, is the source. Any or all of these things could disappear tomorrow. But your needs will not go unmet. For nothing can separate you from the Source (see Rom. 8:35).

3. They looked for evidences of the Spirit's intervention.

The reason we don't look for evidence of God's intervention is that we don't really believe we need it. We plan and pray as if the power of God is reserved for missionaries and preachers. As long as we think our lives don't demand intervention, we will do God's work our way—in our strength.

If you don't think you need the power of God to raise your kids, you aren't paying attention! If you don't think you need His power to remain pure, you are deceiving yourself. You need His intervention every moment of every day. Those who look for it see it. They catch themselves saying, "Only God could have done that. If He hadn't come through for us, I don't know what we would have done."

If God doesn't come through for you today, what will be different? Your answer to that question reveals how consciously dependent you are. It divulges your self-sufficient spirit. If nothing will be different, you certainly aren't looking for much evidence of the Spirit's intervention. You are doing His work your way.

Plan something so big that apart from His intervention, you are sunk! I'm not advocating foolishness. But it certainly would be nice to see a few more Christians move out on the edge every now and then.

4. They were not stressed out.

Probably the most striking characteristics of men or women who are doing God's work His way is their lack of stress. At times it comes across as a lack of concern. But that's not the case at all. Believers who are walking in the Spirit are going to experience peace. Peace and stress cannot coexist. One will replace the other. When we are convinced that God is going to come through for us, stress disappears.

"Wait just a minute," says the skeptic. "You don't know the size of the projects I'm involved in. You don't know the weight resting on my shoulders."

Let me ask you a question. How does the size of your projects stack up against the power of God? Could you possibly tax His strength? The same Spirit that handles my hundred-dollar need can handle your million-dollar one. He's not threatened (or impressed for that matter!). Besides, what has stress ever done for you? It's done plenty *to* you but not much for you.

God sent the Holy Spirit to dwell in you so you could rely on Him. He loves to impress this stressed-out world by moving one of His children into and through a stress-filled environment with perfect peace. That's His way.

Dealing with stress is a matter of perspective and faith. It takes an eternal perspective and God-centered faith. That's a winning combination. Read the stories of the men and women of old. They often faced life-threatening situations. Yet they faced them with perspective and faith of such magnitude that stress found no home in their hearts.

The Spirit-filled life is not a life without responsibility or pressure. It is, however, a life in which God is seen as such a faithful provider that we are free to do what we know to do while trusting Him with those things that are beyond our control. That is the essence of the Spirit-filled life.

5. They spent more time thanking and praising God than requesting things from Him.

The men and women God used did a great deal more thanking than asking. When we do God's work God's way, we won't wake up every morning begging and pleading. We will begin by thanking. True dependency and trust will always erupt in praise. Doubt will constantly dwindle to groveling and bargaining: "OK, God, if You will come through for me this time, I'll never . . ."

God cannot be bribed. And He certainly isn't honored when our relationship is reduced to bartering. He loves praise. *Nothing honors God like praising Him for what He promised before the promise is fulfilled.* That is the ultimate expression of faith.

Judge for Yourself

So, would you say you are doing God's work His way or your way? Are you operating in His strength or yours? If you are like me, you probably go back and forth.

I have found that nothing is accomplished by operating in my own strength. I end up working against myself. Stress depletes my energy. I begin seeing people and resources as a means to my ends. My prayers become a shopping list. Everything seems to move in slow motion.

But on those days when I'm walking and working in the Spirit, things are different. There is a sense of excitement as I look for God to intervene. The pressure rides about two inches off my shoulders. I am free to love people rather than use them. My prayers are filled with thanksgiving and praise. I get more done in less time. And I don't worry about what I don't finish.

Sound easy? It's not. But it is far easier than working in my own strength. I want to encourage you to copy these five characteristics on something you can look at often. Check yourself throughout the day. And begin doing God's work God's way!

———— **THINK ABOUT IT** ————

When I Do God's Work God's Way . . .

- I will be convinced that if God doesn't come through, my project is bound to fail.
- I will view God as my only source for everything I need.
- I will look for evidences of God's supernatural intervention.
- I will not be stressed out.
- I will spend more time thanking and praising God than requesting things from Him.

CHAPTER 12

The Baptism of the Holy Spirit

❋

No ministry of the Holy Spirit has been more misunderstood than the baptism of the Spirit. Growing up, I always heard the baptism of the Holy Spirit described as an experience that took place sometime after salvation. I would meet people from time to time who spoke of "getting the baptism" or "receiving the gift." In asking around, I discovered that the phrases were used to describe the experience of being baptized by the Holy Spirit. Such phrases are still in use today.

I remember the first time I saw somebody "get" the baptism. To be honest, it scared me. In fact, it bothered me so much that I decided I didn't want it! Unfortunately, it was years before I took the time to dig into the Scriptures to discover what God's Word had to say about the baptism of the Holy Spirit. When I did, I reached two conclusions:

1. The Bible is clear and consistent in its explanation of the baptism of the Spirit; the confusion is unnecessary.
2. There is very little similarity between what the Bible teaches concerning the baptism of the Spirit and the experiences of many who claim to have been baptized by the Spirit.

I decided early in my ministry to allow the Bible to determine my conduct and to interpret my experience. By "determine my conduct," I mean the Bible is my standard for living; it is my code of conduct. When I say "interpret my experience," I mean I will always give priority to what the Scriptures say over what my experience may seem to indicate. I will not interpret the Scriptures through my experience. To do so is dangerous. It elevates me to the place of judge and jury over the Bible. I want God to conform my experience to the truth of His Word.

As I mentioned earlier, I know many believers who have had a significant experience following their salvation. Some have attributed this experience to the baptism of the Spirit. It is not my place to judge whether or not something has happened to these people. I feel it is my place, however, to warn them against justifying or explaining their experience at the expense of the integrity of God's Word. With that in mind, let's take a look at what the Bible says about the baptism of the Holy Spirit.

The Testimony of Scripture

John the Baptist got the ball rolling. As the forerunner to Christ, John had the responsibility of preparing the people for His arrival. Four hundred years had passed since the last legitimate prophet had spoken to the Jewish nation. People were suspicious. John had a challenging mission.

John often spoke about the baptism of the Spirit. He continually emphasized that once the Messiah arrived, He would baptize His followers with the Holy Spirit:

> As for me, I baptize you with water for repentance, but He who is coming after me is mightier than I, and I am not fit to remove His sandals; He will baptize you with the Holy Spirit and fire.
> —*Matthew 3:11*

And again, he said,

> And I did not recognize Him, but He who sent me to baptize in water said to me, "He upon whom you see the Spirit descending and remaining upon Him, this is the one who baptizes in the Holy Spirit."
> —*John 1:33; see also Matthew 3:16; Mark 1:8; Luke 3:16*

In all probability, the people of that day had no idea what it meant to be baptized in the Holy Spirit. They might have had theories, but nobody knew exactly what John meant.

Now the plot thickens. Jesus shows up. John recognizes Him as

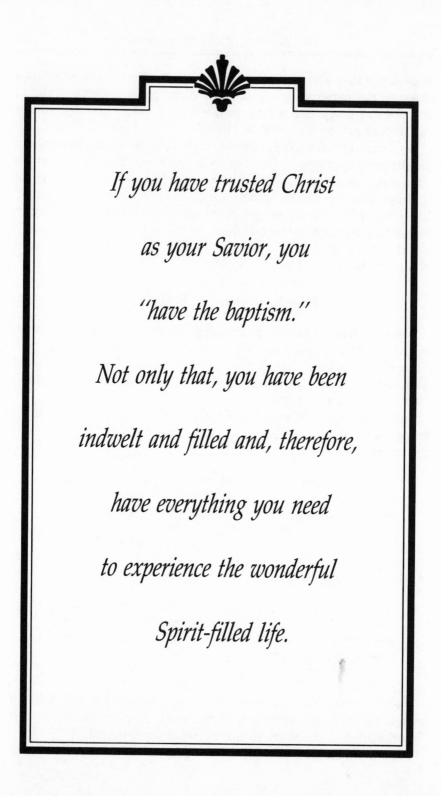

If you have trusted Christ

as your Savior, you

"have the baptism."

Not only that, you have been

indwelt and filled and, therefore,

have everything you need

to experience the wonderful

Spirit-filled life.

the One who baptizes with the Holy Spirit. But nobody gets baptized. For three years we don't hear anything else about the baptism of the Holy Spirit—it seems. Then, finally, the day He ascends back into heaven, Jesus brings it up again.

> And gathering them together, He commanded them not to leave Jerusalem, but to wait for what the Father had promised, "Which," He said, "you heard of from Me; for John baptized with water, but you shall be baptized with the Holy Spirit not many days from now."
>
> —*Acts 1:4–5*

In these verses, Jesus equates the baptism of the Holy Spirit with "what the Father had promised" and, more important, with "[that] which . . . you heard of from Me." Think for a moment. What is He referring to? What had the Father promised? What had they "heard" from Jesus about the Holy Spirit? During His ministry, He never mentioned the baptism of the Spirit specifically. But now He is telling His followers to wait in Jerusalem for the baptism, the baptism that apparently He told them about previously, the one the Father had promised. What is He referring to?

Jesus is referring to a series of conversations He had with His disciples just before His arrest. He promised to send the Holy Spirit after He had departed:

> And I will ask the Father, and He will give you another Helper, that He may be with you forever; that is the Spirit of truth, whom the world cannot receive, because it does not behold Him or know Him, but you know Him because He abides with you, and will be in you.
>
> —*John 14:16–17; see John 15:26*

Notice that He said He would ask the Father to send the Spirit and the Father would do it. Jesus made a promise on behalf of His Father. That is the same as the Father promising the Holy Spirit.

Jesus was describing the baptism of the Spirit. He didn't use the exact phrase. But His comments in Acts 1:5 clearly link the two discussions. He was not talking about two different events—the coming of the Holy Spirit (see John 14) and the baptism of the Spirit (see Acts 1:5). They are one and the same.

Meanwhile . . .

A few days later it all broke loose. The Holy Spirit arrived. But lo and behold, there is no mention of the baptism of the Spirit! The Bible says they were all "filled" with the Spirit. What's going on here?

> And when the day of Pentecost had come, they were all together in one place. And suddenly there came from heaven a noise like a violent, rushing wind, and it filled the whole house where they were sitting. . . . And they were all filled with the Holy Spirit and began to speak with other tongues, as the Spirit was giving them utterance.
>
> —*Acts 2:1–4*

Why doesn't it say, "And they were all baptized with the Holy Spirit"? Isn't that what Jesus promised would happen? Isn't that what John the Baptist predicted? Isn't that what the Father promised?

Absolutely. And that is exactly what happened. They were baptized, filled, indwelt, filled with rivers of living water (see John 7:38–39), and empowered. There is no distinction. It's all the same thing. Jesus, Matthew, John, Mark, Luke—they all used these terms interchangeably to describe the initial coming of the Holy Spirit into the hearts of believers.

Long after the actual day of Pentecost, Luke and Peter added two more figures of speech to the list. Peter was in the middle of preaching to a group of Gentiles when all of a sudden, in Luke's words,

> The *Holy Spirit fell* upon all those who were listening. . . .
> And all the circumcised believers who had come with Peter were amazed, because the *gift of the Holy Spirit had been poured out.*
>
> —*Acts 10:44–45,* emphasis mine

Now we have the Holy Spirit *falling* and *being poured out.* Is this a new ministry of the Spirit? Of course not. It's just another way of describing the initial entry of the Holy Spirit into the heart of a believer.

We know this to be the case from Peter's interpretation of what happened. Notice what he compares the incident to:

> And as I [Peter] began to speak, the Holy Spirit fell upon
> them, just as He did upon us at the beginning. And I remem-
> bered the word of the Lord, how He used to say, "John bap-
> tized with water, but you shall be baptized with the Holy
> Spirit." If God therefore gave to them the same gift as He gave
> to us also after believing in the Lord Jesus Christ, who was I
> that I could stand in God's way?
> —*Acts 11:15–17; see Acts 15:8*

We must allow Peter to call it as he saw it. A group came to faith
and immediately—with no begging, praying, pleading, or
prompting—the Holy Spirit fell. According to Peter, it was the
same thing that occurred in the Upper Room. And it was the same
experience John the Baptist predicted in the beginning.

Now, to really tie it all together, take a look at how the leaders
in Jerusalem interpreted what happened to those Gentiles.

> And when they heard this, they quieted down, and glorified
> God, saying, "Well then, *God has granted to the Gentiles also the*
> *repentance that leads to life.*"
> —*Acts 11:18*, emphasis mine

Why would they bring up repentance and life? Why wouldn't
they say, "Well, then, God has baptized them with the Spirit just
like He did us," or "It looks like God is going to allow Gentiles to
be filled with the Spirit along with us Jews"? Why would they
bring up talk of salvation? Because it all goes together. It is all the
same thing.

The baptism of the Spirit signifies that a man or woman has put
faith in Christ. That is why the apostle Paul could write,

> For by one Spirit we were all *baptized* into one body, whether
> Jews or Greeks, whether slaves or free, and we were all made
> to drink of one Spirit.
> —*1 Corinthians 12:13*, emphasis mine

Every believer has been baptized by the Holy Spirit. Baptism sym-
bolizes our identification with the body of Christ. To be baptized
into the body is to be placed into the body, which happens at the
moment of salvation. Billy Graham concurs:

> In my own study of the Scriptures through the years I have
> become convinced that there is only one baptism with the

Holy Spirit in the life of every believer, and that takes place at the moment of conversion.[1]

The Source of Confusion

You may be thinking, *If it's that simple, why all the confusion? Certainly there must be more to it than that. If not, why are so many Christians convinced otherwise?*

The confusion stems primarily from the delay in Acts between conversion and the baptism of the Spirit. Some believe that to be the normal pattern. So they encourage believers to seek the baptism of the Spirit. After all, the disciples received it later. Paul received it later. The disciples of John received it later (see Acts 19:1–7).

The delay was necessary then because the Holy Spirit could not come until Jesus departed. There was no way around it. Well, there would have been one way. Jesus could have delayed His offer of salvation as well. But that would have made it hard on John the Baptist—not to mention the tens of thousands of Old Testament believers. God's predetermined order of events made it necessary to delay the baptism of the Spirit for those who were saved prior to the day of Pentecost. But something happened on the day of Pentecost that demonstrated God's desire to put an end to the delay.

The First Invitation

The Upper Room phenomena caused quite a stir in the community. Jews from all over were gathered to celebrate Pentecost. When they heard the Galileans speaking various foreign languages, they were amazed. Before long they began asking a critical question: "What does this mean?" (Acts 2:12).

Peter seized the opportunity. He called for their attention and explained in detail what was going on (see Acts 2:14–36). When he finished, the Bible says,

> They were pierced to the heart, and said to Peter and the rest of the apostles, "Brethren, what shall we do?"
>
> —*Acts 2:37*

Peter was ready. He said,

Repent, and let each of you be baptized in the name of Jesus
Christ for the forgiveness of your sins; and you shall receive
the gift of the Holy Spirit.

—*Acts 2:38*

According to Peter, they didn't need to wait to receive the Holy
Spirit. They didn't even need to ask for it. They needed to be
saved. That was the only condition. John Stott writes,

> The 3000 do not seem to have experienced the same miraculous
> phenomena (the rushing mighty wind, the tongues of
> flame, or the speech in foreign languages). Yet because of
> God's assurance through Peter they must have inherited the
> same promise and received the same gift (verses 33, 39). Nevertheless,
> there was this difference between them: the 120
> were regenerate already, and received the baptism of the
> Spirit only after waiting upon God for ten days. The 3000, on
> the other hand, were unbelievers, and received the forgiveness
> of their sins and the gift of the Spirit simultaneously—
> and it happened immediately they repented and believed,
> without any need to wait.
>
> This distinction between the two companies, the 120 and
> the 3000, is of great importance, because the *norm* for today
> must surely be the second group, the 3000, and not (as is often
> supposed) the first.[2]

The only other clear example of a delay between salvation and
the baptism of the Spirit is found in Acts 8. There we find Philip[3]
preaching to the Samaritans and performing signs to validate his
message. A large number of Samaritans expressed interest, and
many were actually coming to faith.

When the apostles in Jerusalem heard about what was happening,
they decided to send Peter and John to Samaria to help with
the work and to check on Philip. When they arrived, they discovered
that the new believers had not received the Holy Spirit. Luke
writes,

> For He had not yet fallen upon any of them; they had simply
> been baptized in the name of the Lord Jesus. Then they began
> laying their hands on them, and they were receiving the Holy
> Spirit.

—*Acts 8:16–17*

Some use this incident to support the idea that the baptism of the Holy Spirit comes by way of laying on of hands. But that is not the point here at all. If that was all there was to it, Philip could have laid his hands on the new believers. After all, God was performing miracles through the hands of Philip (see Acts 8:6). Why didn't he lay *his* hands on this group? Why did they have to wait for Peter and John?

As you may know, the Jews despised the Samaritans. They considered them half-breeds. It wasn't unusual for Jews to travel miles out of their way to avoid going through Samaritan-held territory. Use your imagination. If the Samaritan believers had automatically received the Holy Spirit the day Philip preached to them, what do you think would have happened? There would have been a First Church of the Samaritans and a First Church of Jerusalem. The delay forced the Jews to acknowledge the fact that their God had áccepted the Samaritans just like He accepted them. The delay united the early church.

The significance of this incident is not the delay. Neither is it the relationship between the laying on of hands and the baptism of the Spirit. The significance is that the apostles had to lay their hands on the Samaritan believers. In doing so, they put their stamp of approval on the Samaritan missionary movement.

The Haves and the Have-Nots

About once every two or three months someone will walk up to me and ask me if I have the baptism. I always answer, "Yes." Sometimes I elaborate, "But not in the way you are thinking." What disturbs me most about that question is that it sets up a false dichotomy in the body of Christ. Remember; one of the roles of the Holy Spirit is to enable believers to work together, to build unity in the body. The "do you or don't you" mentality works against the unity of the body. Therefore, it cannot be of the Spirit.

The Bible does not support the notion that one group of believers has the baptism and another group does not: "There are not two levels of believers—gifted and non-gifted, baptized in the Spirit and not baptized in the Spirit."[4] This way of thinking flies in the face of everything the Bible teaches about spiritual gifts and the body of Christ.

I have talked to dozens of sincere believers who claim that the baptism of the Spirit dramatically improved their Christian experience. Their prayer lives are better, they have more boldness, and their hunger for the Word has increased. I say, "FANTASTIC!" I am all for an enhanced Christian experience. "But why," I ask them, "do you have to call whatever happened to you the baptism of the Spirit? Call it something else. You are just confusing the issue." Some have responded by calling it "the second baptism of the Spirit." That's even worse. The Bible never speaks of a second baptism of the Spirit.

As I said in the beginning of this chapter, my job is not to judge the rightness or wrongness of a believer's experience. An experience is an experience. But I cannot stand by silently and watch people misuse the Word of God to validate their experiences. R. C. Sproul says it beautifully,

> I am delighted to hear of increased faith, zeal, earnestness in prayer, and the rest. My concern is not with the meaningfulness of the experience but with the understanding of the meaning of the experience. It is the interpretation of the experience that tends to go against Scripture. Our authority is not our experience but the Word of God.[5]

Andy told me a funny story that illustrates what I am trying to say. Several months ago he began leading a worship service on our new property. Three or four months prior to the starting date he was unable to sleep. He couldn't get the new worship service off his mind. He said he would lie there praying about it until the early hours of the morning. Night after night this went on. After two or three days he started getting up and going into the other bedroom to pray. He was convinced the Lord was keeping him up to pray. When he told me what was happening, he was so excited about what God was doing in his prayer life. "I'm not even tired the next day," he said.

After two weeks of this, his wife got a little concerned. He had been on some medication for the flu, and Sandra thought there might be a connection. She called the doctor. Sure enough, one of the things he was taking was a stimulant. Andy quit taking that particular pill and started sleeping like a baby. So much for his amazing prayer life! I believe God honored Andy's prayers. But the fact remains—Andy misinterpreted what was happening.

I was reminded once again of how easy it is to misinterpret our experiences. We have to be careful. It's dangerous to jump to conclusions. As long as we align the interpretations of our experiences with the teaching of Scripture, we will be fine. But when we use the Bible to sanction the validity of *our* interpretations, we get into trouble. If you have trusted Christ as your Savior, you "have the baptism." Not only that, you have been indwelt, filled, and therefore have everything you need to experience the wonderful Spirit-filled life.

NOTES

1. Billy Graham, *The Holy Spirit* (Dallas: Word, 1988), p. 62.

2. John R. Stott, *Baptism and Fullness* (London: Inter-Varsity Press, 1975), pp. 28f.

3. See Acts 6:5 for background on Philip.

4. R. C. Sproul, *The Mystery of the Holy Spirit* (Wheaton, Ill.: Tyndale, 1990), p. 157.

5. Sproul, *The Mystery of the Holy Spirit,* p. 158.

———— THINK ABOUT IT ————

- What have you been taught about the baptism of the Holy Spirit during your Christian experience?
- Have you ever had a spiritual experience that you misinterpreted? Explain what caused your mistake.
- Why is there so much confusion about the baptism of the Holy Spirit among believers?
- What are the dangers of this confusion?
- Reread 1 Corinthians 12:13 and Acts 2:38. Spend some time thinking about these verses' assurance that if you have trusted Christ as your Savior, you have been baptized in the Holy Spirit.

PART THREE

Looking Ahead

The Holy Spirit's role in decision making

And when they had come to Mysia,
they were trying to go into Bithynia, and
the Spirit of Jesus did not permit them.
—*Acts 16:7*

CHAPTER 13

The Holy Spirit: Our Guide

Not long ago I was photographing in the Bahamas on a little island called Inagua. There is a small commercial port on the island where salt ships dock to load huge quantities of salt for export. As I was watching the activity around the docks, I noticed three large wooden posts. They were lined up several yards apart off to one side of the area where the ships enter the loading area. The posts—or towers—were approximately fifty feet high, and each had a light on top.

Having spent seven years in Miami, I was familiar with buoys and channel markers. So I assumed the posts functioned as some sort of guidance system for the ships. But since they were on land and not out in the channel, I couldn't figure out exactly how they worked. So I asked.

The shape of Inagua forms a natural harbor. For the most part, the water leading into the harbor is too shallow for ships to enter. There is one deep but narrow channel that leads straight into the protected harbor. The three posts guide the salt ships through the channel and ensure they don't veer to the left or right (or for you purists, port or starboard). As the freighter's captain begins to make his way through the channel, he aligns the three posts so it looks from his perspective as if there is only one post. In this way, he knows he is in the channel.

Spiritual Markers

One of the primary roles of the Holy Spirit is that of a guide. Yet it is not always easy to discern His voice. People often ask me, "How do I know who is talking to me? How can I tell the difference between my thoughts and God's?" In the following chapters we are going to look at some spiritual markers that will always line up when the Holy Spirit is guiding us. Since God is not the author of confusion, He does not want us to be confused about an area as vital as this one. So He has given us some clear channel markers to ensure that we stay right on course with His will for our lives.

Before we jump into an in-depth look at each marker, I want to pause and focus your attention on something Jesus said concerning the Holy Spirit as a guide. In talking to the disciples about this very issue, Jesus said,

> But when He, the Spirit of truth, comes, He will *guide* you into all the truth; for He will not speak on His own initiative, but whatever He hears, He will speak; and He will disclose to you what is to come.
>
> —*John 16:13*, emphasis mine

This verse speaks volumes, but we need to consider four key truths before we go any further in our discussion.

1. The Holy Spirit will guide us.

The emphasis is on the word *guide*. Jesus doesn't promise that the Holy Spirit will *control* us. He doesn't promise that He will *drive* us. He doesn't say that the Holy Spirit will *force* us to do anything. He says He will *guide* us.

Granted, there are times when I wish the Holy Spirit would control me. For instance, when I am tempted. Or when I become so task oriented that I become insensitive. Or when it's a beautiful Saturday afternoon and I need to study, but everything in me wants to grab my camera and head for the mountains. Life would be much easier—and I would be a much more enjoyable person—if the Holy Spirit would reach out and take control of me.

But that is not the case. He is our guide, not our controller. At no point do we lose our ability to choose to follow His leading. Consequently, we are always responsible for our words and actions.

2. The Holy Spirit is a trustworthy guide.

The Holy Spirit is called the Spirit of *truth*. He guides believers into truth and according to what is true. That makes Him a trustworthy guide.

The Holy Spirit helps believers discern between what is true and what is not; what is wise and what is foolish; what is best and what is simply OK. Each day is full of decisions. Most of our decisions concern issues not clearly spelled out in the Scriptures, for example, where to attend school, whether to hire a particular applicant, how much to budget for vacation, on and on it goes.

As you are barraged with the details of everyday living, the Holy Spirit will guide you. He will give you that extra on-the-spot sense of discernment you need to make both big and small decisions. And the wonderful thing is that as you develop a greater sensitivity to His guidance, you will worry much less about the decisions you make. Why? Because the Holy Spirit is a trustworthy guide.

3. The Holy Spirit is God's mouthpiece to believers.

The Holy Spirit does not speak on His own. Like Christ, this member of the Trinity has willingly submitted to the authority of the Father. Everything He communicates to us is directly from the Father: "He will not speak on His own initiative."

God has chosen to communicate to His children through the Holy Spirit (see Acts 11:12). He is God's mouthpiece to believers. When God chooses to speak directly to you, it will be through the Holy Spirit.

When you think about it, this really makes perfect sense. After all, where does the Holy Spirit reside? In you! And in me! Therefore, He is the perfect candidate for communicating God's will to Christians. Living inside us, He has direct access to our minds, emotions, and consciences.

4. The Holy Spirit speaks.

The question of whether God still speaks today is one that has spawned numerous books, articles, and lectures. It is not my purpose to present a tightly woven argument about why I believe God still speaks today. Suffice it to say, I do believe God, through the Holy Spirit, communicates directly with believers. No, I don't write these revelations in the back of my Bible and call them inspired. Neither do I run around telling everybody what "God told me."

My experience (as well as the experience of many godly men and women) is that the Holy Spirit, at the prompting of the heavenly Father, still communicates with believers today. In the following pages I will describe several occasions when I feel the Holy Spirit spoke to me. None of them were audible. But that shouldn't come as much of a surprise. The Holy Spirit indwells me. He doesn't need my ears. What He needs is a listening heart and a renewed mind.

The book of Acts records several occasions when the Holy Spirit spoke to Paul and Peter (see 11:12; 13:2; 16:6; 20:23). It can't be denied that those men had a special gift and call upon their lives. They were apostles, men handpicked by Christ to take the gospel to the world. But the same Holy Spirit that indwelt those men indwells every believer. Just as they needed divine direction at critical times in their lives, we need it today.

In his letters to the Christians in Rome and Galatia, the apostle Paul refers to believers as "led by the Spirit" (Rom. 8:14; Gal. 5:18). It would be difficult to lead someone you were not communicating with. The same is true for the Holy Spirit. If we are going to be led by the Holy Spirit, we can only assume He is more than willing (and able) to communicate with us.

Confessions

I have not always looked to the Holy Spirit for guidance. It wasn't because I didn't think He was trustworthy. And it wasn't because I didn't think He was able. To be honest, for a long time I wasn't convinced that God was interested in guiding me. I wasn't convinced that God really cared about my everyday decisions. Decisions that affected our church were one thing, but most decisions are hardly that monumental. I had a difficult time believing that God took interest in the details of my life. At times I have felt a little guilty bothering Him with the mundane decisions that fill my time.

Maybe you have had similar doubts. I talk to Christians all the time who struggle with this issue: "Does He really care where I go to college? Does it really matter which job I take? Does it make any difference which house we buy? Does God really care about where our kids attend elementary school?" I would catch myself thinking, *How could the God of the universe—who is watching events in important places such as Washington, the Middle East, and Moscow —how could He really take my puny decisions seriously?* So, I went to Him with the big things and did my best to handle the little things on my own. Don't get me wrong. I prayed about the small things. I always prayed. But I didn't really expect any divine guidance, so I didn't look for any. I just took everything in stride and did the best I could.

Then one day a very familiar passage of Scripture took on new significance for me:

> Humble yourselves, therefore, under the mighty hand of God,
> that He may exalt you at the proper time, casting all your
> anxiety upon Him, because He cares for you.
> —*1 Peter 5:6–7*

Suddenly, it dawned on me. If God encourages me to unload on Him all the things that are worrying me, it must be for a reason. According to this passage, the reason is, *He really cares about me.* He's not too busy to care about the things that concern me.

If you have kids, you experience this phenomenon all the time. They come running in with what they believe is a major crisis. But to you, in your adult world, it is no crisis at all. How do you respond? You bend down and listen intently. You take them in your arms and assure them that everything will be all right. When you can, you work to help them solve their problem. Why? Because of the nature of the crisis? No! Because it affects someone you care for.

When you are concerned, God is concerned. Jesus echoed this idea in the Sermon on the Mount when He said,

> Do not be anxious then, saying, "What shall we eat?" or
> "What shall we drink?" or "With what shall we clothe our-
> selves?" . . . for *your heavenly Father knows* that you need all
> these things.
> —*Matthew 6:31–32*, emphasis mine

How comforting! He knows what we need. He notices even the smallest details. The principles we will be discussing apply to every facet of your life. God is concerned about your job, your house, your kids, your vacation, your choice of church, your finances, and even your hobbies. If it matters to you, it matters to God. Why? Because YOU matter to God.

——————— **THINK ABOUT IT** ———————

- Describe an experience you've had when you were certain that the Holy Spirit was speaking to you.
- Can you recall a time when you ignored the Holy Spirit's guidance?
- Do you believe that anything that matters to you matters to God?
- Do you live as though you believe it?
- Review for a moment the four truths presented in John 16:13:
    - The Holy Spirit will guide us.
    - The Holy Spirit is a trustworthy guide.
    - The Holy Spirit is God's mouthpiece to believers.
    - The Holy Spirit speaks.
- Are you willing to try casting *all* your anxiety upon God during the coming week?

CHAPTER 14

Preparing to Hear: The Principle of Neutrality

In the past two years our church and television ministry have undergone some wonderful changes. We have changed our location. We have changed our organizational structure. We have redefined our purpose and objectives. We have even changed some key staff members and job descriptions.

Change, however, is never easy. There is always a group who wants to move too fast. At the same time there are well-meaning saints who subscribe to the philosophy of "if it ain't broke, don't fix it!"

Changes mean decisions, decisions that, in our case, affect hundreds of families. Over the past two years, as I have labored to know God's will concerning our church, I have learned a great deal about the Holy Spirit's involvement in decision making. Not surprisingly, I have found that these principles hold true not only in big decisions but in the daily decisions that fill our lives.

During this exciting and yet somewhat tumultuous period in the life of our church, we were forced to come up with a short-term solution for our space problem. Moving was the ultimate answer. But it would be two and a half years before we moved. In the meantime we were bursting at the seams, and it was hard to imagine leaving things in their present state for very much longer. We had discussed every option imaginable—holding three morning services, conducting a Saturday evening service, rotating groups of people through the overflow rooms. The discussions were endless and the conclusions far from conclusive.

171

The problem was that adding a service meant that I would need to preach three times on Sunday morning or twice on Sunday morning and once on Saturday night. I had already tried preaching three times on Sunday morning for a brief period two years earlier, and it about killed me. After only three months, I was actually dreading Sunday!

Despite my past experience, in June of 1991 we decided that beginning in the fall of 1991 we would begin three Sunday morning services. The difference between this time and the last time we tried it would be that my son, Andy, would take the Sunday evening service. That way, when I was finished on Sunday morning, I was really finished. I wouldn't need to gear back up for another sermon that night.

Another advantage to this plan was that it would cut down on my preparation time. I would need to prepare only one sermon for Sunday instead of two. Preaching three times on Sunday morning would be tough, but I knew I only had to do it for two and a half years, so there *was* light at the end of the tunnel.

Everybody was excited about the change. It looked great on paper. It would allow us to keep growing without forcing so many people to sit in our overflow rooms. Every department began preparing for the change. We put together a churchwide leadership recruitment program in anticipation of the new people our third service would attract.

There was one problem, however. Our plan was the result of a whole lot of discussion but very little prayer. Every time I would walk away from one of our meetings I would feel good about having found a short-term solution to our problem. But whenever I sat down alone and thought about it, something just wasn't right. I couldn't put my finger on it. Again, it looked great on paper. We weren't violating any scriptural principles. But somehow I just couldn't get excited.

First Things First

During this time, we saw God work in a powerful way to solve a similar problem at "In Touch," our radio and television ministry. In that particular situation, the dilemma was resolved while we were on a three-day prayer retreat. I will share the details in the next chapter. Suffice it to say that after I saw God work in such a mighty way in response to our prayers, I thought it would be a good idea if our pastoral staff spent some concentrated time in prayer as well.

I shared with my associate pastors the details of how God worked to solve the problem at "In Touch." I suggested we go away as a church staff and pray for a couple of days. They were in total agreement with the suggestion. The only hitch was that it would be August before we could all get together. Our new Sunday schedule was to begin on the last Sunday of the same month. So much had gone into getting ready for the change that I knew if we came back with an alternative, it would be very discouraging to our staff and volunteers. But August was as soon as we could get away, so we went ahead with our planning while anticipating our prayer retreat.

By the time we left for our retreat, everything was in place to begin a third service and a third Sunday school. Announcements had been made. Publicity had been printed. Teachers and outreach leaders had been recruited. Everything was on go. I still didn't have real peace about it, but it didn't appear that we had any choice—other than to sit and do nothing.

When we arrived at the retreat center, we immediately set about praying. We all knew what we *should* pray, "Lord, show us what to do about our space problem." But so much had already been done—our plans were so far along—it was hard to pray that and mean it. What we really wanted to pray was, "Lord, bless our plans!"

As badly as we hated to admit it, we had come to God with an agenda—*our* agenda. Granted, it was a good plan. We had given it a great deal of thought and discussion. And it might have worked. But God had something different in mind.

We Were Not the First

Sometime early on in our praying, one of the men read a verse that really hit home with me. The context was a situation not unlike ours. The disciples, who were headquartered in Jerusalem, were trying to make a decision about what to expect of Gentile believers insofar as the law was concerned. They didn't want to heap unrealistic or needless expectations upon these babes in Christ. On the other hand, they didn't want the Gentiles doing things that would offend the Jewish believers and thereby divide

The Holy Spirit is a

wonderful communicator.

But He does not speak

for the sake of passing along

information.

He speaks to get

a response.

He waits for us to become

neutral enough to hear

and eventually obey.

the church. And you better believe everybody at their meeting had an agenda!

When they finally reached a conclusion, they wrote a letter with their suggestions concerning this delicate issue. The list of requirements that the group decided upon is introduced in the letter with the following statement, the statement one of my associates read during a break in our prayer meeting:

> For it seemed good to the Holy Spirit and to us to lay upon you no greater burden than these essentials.
> —*Acts 15:28*

I don't know how many times I have read that passage. But its significance had never registered with me before. Somehow the disciples were able to state their opinions on the matter, discuss their differences on the subject, and yet remain open to the Holy Spirit's promptings. In the end, they were convinced, as a group, that the Holy Spirit had led them to their conclusion. It *seemed good* to Him. They were aware of His presence and guidance throughout the decision-making process.

Upon hearing that verse we immediately began to ask the Holy Spirit to make His will known to us as we prayed and talked together. It occurred to us that we needed to arrive at a conclusion that *seemed good* not only to us but to Him as well. Once we decided to make that our priority, we were forced to lay down our personal agendas. We knew we had to be *neutral* about the whole issue. We realized that we were never going to find out what pleased the Holy Spirit until we cared more about hearing from Him than we did about getting our way.

That was really tough for me. I became aware of my agenda. I realized I just didn't *want* to preach three times on Sunday morning—and that was all there was to it. Before I could hear from the Holy Spirit, I knew I had to get neutral. It wasn't long before some of the other pastors there began confessing that they, too, had an agenda that they needed to surrender in order to be completely neutral before God.

As we prayed and enjoyed fellowship together those two days, God slowly broke us all down to the point that to the man, we really wanted to know what pleased the Holy Spirit more than we wanted our way. The process united us as a staff—so much so that we were excited about what God had in mind long before He ever made His will known to us.

On our last evening together we finally received clear direction about the fall. It seemed good to us and the Holy Spirit that we were *not* to start a third morning worship service. How did we know? We just didn't have peace about moving ahead with our plans. At the same time, we didn't have peace about any of the other options we discussed, either. They still looked good on paper. And we may adopt one or more of those strategies in the future. But at that time (and at this present time as well) we knew it just wasn't the thing to do.

We left the retreat center with some unanswered questions. We left there with no strategy for dealing with our overflow crowds. But we left there with the assurance that we were doing the right thing. And we left there united.

Shifting into Neutral

The Holy Spirit speaks to neutral hearts. By that, I don't mean passive or indifferent hearts. God gave us the ability to dream dreams and make plans. Many of the Old and New Testament leaders were men and women of vision and ambition.

By neutral, I mean *being consumed with discovering what pleases the Holy Spirit rather than working to convince Him of the wisdom and brilliance of our plans.* I'm afraid many of us pray with the goal of talking God into things rather than trying to discover His will. Consequently, we never hear from Him. Jesus understood the importance of neutrality. He modeled it for His disciples when He prayed. "Thy kingdom come, Thy will be done." The implication was, "Father, whatever You want, that's ultimately what I want." Then again in the Garden of Gethsemane, on the night of His betrayal, He prayed,

> My Father, if it is possible, let this cup pass from Me; *yet not as I will, but as Thou wilt.*
> —*Matthew 26:39*, emphasis mine

To say Jesus had strong feelings about which way He wanted the Father to go in this matter would be to make the understatement of all time. He didn't want to die. But even with His life on the line, He was able to remain neutral enough to hear from the Father and accept His decision.

The Real Issue

From God's perspective, the content of our prayers takes second place to the question of whether or not we are willing to obey Him. *His ultimate goal is hearts and minds that are in complete harmony with His kingdom agenda.* His plan for you and me is to move us to the place where we can sincerely say with Christ, "Thy kingdom come [regardless of how it interferes with my plans], Thy will be done [in spite of what I expect or desire]."

The neutral heart is the one that is able to keep its own hurts and burdens and requests in proper perspective. The neutral heart, the one the Holy Spirit speaks to and through with ease, is the one that seeks to discover God's perfect will. The neutral heart always approaches the throne of grace with its own agenda in the background.

Who Is Doing the Talking?

One reason it is so important to approach God with a neutral heart is our uncanny ability to confuse our will with His. If you are a parent, you know how easily your children can confuse the phrase, "I'll think about it" with "I promise." You know the situation. Your kids ask you if you will take them such and such a place on a particular day. You respond, "I'll have to think about it," or "We'll see." Then you promptly forget about the whole thing, but they don't. The day rolls around, and they are all excited about the trip you promised them. "I never promised. I said I'll think about it," you tell them. But they are convinced that you promised to take them.

Why does this happen? Here's my theory. When kids (or adults for that matter) really want to do something, there is such a buildup of emotional momentum that any answer except "absolutely not" is interpreted as "yes." If you don't refuse, then you promised. Not because you actually promised but because the momentum was moving in that direction. They take any hope of "yes" to an extreme. The more time between the request and the event, the greater the anticipation and the excitement. As the excitement builds, the promise (which wasn't actually a promise) becomes etched in stone. Time erases any trace of doubt from their minds.

I am convinced we do the same thing with God. We approach Him with requests that are emotionally charged. We want whatever it is so much we can taste it. We couldn't hear a "NO!" if our lives depended on it. So we assume a "yes!" response. And if God says, "Yes," that is an unalterable promise. It's going to happen no matter what anyone says.

When things don't work out—the person God *promised* me I was going to marry marries someone else, the job God *promised* me falls through—we become disappointed with God. The world is full of people who abandoned the faith because God didn't come through for them. In every case, however, the problem was not God. The problem was misplaced faith in a promise God never made.

I believe God has spoken to me on several occasions. Our decision to move the church was one of them. As confident as I am that God spoke to me, I am equally confident that I have the potential to read my will into His; I am capable of misunderstanding God. For this reason, you will never hear me flaunting the fact that God spoke to me. God always keeps His promises. When things don't work out the way I expect them to, I just assume that my timing is wrong or that I misunderstood the Father's will.

The Fear Factor

Shifting into neutral as we approach the throne of grace can be a terrifying thing: "What if God's will for me is something I don't want to do?" "What if He says, 'No'?" At first glance it appears that there might be something to the notion that what we don't know can't hurt us. But that is not the case at all. Missing God's will is a tragedy second only to missing His offer of salvation. God has a kingdom niche carved out just for you. There are people He wants you to meet, lives He wants you to influence. He is tailoring your personality in such a way that you will hit it off with unsaved men and women who otherwise would never have the opportunity to experience a relationship with a believer. You are the instrument God wants to use to change someone's distorted perception of Christianity. You will be the one God uses to reshape someone's thinking and thereby prepare the way for salvation.

That is, if you are willing to make the discovery of His will your priority.

To miss God's will is to miss out on the most exciting adventure this life has to offer. God's will is not something we should fear. In fact, just the opposite is true; we should fear missing it!

Think about it. Isn't it when you and I *miss* God's will (either accidentally or on purpose) that life becomes complicated, confusing, and oftentimes painful? What has led to the greatest disappointments in your life, obeying God or disobeying Him?

Like most people, I made choices in the past that I look back on with deep regret. Several of those decisions continue to affect my life to this day. Without exception, the decisions were contrary to the will of God for my life. Some were motivated out of a desire to have my own way. Others were made in ignorance. But in every case I have lived to regret them.

On the other hand, I have never regretted moving in tandem with God's revealed will for my life. It doesn't always make sense *initially*—as you may well know! But it always makes sense *eventually*. If we are going to fear something, we ought to fear missing His will, not discovering it.

Barriers to Neutrality

Why, then, do we sometimes feel threatened by the notion of putting aside our agenda and approaching Him from the standpoint of neutrality? It goes back to something I talked about earlier. Neutrality before God threatens whatever or whoever functions as the central focus of our lives. In other words, until Christ is Lord, the knowledge of His will, will always seem like a threat —because it is a threat. It threatens the thing, the relationship, the plans, the career, or whatever at that moment sits on the throne of our lives. And that is precisely why God demands neutrality. He wants to be Lord!

Surrendered men and women who have given over control of their lives to the Savior welcome the Father's will. They are not afraid of the Spirit's leading. They are not threatened. Why? Because Jesus is not threatened by the will of the Father. And when Jesus sits as Lord upon the throne of a life, He is never threatened by the will of the Father from that vantage point, either.

The Holy Spirit is a wonderful communicator. But He does not speak for the sake of passing along information. He speaks to get a response. And He knows when our agenda has such a large slice of our attention that it is a waste of time to suggest anything to the contrary. When that is the case, He is often silent. He waits for us to become neutral enough to hear and eventually obey.

Are you at one of those stages in life where you need direction? Wisdom? An answer? Maybe the Holy Spirit is waiting on you to shift into neutral. Once you do, He knows, and you know, that His agenda has become the priority of your life. When that happens, obedience comes much easier. And with obedience comes the peace that surpasses all comprehension.

As I sit here at my desk finishing this chapter, I still don't know what we are going to do about our space problem at church. I believe, however, that God has a solution for our problem. We don't have peace about any of our plans—yet. So in the meantime I plan to keep praying and stay neutral.

THINK ABOUT IT

Are you in the midst of making a big decision—a personal decision or a business decision? Let me make the following suggestions concerning becoming neutral:

- Write on a sheet of notebook paper or an index card your personal preference in the decision you are making.
- Go to a quiet place where you will be uninterrupted, and get on your knees. Ask God for His help in making you absolutely neutral in regard to this decision.
- Tear up that piece of paper, thus acknowledging your willingness to become neutral.
- Continue praying until you are convinced that your hands are open and you are neutral.

Don't use this time of prayer to try to talk God into your plan. You will defeat the whole purpose of the project. Become neutral, make the decision that God desires for you to make, and experience the joy in knowing that you are on your way to discovering the will of God.

CHAPTER 15

Marker 1: Peace

The Holy Spirit uses several spiritual markers to indicate and confirm His will. The first one is the marker of peace.

The Winds of Change

As I indicated in the previous chapter, the past two years have been a time of transition for our church and television ministry. The majority of the changes revolved around our decision to relocate the church.

We sold all of our downtown property in the fall of 1990. The group who bought it allowed us to occupy our main buildings until the spring of 1994. That would give us a chance to build a new building while continuing to have a place to carry on the ministry. The building that housed "In Touch," our radio and television ministry, was not included in that arrangement. According to the contract, we had to vacate that location by July 1991.

In April of that same year we found a building we thought would be perfect. The only problem was that it cost $2.7 million. Several of our board members and executive staff felt good about the location and the price. They suggested we go ahead and borrow the money to purchase the building. Others of us, however, did not have peace about the price or borrowing the money.

One Wednesday afternoon in April a group of us were sitting around a conference table discussing our move and getting nowhere. It was as if we were in a fog. We needed divine direction, and I knew we were not going to receive any sitting around a table. I asked my secretary to call Unicoi State Park to see if we could book some cabins for the following week. She gave me a funny look as she left the room to make the call. It was her way of reminding me that to reserve cabins at Unicoi, we should have called four to six months in advance. Ten minutes later, however, she returned and reported that we were all set.

On the morning we left for Unicoi I asked a friend to begin negotiating the price with the owner of the building. I told him to do his best to get the price down to $2 million.

I made one more call before I started out for Unicoi. I instructed our church administrator to contact the group who had bought our property and ask them if we could stay in the building until January. He said he would do his best.

The cabins were about a two-hour drive from Atlanta, so I had some time to think and pray. During the trip, a passage of Scripture came to mind:

> This is the word of the LORD to Zerubbabel saying, "Not by might nor by power, but by My Spirit," says the LORD of hosts.
> —*Zechariah 4:6*

I took that as a sign that God wanted to do something we didn't know about. As I drove through the mountains of north Georgia, I kept praying, "Lord, whatever You have in mind, please don't let us miss it!"

For two days we did very little talking and a whole lot of praying. We cried out to God in desperation. We had a deadline. We also had a plan. But we couldn't get corporate peace about moving ahead with the purchase of the building.

Good News!

During a break, I called our administrator and discovered we were granted an extension on time. We didn't have to move until January. That was great news. Then the board member who was negotiating with the owner of the building called to tell me we could get the building for $2 million. There was only one problem. The building had a tenant whose lease would not expire until after

January. Moving them out early would cost us extra. We just kept praying.

When we left Unicoi two days later, we still didn't have any clear direction about how to purchase the building. But we were committed to waiting on God. We were confident that God had something in mind other than borrowing the money. In fact, we were so confident, we were talking as if everything had already been worked out.

When I arrived home Tuesday evening, I had a message to call a man I had never met. He lived in another state. The message said he was an "In Touch" viewer who was interested in helping the ministry. I called him back—immediately! He said, "Dr. Stanley, I have had you and your ministry on my mind the past several days. I notice that you never ask for money on the broadcast, and I was wondering if you have any needs."

I didn't know whether to laugh or cry. I explained our situation with the building. Then I told him about our prayer meeting. He asked me how much the building was going to cost. I told him I thought we could get it for $2 million. He said, "I think I can handle that." And he did. We closed about ninety days later.

The Peace Principle

The absence or presence of peace is often the first indication that the Holy Spirit is up to something. (You'll recall that peace is a fruit, or expression, of the Spirit.) I had no peace whatsoever about borrowing $2.7 million. I couldn't explain it. It wasn't a reasonable thing in light of our deadline. Borrowing to buy property would not have violated any of my personal convictions. But Someone on the inside of me was saying, "No!" Strangely enough, once we decided to wait and let God handle it, my peace returned.

Inner peace is a difficult concept to define, but it is easy to identify its absence. Like joy, it goes beyond mere emotion. And it certainly transcends circumstance. Peace is the ability to lie in bed at night, look up at the ceiling, and know everything is going to be all right when everything really isn't all right. Peace is an inner settledness.

The apostle Paul was right on target when he spoke of it as that "which surpasses all comprehension" (Phil. 4:7). Both the presence and the absence of peace oftentimes do not make sense—humanly speaking. Peace defies human comprehension.

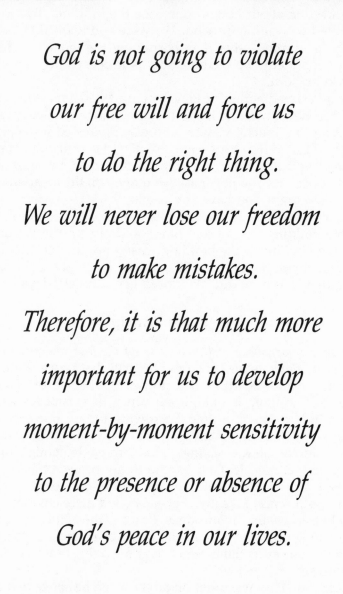

God is not going to violate

our free will and force us

to do the right thing.

We will never lose our freedom

to make mistakes.

Therefore, it is that much more

important for us to develop

moment-by-moment sensitivity

to the presence or absence of

God's peace in our lives.

To Buy or Not to Buy?

A young man in our church was looking for his first house. Jim has a modest income, yet he is one of the most generous people I know. His real estate agent was a Christian, and she knew how important it was to Jim to find the house God had for him.

After about four months of searching they discovered what looked like a great deal. The house was everything Jim was looking for—plus a pool! It was too good to be true. But Jim couldn't get any peace about it. He agonized over it several days while his agent shook her head in unbelief. It didn't make any sense to anyone. Several of Jim's friends really pushed him: "Come on, you're just scared. Everybody goes through this with the first house." But Jim stuck to his guns and told his agent to keep looking.

Six weeks later they found another great deal. Jim had peace that it was the house for him. His agent was relieved. As the negotiating began, Jim prayed his way through every offer and counteroffer. Finally, the two parties were within $3,500 of each other. To everyone's amazement, Jim told his agent to make one final offer, and that would be his last. After the owners made a counteroffer, the two parties were within $2,500 of each other. Jim wouldn't budge. None of his friends could believe that he was willing to lose the house over what amounted to $18 a month! But he didn't have peace about going any further.

Reluctantly, his agent announced to the owners that her client was not going to counter again and the deal was off. Everybody thought Jim was just afraid. But Jim was confident he had done the right thing.

Two days later the owners of the house came back to Jim's agent and countered again. Jim prayed and felt perfect peace about moving ahead in the negotiations. He is now a home owner. And of course, everyone congratulated him on being a tough negotiator. But Jim doesn't see it that way at all. From his perspective it was a matter of being sensitive and responsive to the peace "which surpasses all comprehension."

Don't Worry . . .

We need peace when we are on the right track, but others tell us we are wrong. Peace, as administered through the Holy Spirit, assures us that we are in step with God's will for our lives.

Look at the context for Paul's description of peace:

> Be anxious for nothing, but in everything by prayer and supplication with thanksgiving let your requests be made known to God. And the peace of God, which surpasses all comprehension, shall guard your hearts and your minds in Christ Jesus.
>
> —*Philippians 4:6–7*

I love these verses. "Don't worry. Pray!" Paul says. And notice the immediate result—peace. Even before our prayers are answered, there is peace. Before we have any idea how things will work out, there is peace. Why? Because by our crying out to God and unloading our cares and burdens on Him, He is assured of (and we are reminded of) our dependence on Him. And that is His priority; that is what pleases Him.

Paul describes the role of peace as that of a guard. The picture here is peace as a soldier guarding our hearts (emotions) and minds. The idea is that peace—if we can personify it for a moment—will inform us of who is influencing our hearts and minds. When the wrong influences tamper with our emotions and minds, peace informs us through a sense of foreboding or hesitancy. We lose our peace. We can't always put our finger on it, but something is just not right.

If you have ever been in the role of a counselor, you can probably relate to what I am talking about. Oftentimes in counseling, someone will be talking, and I will get what I call a *check* in my spirit. That is my way of saying, "I lose my peace." In those cases I believe the Holy Spirit is guarding my mind against error or deception or perhaps just a slight distortion of the facts.

On the other hand, the Holy Spirit will oftentimes give us peace —or the go-ahead—about something that from a purely circumstantial perspective makes no sense at all. Why pray about whether or not to buy a building when you have no money? Isn't that getting the cart before the horse? Humanly speaking, it sure was. But we had peace about pursuing it. And it proved to be the right decision.

I have talked to countless people who have gotten themselves into major financial and marital messes by ignoring the Holy Spirit's warning. They say things like, "You know, pastor, when he asked me to marry him, I knew something wasn't quite right. But since I couldn't put my finger on it, I went ahead anyway." Or "I knew there was something funny about that deal, but everybody around me thought it looked good, so I went for it."

A Financial Nightmare

A close friend came to me with the most complicated financial problem I have ever heard in my life. Space (and your interest) does not permit me to outline the whole thing here except to say he made one unwise decision that led to a series of unwise decisions, and he was on the verge of losing everything. My heart went out to him in the deepest way as he related his situation in detail. Somewhere toward the end of his story, he said, "When I was in the middle of deciding [his first big decision], I talked to a wise friend of mine, and he gave me some good insight on my situation. I really had peace following his suggestion. But later on I started thinking about what he said, and I don't know why, but I didn't follow his advice."

As he finished his story, he asked what so many Christians ask, "Why would God let me do something so foolish? Why didn't He stop me?" I reminded him of his conversation with the man who gave him the good advice. I said, "Remember the peace you mentioned? That was the Holy Spirit confirming the truth and wisdom of your friend's advice. But you ignored it. God, through the Holy Spirit, tried to stop you, but you wouldn't listen."

As much as God loves us and wants to keep us out of trouble, He is not going to violate our free will and force us to do the right thing. *We will never lose our freedom to make mistakes.* Therefore, it is that much more important for us to develop moment-by-moment sensitivity to the presence or absence of God's peace in our lives.

The logical question to ask at this point is, How? How do I go about developing this kind of sensitivity to the Holy Spirit? In the next couple of chapters we are going to address that question. But for now think of it like learning a foreign language.

I'll never forget my first Spanish class or my teacher, Mrs. Flowers. She walked in, said hello, and then started rattling off the biggest bunch of gibberish you've ever heard in your life. We all looked at each other like, "Is this the right class?" Finally, after what seemed like an eternity, she started speaking English again.

She informed us that at the beginning of each class she would ask a series of questions in Spanish. Within a few weeks each of us would be able to understand and answer in Spanish. I wasn't convinced.

The first few days were murder. I strained to pick out a word here and there. After a couple of weeks, I was able to understand some phrases. And sure enough, halfway through the semester just about everyone in our class was answering her questions.

If you have studied a foreign language, you know the process. And furthermore, you know from experience that the more time you spend with a language, the more familiar it becomes. The same is true in learning to discern the voice of the Holy Spirit. The more you listen and determine to obey, the more familiar you will become with Him; the easier it will become to distinguish His voice from the other voices that vie for your attention.

Let me give you one more tip as you begin your journey. I learned a long time ago that *we see what we are looking for.*

Years ago, my son, Andy, was snorkeling with a friend in about nine feet of water. Earlier that day he had expressed a desire to find a sand dollar. But as our day of diving was about to end, there were no sand dollars in our bucket of treasure. As Andy made his way back to our dinghy the last time, his snorkel disappeared for a moment and then reappeared. I didn't think anything of it.

As he pulled up to the side of the boat, however, I could see that he was holding something gently in his hands. "Dad," he said, "take a look at this." On the tip of his index finger was the smallest sand dollar I have ever seen in my life. It was tiny. And it was perfect, not a flaw. Our guide, who had lived in that area his entire life, said he had never seen one that small, either.

"How in the world did you see it?" I asked.

"I don't know," he said. "I guess I was just looking hard."

Andy found the sand dollar because that was exactly what he was looking for. What are you looking for? Whatever it is, that is what you are most likely to find. When you begin looking for the Holy Spirit, when you begin tuning in to the absence or presence of His peace, you are going to be overwhelmed by the consistency of His presence. You are going to be amazed at His willingness to lead. And best of all, you are going to be assured of the love of your heavenly Father. It is a love that reaches into every detail of your life.

———— THINK ABOUT IT ————

If you are in the middle of making a decision, now would be a good time to apply what you have learned in this chapter. Evaluate your situation with these questions:

- As you think through your options, is there one in particular you really have peace about?
- Is there one that looks good on the surface, but as you think about yourself following through with it, something just doesn't seem right?
- Do any of your options conflict with the Word of God?
- Is there an option that scares you, but when you pray about it, you really have peace?
- Is there an option that disturbs you but your friends are encouraging you to follow?
- Do you have a feeling you know what God would have you do, but you really don't want to face it?

CHAPTER 16

Marker 2: The Conscience

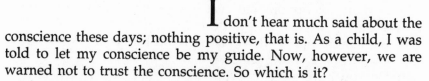

I don't hear much said about the conscience these days; nothing positive, that is. As a child, I was told to let my conscience be my guide. Now, however, we are warned not to trust the conscience. So which is it?

I have never read a book—or even a chapter in a book—about the conscience. I have never heard a sermon on the subject. Yet my conscience is a constant companion. It has something to say about every decision, invitation, thought, word, and deed. So how am I to respond? As a Christian, how seriously should I take the promptings, warnings, and accusations of my conscience?

The conscience has been condemned by many as an untrustworthy source of information, an uninformed guide. Nothing could be further from the truth. *The Holy Spirit uses the conscience as a primary avenue of communication.* The term *conscience* appears thirty times in the New Testament. And in almost every instance, it is spoken of in a positive light.

The conscience is that inner capacity within each of us to discern right from wrong, wise from unwise. One author defines it this way:

> The conscience is that faculty by which one distinguishes between the morally right and wrong, which urges one to do that which he recognizes to be right and restrains him from doing that which he recognizes to be wrong, which passes judgment on his acts and executes judgment within his soul.[1]

Everyone has a conscience (see Rom. 2:14–15). We all have an inner sense of what is right and wrong. God has placed in each person's heart a moral barometer that is constantly accusing or defending motives and actions.

For some, this inner judge operates at a very primitive or uninformed level. But it operates just the same. Others suffer from what the Bible refers to as a *seared* conscience (see 1 Tim. 4:2). A seared, or callous, conscience is one that has been ignored so long that it cannot be felt. It's there but has been rendered ineffective through neglect.

The Conscience and the Holy Spirit

Once a person becomes a child of God, the conscience takes on new significance. It becomes a divine tool. It functions as a megaphone in the hands of the Holy Spirit. It becomes the means through which the Holy Spirit reveals the will of God to the mind.

In his book to the Romans, Paul directs his reader's attention to the unique relationship between the Holy Spirit and the conscience:

> I tell the truth in Christ, I am not lying, my conscience also bearing me witness in the Holy Spirit, that I have great sorrow and continual grief in my heart.
> —*Romans 9:1–2* NKJV

In the following verses Paul made a radical statement. He was so burdened over the lost condition of Israel that he was willing to forfeit his salvation for their sake. Paul was willing to trade places with the nation of Israel (see Rom. 9:3–5).

That was an extreme statement. So Paul felt it necessary to assure his readers that it was something he had thought through. He was genuinely willing to lose his salvation if in his doing so, Israel would acknowledge Jesus as their Messiah. To remove any doubt of his sincerity, Paul began his discourse with the statement quoted above.

So, what did he mean by "my conscience also bearing me witness in the Holy Spirit"? Paul had a clear conscience concerning his extravagant claim. He didn't feel that he was exaggerating in the least. Nothing inside made him doubt his sincerity. As far as he could tell, it was not for effect; it was the truth. Also, he believed his conscience was tuned in to the Holy Spirit in such a fashion that his clear conscience was an indication of the Holy Spirit's approval.

Let's turn it around. Paul believed that if he had been stretching the truth for the sake of making his point (in other words, lying), the Holy Spirit would have been displeased and would have shown His displeasure by disturbing Paul's conscience. Since his conscience was clear, Paul assumed everything had been cleared by the Holy Spirit. Paul trusted his conscience.

A Closer Look

The conscience functions somewhat like a computer. A computer is programmed to respond in specific ways to specific incoming information. Also, it responds to incoming information based on the commands it has been programmed to follow. When I click my word processing application, my computer knows to open my word processor. When my computer receives the *copy* command, it copies whatever I have selected to copy. Computers are smart, but for the most part, they are simply responders.

The conscience is a responder as well. It responds to certain input the way it has been instructed to respond. God has programmed every man and woman's conscience to respond in particular ways to certain data. Paul described it like this:

> For when Gentiles who do not have the Law do *instinctively* the things of the Law, these, not having the Law, are a law to themselves, in that they show the work of the Law *written* in their hearts, their *conscience* bearing witness, and their thoughts alternately accusing or else defending them.
> —*Romans 2:14–15,* emphasis mine

God has written, or programmed, His moral code into the heart of every man and woman. We are born with it. When a person's actions or thoughts are contrary to that code, the conscience responds by sending a "NO" message to the brain. On the other hand, when a person decides to go along with the preprogrammed moral code, the conscience says, "GO."

We experience this phenomenon every day. Sometimes it comes as an inner hesitancy. At other times, it is just plain old guilt. Then there are times when an opportunity to do good comes along, and something on the inside urges us to follow through. That *some-*

thing is the conscience. Notice, Paul says our thoughts sometimes *defend* or point out the legitimacy of certain actions (see Rom. 2:14–15). When that happens, if the actions are in line with the law of God written in our hearts, the conscience gives us the go-ahead.

Reprogramming the Conscience

When you became a Christian, a change began to occur in your conscience. The *basic* moral code that everyone is born with was overhauled or reconditioned. The Spirit of truth took up residency in your heart. Then, whether you were aware of it or not, He immediately set about to complete the programming of your conscience. Whereas before you had a general sense of right and wrong, the Holy Spirit began renewing your mind to more specific and complete truths (see 1 Cor. 2:10–13).

You participate in this renewal process every time you read your Bible, attend worship, memorize a verse, or pray. The Holy Spirit uses all this input to reprogram the data base through which your conscience evaluates every opportunity, thought, invitation, word, and deed.

As this process continues, your conscience tunes in with the moral code of the Holy Spirit—a code reflecting the moral and ethical standards of God. This process sensitizes you not only to God's moral standards but to the will of God as well.

That is why new Christians are often offended by things that just days previous to their salvation didn't bother them at all. Sometimes it is a sudden change. At other times it is gradual.

Before his conversion, a talented musician in our church played in clubs around Atlanta. His testimony is a beautiful example of how God, by sensitizing the conscience, leads a person to change life-style.

Ron was saved sitting on the edge of his bed watching "In Touch." After the message, I asked those who wanted to trust Christ as their Savior to pray the sinner's prayer with me. He did. And almost immediately he felt an irresistible urge to begin reading the Bible. That and regular church attendance were really the only visible evidences of his conversion.

About two months later he reported to me that he had quit drinking.

"Why?" I asked.

"I'm not sure," he said. "It just doesn't feel right anymore."

The conscience is one of the

Holy Spirit's primary tools

through which He

communicates

with believers.

Don't ignore the warnings

and promptings of

the conscience.

To do so is to run the risk

of missing God.

I knew then that the Holy Spirit was at work, raising the sensitivity level of Ron's conscience.

It wasn't too many weeks later that he cornered me to let me know he was going to quit his band. I was shocked—and concerned. He was making good money. To be honest, I was afraid if he quit, he wouldn't make it financially. If that happened, I thought he might conclude that God had let him down. Oh, me of little faith!

"Why do you want to quit the band?" I asked.

"I don't feel comfortable there anymore. In fact, I hate going in those places. I don't enjoy the people, the atmosphere—nothing about it is appealing."

"But what will you do about a job?" I asked.

"I don't know," he said with a laugh.

I realized I was more worried about it than he was. So I decided to get out of the way and let the Holy Spirit continue.

A few months later he burned the final bridge.

"I told Teri we couldn't go out anymore."

"Why?" I asked, as if I didn't know by now.

"She's not a Christian, not like I am. She doesn't understand these changes. And besides, she's not good for me."

I had to hold back the tears. The Holy Spirit never ceases to amaze me. I never had to say a word about any of those things to Ron. Besides, I never felt the freedom to say anything.

The Holy Spirit went right to work, sensitizing his conscience to the truth, to God's standard of holiness. As his conscience was renewed, it began troubling him. Soon it became apparent to Ron that something wasn't right. Things that were at one time a part of his routine now made him feel uneasy, awkward, even guilty. Why? What had changed? His conscience was tuned in to the Holy Spirit. The Holy Spirit, through Ron's conscience, was speaking.

The Holy Spirit uses the conscience to do three things in particular.

1. The Holy Spirit uses the conscience as an instant warning device.

I have a bad habit. In talking with other men, I find that I am not alone. When the empty gas tank light on my dashboard comes on, I keep driving. More than once I have lost this little game. The consequences are embarrassing and sometimes dangerous! The warning light on my dash is there for a reason. And I am not being sensible when I ignore it.

In much the same way, the Holy Spirit tries to warn us of moral and physical danger. One great example is found in the book of Acts. In talking to the elders from the church at Ephesus, the apostle Paul said,

> And now, compelled by the Spirit, I am going to Jerusalem, not knowing what will happen to me there. I only know that in every city *the Holy Spirit warns me* that prison and hardships are facing me.
>
> —*Acts 20:22–23* NIV, emphasis mine

The Holy Spirit has a divine perspective on our lives. He can see trouble coming miles down the road. Often He will try to warn us. I believe He uses the conscience to do so.

Several years ago we needed to fill a particular staff position. We had been without someone for several months so the pressure was on. A pastor friend called and highly recommended a fellow. According to my friend, this man had all the proper credentials and had expressed an interest in joining our staff. I had one of my associates call him and arrange a visit to Atlanta.

When we finally met face-to-face, I had a check in my spirit. The Holy Spirit gave me a stern warning. I had nothing to base it on. Humanly speaking, it was an unfair assessment. But I knew I should not hire him.

Unfortunately for me, just about everybody on our staff took an instant liking to this fellow. In fact, I have never known anyone to be so readily accepted. I reconsidered my feelings: "Maybe it was something personal. Maybe I was just in a bad mood when we met." Round and round I went. When I would pray, I knew that hiring him was the wrong thing to do. But when I would just sit and think about it, I couldn't come up with any reason not to allow him to join our staff.

I let the situation drag on for three months. Finally, the pressure got to me, and I approved him for the position. Less than a year later I had to let him go. The Holy Spirit warned me, but I didn't listen. My conscience was sending me strong signals, but I ignored them. And I regretted it.

I'm sure you have had the same experience. Maybe you have been invited to a party or another social function and felt funny about accepting the invitation. You found yourself saying, "No," but were not sure why. Or maybe you accepted the invitation and later regretted it; you wished you had taken your initial apprehension more seriously.

If you are a parent, you have probably felt this same uneasiness upon being introduced to certain "friends" of your son or daughter. Something on the inside sent up red flags: "This is not someone my child should spend time with."

More than likely your child reacts, "You just don't want me to have any friends" or "I guess you want to pick out all my friends." It is a no-win situation. Why? Because you don't have any real reason. It is just a sense you have—holy sense! So when your child asks, "What's wrong with him?" you don't have a good answer. But if you are walking in the Spirit, you probably have the right answer.

"But wait," you say, "you mean to tell me that the Holy Spirit is making me feel that way?" Absolutely. "But don't all parents have that extra sense?" I believe they do. But a Spirit-filled parent has additional help—the Holy Spirit, who has the advantage of inside information on everybody and can fine-tune a believer's ability to discern the spirit of another person. That brings me to the second way the Holy Spirit works through the conscience.

2. The Holy Spirit energizes the conscience to function as an accurate evaluator and discerner.

The conscience, once it is empowered by the Holy Spirit, can correctly discern or evaluate what is and what is not of God. In the apostle Paul's second letter to the believers in Corinth, it is apparent that he was not sure of their confidence in his ministry. He was sure God had approved what he was doing. But he really wanted the Corinthians to trust him as well. From that context he made this statement:

> Therefore knowing the fear of the Lord, we persuade men, but we are made manifest to God; and I hope that we are made manifest also in your *consciences*.
> —*2 Corinthians 5:11*, emphasis mine

The term *manifest* means "clear," "obvious," "apparent," or "self-evident." Paul was arguing, "It is clear to God what I am up to. I hope your consciences will make it equally clear to you." Paul

asked his readers to evaluate his ministry based on the message
they received from their consciences. He believed their consciences would line up with the truth. He believed the conscience
was an accurate discerner/evaluator (see 2 Cor. 4:2).

The Deal of a Lifetime

When I was first starting out in the ministry, a businessman
offered me an opportunity to invest in his company. He assured
me it was a very low-risk investment. He knew I didn't have
much money, and it was his way of helping me out. I didn't have
any reason to doubt his sincerity so I took the paperwork home to
my wife, Anna, and we read it together.

At first, neither one of us had any reservations. But a couple of
days later I was in my study praying about something else, and
suddenly, the business venture popped into my mind. I immediately had an uneasy feeling about the whole thing. From then on,
anytime I thought or prayed about it, I had misgivings. When I
would try to argue the point, my conscience would bother me. I
knew that the moment I gave him a check, I would feel guilty. I
could feel the guilt beforehand.

Anna had the same premonition. When she shared how she felt,
that settled it for me. We thanked the gentleman for his interest
and politely declined his offer. Years later we heard through the
grapevine that he was forced to declare bankruptcy. Everybody
who had invested with him lost the entire investment.

All of us will be given opportunities to participate in things that
are not God's will. They are not necessarily bad things. They just
aren't God's best for us at the time. If not for the work of the Holy
Spirit in our lives, we would have no way of knowing. That is
why it is so important to develop sensitivity to the Holy Spirit. We
must go beyond evaluating things based on their moral or ethical
merit alone. There is more to decision making for the child of God
than that. We must allow the Spirit-filled conscience to discern.
Only then can we know what is and what is not of God.

Friends?

I considered Steve Moyer one of my closest friends. We worked
together on several ministry-related projects. Our interaction covered a span of more than six years. During that time, I entrusted

him with more and more responsibility. He seemed to handle it fine. I was constantly telling people what a great help he was to our ministry and to me personally.

In time I began to sense a wall developing between us. More than once I went to him to make sure I hadn't done anything to offend or insult him. He would always assure me that everything was fine. Somehow I was never convinced.

The Holy Spirit kept impressing on me a need to deal with the growing tension between us. My conscience bothered me. I felt guilty every time I saw Steve. I knew I needed to approach him about what I was sensing, but it never seemed to do any good—so I would put it off.

For two years I was sure there was a problem, but I could never put my finger on it. When we would talk, he would smile and assure me he was fine, but he wouldn't open up. I knew he was hiding something. But I never pressed the issue. That was my mistake.

One day, with no warning, he called to inform me that he was resigning. I was both shocked and relieved. He sounded so distant. He wasn't the same warm fellow I had known in years past. Something was definitely wrong. Again, I tried to probe. And again, I got nowhere.

When he finally left, we discovered the problem. He had gotten into financial trouble. As is often the case, his personal problems spilled over into his relationships at work. He had alienated his staff. He had made several unwise decisions in regard to ministry finances. We really had a mess on our hands.

As the saying goes, hindsight is always twenty-twenty. Had I really pushed him earlier, I would have saved the ministry considerable headaches. My conscience tried to warn me, but I relied too heavily on what my mind was telling me (as well as my emotions). I waited. And I was sorry.

3. The Holy Spirit energizes the conscience to function as a judge and jury.

The third way in which the Holy Spirit works through the conscience is the one with which we are most familiar. The Holy Spirit uses the conscience to convict us of sin.

If you have been a Christian very long, you are probably familiar with this passage where Jesus refers to the convicting work of the Holy Spirit:

> And He [the Holy Spirit], when He comes, will convict the
> world concerning sin, and righteousness, and judgment; con-
> cerning sin, because they do not believe in Me; and concern-
> ing righteousness, because I go to the Father, and you no
> longer behold Me; and concerning judgment, because the
> ruler of this world has been judged.
>
> —*John 16:8–11*

Now compare what Jesus said about the Holy Spirit with what
Peter and Paul said about the conscience.

Peter stated,

> Always be ready to give a defense to everyone who asks you
> a reason for the hope that is in you, with meekness and fear;
> *having a good conscience*, that when they defame you as evildo-
> ers, those who revile your good conduct in Christ may be
> ashamed.
>
> —*1 Peter 3:15–16* NKJV, emphasis mine

Peter viewed the conscience as a trustworthy indicator of the presence or absence of sin. A good or clear conscience suggested no
sin.

Paul communicated the same idea in his second letter to the
believers in Corinth when he wrote,

> For our boasting is this: *the testimony of our conscience* that we
> conducted ourselves in the world in simplicity and godly
> sincerity, not with fleshly wisdom but by the grace of God,
> and more abundantly toward you.
>
> —*2 Corinthians 1:12* NKJV, emphasis mine

Like Peter, Paul viewed the conscience as a trustworthy source of
information regarding the presence of sin (see Acts 24:16). Jesus
said the Holy Spirit would convict of sin. Peter and Paul looked to
the conscience for evidence of that conviction. The conscience,
then, is the realm in which the Holy Spirit carries out His convicting work. When the conscience is stirred, chances are, the Holy
Spirit has spoken.

There is a reason I have gone to such great lengths to explain
this relationship. Many Christians aren't sure when the Holy
Spirit speaks to them. Yet these same believers would readily admit that they have a very active conscience. When believers feel

the prick of conscience, there is a good chance that they are hearing from the Holy Spirit!

Do you see how practical the Spirit-filled life is? It is not a mystery that can be grasped only by some elite subset of Christians. The Spirit-filled life is not reserved for those who are more "in tune" with the "deeper" things of God. The Spirit-filled life is for all Christians.

A Perfect Introduction

Another reason for stressing the relationship between the conscience and the Holy Spirit is that it is a wonderful way to introduce children or new believers to the ministry of the Holy Spirit. The idea of hearing from God is difficult for children and new converts to grasp (it's difficult for many old converts as well!). But everyone is familiar with the conscience. That makes it the perfect place to begin when explaining how the Holy Spirit communicates with His people.

The Spirit-filled life is a life in tune with the Holy Spirit. The conscience is one of the Holy Spirit's primary tools through which He communicates with believers. For that reason, the conscience is to be taken seriously. Don't ignore the warnings and promptings of the conscience. To do so is to run the risk of missing God.

Join with the apostle Paul in striving to keep your conscience clear before God (see Acts 24:16). A clear conscience is evidence of a life in harmony with the Holy spirit. And that, my friend, is what the wonderful Spirit-filled life is all about.

NOTE

1. A. M. Rehwinkel, *The Evangelical Dictionary of Theology,* edited by Walter A. Elwell (Grand Rapids, Mich.: Baker, 1984), p. 267.

―――――――― THINK ABOUT IT ――――――――

• Do you consider your conscience a valid guide, or have you been ignoring it and viewing it as untrustworthy?
• If the conscience is that inner capacity within each of us to discern right from wrong, wise from unwise, will you begin taking seriously those warning signs?
• How committed are you to reprogramming or sharpening your conscience through actively studying God's Word, attending worship services, memorizing Scripture, and praying for discernment?
• Review the three particular ways the Holy Spirit uses your conscience:
    1. As an instant warning device.
    2. As an evaluator and discerner.
    3. As a judge and jury.

CHAPTER 17

Marker 3: The Word of God

---❧---

A third tool the Holy spirit uses to reveal His will is the Bible. Of all the ways the Holy Spirit reveals Himself, this is the most objective and, for that reason, the most valuable. Don't misunderstand. I am not discounting the merit of the peace of God or the accuracy of the conscience. Certainly, my illustrations demonstrate the significant role these instruments play in my life. But to be honest, they take a back seat to the Scriptures when it comes to helping me discern the will of the Holy Spirit. As we take a closer look at the relationship between the Scriptures and the Holy Spirit, I think you will understand why.

The Source

Believers generally accept that the Bible is the Word of God. I like the term *inerrant*. I believe the Bible is the inerrant Word of God. That is, it is without error in its original form. Everything the Bible states as true is true. We could add to this description terms like *infallible, inspired,* and *verbally inspired*. But I think you get my point.

Although it is true that most Christians believe in the reliability of the Bible, it is not true that most believers understand the source of our Bible. "But," you ask, "didn't God inspire men to write the Bible?"

Yes. But there is more to it than that. The Holy Spirit worked through men to pen the holy Scriptures. The Bible is the work of the Holy Spirit.

The verse most often used to substantiate this claim is found in Peter's second letter:

> But know this first of all, that no prophecy of Scripture is a matter of one's own interpretation, for no prophecy was ever made by an act of human will, but men moved by the Holy Spirit spoke from God.
>
> —2 *Peter 1:20–21*

Peter is referring here to the Old Testament. He is describing, however, the process through which the thoughts of God found their way to pen and paper. This same process is used to bring about the creation of the New Testament.

This reference is not the only one to attest to the Spirit's involvement in the origination of the Scriptures. The Bible is full of references to the Holy Spirit's work in bringing us our Bible (see 2 Sam. 23:2–3; Isa. 59:21; Jer. 1:9, Matt. 22:42–43; Mark 12:36; Acts 1:16; Hebr. 3:7; 10:15–16).

In light of what we discovered earlier in the gospel of John, this makes perfect sense. Remember? Jesus said the Holy Spirit would be God's mouthpiece to man (see John 16:13). Jesus said He (the Holy Spirit) would bring thoughts to our minds. He would remind us of truth. Therefore, it should not be surprising to find the Holy Spirit serving once again as the Father's messenger to man, this time bringing with Him the timeless, unchangeable truth of the Old and New Testaments.

Time with the Word

Two important implications emerge from all of this. First, *if you want to know what the Holy Spirit thinks about something, read the Bible.* The Scripture is His thoughts on paper. It doesn't get any clearer than that. You and I are not left to discern the mind of the Spirit through the presence or absence of peace and the voice of conscience alone. We have His thoughts on paper! I would go so far as to say that *you will never be able to accurately identify the peace of God or the voice of God without some understanding of the Word of God.*

The fact that we have the mind of God on paper is great news.

As sensitive as I try to be to the voice of the Spirit, sometimes I miss Him. There are so many other things influencing my thoughts and emotions. I, for one, need things spelled out for me in black and white (pen and ink).

The most balanced Christians I know are those who spend time in God's Word on a daily basis. The most unbalanced Christians I know are those who do not. It is that simple.

I know people who wear their Christianity on their sleeves. Yet these same folks are some of the poorest excuses for Christians I know. Their lives are governed by their emotions. One day they are up; the next day they are down. They make bad decisions. Their relationships are always in turmoil. Their marriages are a mess. And yet every other word has something to do with God. "Praise the Lord" this and "Praise the Lord" that. I am tempted to ask them not to mention Christ for fear that they will drive people away from the faith.

Upon closer examination I have found that these folks have never developed the habit of spending quality time reading God's Word. They have heard every tape, attended every seminar, and read every how-to book, and they listen to nothing but Christian music. But they are neglecting the primary source of wisdom and direction available to believers. Consequently, there is something missing in their lives. They rely exclusively on the subjective and are void of the objective.

You and Your Bible

How about you? How much time do you spend reading and studying God's Word? Notice, I didn't ask how often you attend church or Bible study. Neither did I ask how much time you spend praying. How much do you read your Bible?

"But I don't understand the Bible," you say.

That is a poor excuse. Besides, it's not even true. There may be parts of the Bible you don't understand. But that is no reason to give up reading it entirely.

My son, Andy, serves with me at First Baptist as our youth pastor. When teenagers tell him they don't read their Bibles because they don't understand it, he responds with this scenario. He tells the teen to imagine that the best-looking and most popular guy (if he is talking to a girl) or girl (if he is talking to a guy) in school walks up and says, "I am having a party at my house this weekend. I want you to be my special guest." (For this illustration, we'll assume a girl is to be the guest.)

Andy asks her to imagine that this guy is someone she has had a crush on for a long time. He is someone she is really crazy about but, at the same time, someone she never dreamed would have anything to do with her.

He continues, "After he invites you to the party, he hands you a folded-up piece of paper and says, 'Here is a map to my house. I'll see you Friday night.' You stand there in a daze. You can't believe this person even talked to you, much less invited you to the party. Finally, you snap out of it and begin unfolding the map. At first you think you are holding it upside down. When you turn it over, however, it is just as confusing. The map doesn't make any sense to you at all."

At that point Andy puts the ball back in the student's court. He asks, "So what would you do? Would you throw the map away and say, 'Well, I guess I can't go to the party; I just can't understand the map'? Or would you do everything in your power to figure it out?"

I think you get the point. No normal teenager would throw the map away. She would go to any extreme necessary to figure it out. Why? Because she is motivated.

When people tell me they don't read the Bible because they don't understand it, they are really saying, "I don't understand the Bible, and I don't consider it important enough to make any effort to remedy my ignorance." Generally speaking, *the problem is not education or information; it is motivation.*

Good Ol' Cousin Ed

Let's change the illustration. A distant cousin leaves you a large sum of money. His attorney writes you to inform you of your good fortune. To collect the money, you must fill out a lengthy and complicated form. In fact, after an hour of working on it, you realize that it is over your head. What do you do? Throw it away and write Cousin Ed's attorney telling him you can't accept the money because you didn't understand how to fill out the form? I doubt it. Instead, you would get some help. You would do whatever you had to do to figure it out. Why? Motivation.

The Bible is more valuable than a map to a party. It is worth far more than a few thousand dollars left by a departed relative. The

Bible is the mind of God in print. It gives men and women a purpose for living. It explains the mysteries of creation, suffering, heaven and hell. The Bible holds the keys for attaining and maintaining real success. It contains the blueprint for successful marriage and family relationships. The Scriptures contain the story of salvation, a story that reaches back to the beginning of time and extends into eternity.

Is there really a good excuse for a Christian not to read the Bible? When you think about all the reading and study aids available today, our excuses disappear completely.

Let me put it another way. If you can read this book, you have no excuse for not reading your Bible. If you can read this book and you are not reading your Bible, you will never experience the Spirit-filled life with any consistency. Your Christian experience will for the most part be a subjective search for truth within the limited realm of your thoughts. Your conscience will never be a totally reliable guide since you are not renewing it to the truth of the Holy Spirit. And the peace of God will elude you. The Bible is the Holy Spirit's most objective way of communicating with His people. It is the only way to know anything about Him. There is NO substitute. *If you want to know what the Holy Spirit thinks about something, read the Bible.*

Follow the Leader

A second important implication emerges from the Holy Spirit's involvement with the creation of the Bible: *the Holy Spirit will never lead you where the Word of God forbids you to go.*

Now, that may seem rather obvious. But I am constantly amazed at the decisions believers justify by claiming they were led by the Spirit.

A man came into my office one summer and told me the Spirit had led him to divorce his wife. When I asked why, he said it was because she was an unbeliever. She was hindering his spiritual progress. He had prayed and prayed and finally received peace about filing for divorce.

I picked up my Bible, turned to 1 Corinthians 7, and read him these verses:

> If any brother has a wife who is an unbeliever, and she consents to live with him, let him not send her away. For the

unbelieving husband is sanctified through his wife, and the
unbelieving wife is sanctified through her believing husband.
—*1 Corinthians 7:12–14*

He assured me he had read the verses. Then he assured me that
God had released him of his obligation to his wife. He was wrong.
How could the same Holy Spirit who moved Paul to instruct believing husbands to remain married to their unbelieving wives
turn around and tell this man to do something different?

We must always allow the Word of God to stand as judge over
our thoughts, feelings, and impressions. When we feel impressed
to do *A* but the Word of God says to do *B*, we better do *B*. No
matter how strongly you feel that the Holy Spirit is leading you,
remember, *the Holy Spirit will never lead you where the Word of God
forbids you.* Never! There are no exceptions.

A False Dichotomy

Part of the conflict we experience in trying to discern the voice
of the Holy Spirit stems from a misunderstanding. Somewhere
along the way we were taught that there is a conflict between
what is spiritual and what is logical and reasonable.

I will never forget a conversation I had with one lady in our
church. She just kept shaking her head and saying, "Dr. Stanley,
you just don't understand. You are being too logical. You need to
be more spiritual." Like many Christians, this well-meaning lady
saw a division between the spiritual world and the world of reason and logic. *No such division exists.*

Certainly, there are times when the will of God *seems* to go
against what is reasonable. But when all the facts are known, such
is not the case at all. It didn't seem reasonable for Joshua to march
around Jericho. But when all was said and done, it made perfect
sense—God was making a point about His power and His love for
His people.

God created reality. He also created the laws of logic. Then He
created our multifaceted brains with the ability to use these laws
to understand and discover reality. The spirit world functions in
accordance with these same laws. If it didn't, God would have no
way of communicating with man. If there is a difference between
spiritual reality and reality as we know it, how could God get
spiritual truth into our unspiritual world? There must be a con-

nection of some kind. There must be a common bond, or the two worlds would remain mutually exclusive. God would not be able to communicate with man.

In the last chapter I told a story about hiring a man I had reservations about from our first encounter. I said I had no *reason* not to hire him. From my perspective, there was no logical explanation about why I shouldn't hire him. But in reality, there were several reasons. And the Holy Spirit knew them all! So what did *He* do? He gave me an uneasy feeling about the whole thing. What did *I* do? I ignored His warning and hired the guy because I didn't have any hard and fast reason not to.

You see, there was no conflict between the spiritual and the logical. What was spiritual was logical. My problem was that I didn't have all the facts. So I made the wrong decision.

My point? God chose to communicate His truth in human language. Then He took it a step further; He had men write it down. If spiritual truth can be accurately communicated through language, spiritual truth and reality must work within the confines of logic and reason as we know them. Why? Because human language functions according to prescribed rules, rules that were set down by finite men. If there is a conflict or contradiction between what is spiritual and what is logical, we have a real problem. God's truth must have been distorted once it was forced into the confines of human language—with all its logical rules and structure. If that is the case, what the Bible says is not really what God meant. But since Christ quoted the Old Testament as a source of reliable—God-breathed—information, we know that eternal truth can be communicated within the structure and rules of language.

The fact that Christ attempted to communicate with man through language supports this point as well. Jesus believed that language was an adequate form through which to pass along spiritual truth. He saw no conflict between the spirit world and the world of logic as we know it.

Regardless of the fact that the Holy Spirit and the Word of God exist in different realms, they will not conflict. After all, the Holy Spirit gave us the Scriptures.

The Word of God Stands

A couple came to see one of our pastors for premarital counseling. They had a date set, the chapel reserved, a dress made, and a caterer lined up for the reception. They were ready. In the course of his conversation with the couple, my associate discovered that they were living together. In fact, they had been living together for two years. Both claimed to be Christians. Each had a convincing story about coming to know Christ. Yet they saw no problem with their premarital arrangement.

When Jim asked them about it, the young woman responded, "Well, we love each other. And the Bible says that love is the most important thing. So we figured it didn't matter. I mean it's not like we are immoral or something. We are very faithful to each other."

The more they talked, the more confusing it became. They really believed they were in God's will. They had peace about it. Their consciences didn't bother them in the least. They could not understand Jim's concern. The couple honestly believed the verses dealing with premarital sex didn't pertain to them; their situation was different.

Without putting it in these terms, this couple believed there is a dichotomy between the spirit world and the world of principle and reason. They were taking their cue from what they felt, what they *sensed* God was approving. They were ignoring the objective, clear teaching of God's Word. They were mistaken.

Peace or no peace. Guilty conscience or no guilty conscience. The Word of God stands. It is the final authority for the Spirit-filled believer. The Spirit-filled life is a life lived in accordance with the teachings of the Scripture—whether one feels like it or not and whether it bears witness with one's spirit or not.

The Illumination of the Holy Spirit

The Holy Spirit's involvement with our Bible goes beyond inspiration. Today He is involved in a ministry of *illumination*. In this unique ministry the Holy Spirit opens the spiritual eyes of the believer so that he or she may understand the things of God as recorded in Scripture. Dr. Charles Ryrie provides a helpful definition:

> It [illumination] is generally thought of in connection with the ministry of the Holy Spirit which makes clear the truth of the written revelation in the Bible. In reference to the Bible, *revelation* relates to its content, *inspiration* to the method of record-

ing the material, and *illumination* to the meaning of the record.[1]

Paul explained the Spirit's ministry of illumination this way:

> For to us God revealed them [the mysteries of God] through the Spirit; for the Spirit searches all things, even the depths of God. Now we have received, not the spirit of the world, but the Spirit who is from God, that we might know the things freely given to us by God.
> —*1 Corinthians 2:10–12*

Paul does not say that God revealed things through the Word alone. The truths of God are revealed through the work of the Spirit. The Holy Spirit is constantly working to *reveal* the thoughts and truth of God. He does that by opening the minds and hearts of believers so that we can understand the thoughts of God as we have them recorded in Scripture.

Have you ever had a verse of Scripture jump off the page and affect you in a way that takes you totally by surprise? Have you ever read a passage that is very familiar to you, but you gain new insight from it? Have you ever been in a pressure situation and from out of nowhere a verse comes to mind that brings you comfort or renewed perspective? Or how about those times when everything is falling apart and you throw open your Bible and BAM! There it is—a verse tailor-made for your situation.

When these things happen, they are not coincidental. More than likely the Holy Spirit is at work—illuminating our minds, opening our eyes, infusing our hearts with the specific truths we need for the moment. Unfortunately, we never realize that the Holy Spirit is at work. We never pause to thank Him. We just take the truth and run.

The Holy Spirit's ministry of illumination underscores once again how important it is for us to spend time in God's Word. Spirit-filled believers pore over the Scriptures with a burning desire to fill their hearts and minds with truth, not for the sake of some academic pursuit (although there is certainly a place for that) but with the goal of seeing God affect their lives.

Dr. Billy Graham agrees:

> This has been my experience as I have studied the Scriptures. Things I may have known intellectually for years have come

alive to me in their fuller spiritual significance almost miraculously. As I have studied the Scriptures, I have also learned that the Spirit always lets more light shine from the Word. Almost every time I read an old, familiar passage I see something new. This happens because the written Word of God is a living Word. I always come to the Scriptures with the Psalmist's prayer, "Open my eyes, that I might behold wonderful things from Thy law" *(Psalm 119:18).*[2]

The motto of one of our Atlanta AM radio stations is, "If you miss a day, you miss a lot." I can't think of a more appropriate motto for a Christian when it comes to spending time in God's Word. To miss a day is to miss out on an opportunity for the Holy Spirit to speak directly to you. And to miss out on that is to miss a lot!

Progressive Illumination

The Spirit-filled life is a life of continual growth. Anybody who has trusted Christ as Savior has the potential of living a Spirit-filled life. But a person's spiritual maturity (which should be a reflection of the amount of time as a Christian) will dictate the nature of their Spirit-filled experience. This fact makes the ministry of illumination all that much more important.

Although the Word of God never changes, our understanding of it will. Our ability to understand God's Word and our willingness to apply it are tied in to our maturity. For that reason, we need a tutor to guide us and enlighten us as we work our way through the Scriptures. But not just any tutor. We need one who is sensitive to where we are in our spiritual pilgrimage, one who won't go too fast or too slow. We need a tutor who will direct our attention to those things we are ready for. And we need one who won't let us slide by lessons that are difficult to learn.

Since spiritual maturity is a process, and we are all at different places in that process, it makes sense that each of us needs a *personal* tutor to guide us. God gave us the Holy Spirit. That is another reason the Bible refers to the Spirit-filled life as a life *led by the Spirit* (see Gal. 5:25). A good leader is sensitive to the progress of those he or she is leading. And the Holy Spirit is an excellent leader.

All that is to say, it wasn't enough for the Holy Spirit to inspire men to write the Bible. He knew each of us would need someone to lead us through the text as well. So every time a believer opens his or her Bible, the Holy Spirit goes to work to illuminate the Scriptures. In that way He is able to minister to each of us, at the right pace, according to our particular needs.

A Word of Warning

In the spring of 1982 a woman marched into my office and informed me that God told her to divorce her husband. She knew my stand on divorce and consequently was defensive from the very outset of our conversation. Before I had a chance to respond, she picked up a Bible from my desk and turned to the verse God had given her as confirmation. I can't remember the verse. I do remember that it had nothing to do with divorce—at least not in its original context.

I did my best to reason with her. I even got her to talk about the "other" reasons why she thought a divorce was necessary. She felt that her husband was a loser. He was not a good provider. She didn't think he was a good role model for the kids. And to sum it all up, she just didn't love him anymore.

She had a convincing case, humanly speaking. But the longer we talked, the more evident it became to me (and I think to her as well—although she never admitted it) that the situation had nothing to do with God. She was miserable and wanted out. Since she was a Christian, she felt that she needed to spiritualize her decision so she went verse hunting. By that, I mean she got her Bible out and started looking for something that would support her decision.

That is why the Spirit-filled life begins with surrender to the lordship of Christ. Surrendered Christians approach the text with humble hearts, not hidden agendas. Spirit-filled believers come to the Scriptures with teachable spirits. They don't view Bible study as simply a fact-finding mission. They see it as an opportunity to peer into the mind and heart of God.

Reading Tips

Here are some tips for studying the Bible.

1. Look for principles.

We would all do well to become more principle centered in our Bible reading. Most of us are *promise* centered. That is, we are always on the lookout for something else God must do for us.

When it comes to decision making, principles are far more helpful than promises. My experience has been that the Holy Spirit brings principles to my mind far more often than promises.

A principle is like an equation. If you do *A*, you can expect *B* to happen. If you don't do *A*, you can be confident of *C*. Here are some examples:

- We always reap what we sow (see Gal. 6:7).
- The people you spend time with will influence the direction of your life (see Prov. 13:20).
- The person who hates to be corrected will eventually make stupid mistakes (see Prov. 12:1).
- Liars are always found out (see Prov. 12:19).
- What you hold on to will diminish, but what you give will be multiplied (see 2 Cor. 9:6).
- God always provides for the needs of the generous (see Phil. 4:19).

Principles are timeless truths. They apply to everyone at all times. They are like the laws of nature. They can be ignored but not broken. The Bible is full of them. One writer states,

> Principles are timeless, universal laws that empower people.
> . . . Principles have infinite applications, as varied as circumstances. They tend to be self-validating, self-evident, universal truths. When we start to recognize a correct principle, it becomes so familiar to us, it is almost like "common sense."[3]

Just about every decision you make will intersect with one or more principles of God's Word. They are that comprehensive. From friends to finances, there are principles to guide you, and the principles are handed down through the Holy Spirit.

On many occasions people have come to me for counseling with what they considered unsolvable problems. As they related their situations, principle after principle flooded my mind. When they finished, I applied the principles of Scripture to the problem. Generally speaking, they walked away thinking I was brilliant. I say "generally speaking" because there were some who, after hearing my answer, shook their heads and said, "I should have known that. It's right there in the Bible." And they were right. They should have known.

God has spoken. He has anticipated our questions as well as our frustrations. He knew the decisions we would be faced with before we did. To help us navigate the never-ending series of crossroads, He has provided us with principles.

The problem is not that God won't give us answers to our questions. The problem is that we haven't taken the time to look them up! We haven't done our homework. Again, God has spoken.

Nowhere is this truth made any clearer than in Paul's letter to the Romans:

> And do not be conformed to this world, but be transformed by the renewing of your mind, that you may prove what the will of God is, that which is good and acceptable and perfect.
> —*Romans 12:2*

Notice the relationship between renewing the mind and *proving* what the will of God is. The term *prove* means "to discern or sort out." The idea is that men and women in the process of renewing their minds will be extra sensitive to what is of God and what is not. They will be able to distinguish the will of God from their own desires.

The term *renew* means "to make something new." Renewing something is usually a two-step process. The first step involves taking off the old. The second step involves putting on the new. If you have ever painted a car or refinished a piece of furniture, you are familiar with how this process works. Before you can put a new finish or a new coat of paint on a car, you must first remove the old one.

Renewing the mind works much the same way. It is an ongoing process wherein we strip away our old ways of thinking and replace them with the principles of God's Word. The reward for staying involved in this process is greater sensitivity to God's will.

The principles of God's Word have been more instrumental in giving me direction for my life than anything else. Their value lies not only in their source (the Holy Spirit) but in their objectivity as well. Several years ago I made a decision that at the time seemed like a great thing to do. Anna and I prayed about it, and both of us felt real peace in our hearts. It turned out to be a disaster. I was devastated. I couldn't figure out why God would *lead* us to do something that would cause such confusion and stress in our family. Months later I was thinking about the situation, and out of nowhere a verse I had memorized years ago popped into my mind. The Holy Spirit let me know in no uncertain terms that I had violated a principle.

When I shared with Anna what had happened, we both agreed that the peace we experienced was probably the peace that comes with getting what we want rather than the peace of God. We both learned a fundamental lesson through all of that. *Principles always take precedence over peace.* If you have peace about something that violates a principle, rest assured, it is not the peace of God. The peace of God will never conflict with the principles of God.

I cannot overemphasize the importance of knowing the principles of Scripture. They are God's guidelines for living. No one has ever come to me with a problem that was not the result of someone's violating a principle. Principles are the clearest avenue for knowing God's will. Learning principles is as spiritual an exercise as praying or fasting. And it is equally necessary if we are to experience the wonderful Spirit-filled life.

2. Read with the context in mind.

The best way to guard against the trap of reading into the Scriptures what you want to see is to *read with the context in mind.* Read the Bible as you would any other piece of literature. "But wait," you say, "I thought the Bible was a special book." It is. But remember, God views human language as an adequate medium through which to communicate spiritual truth. That means the normal rules of sentence structure, subjects, verbs, and so on apply to the Bible.

You don't need to read into the text more than is there. Don't look for the *hidden* or *deeper* meaning. Just take it for face value. Many people miss the obvious in their attempt to discover the *real* meaning.

Don't read with the goal of finding something too specific. Why? Because you always will. If you read with an agenda, your findings will always be suspect. You won't know if what you find is a product of the illuminating work of the Spirit or your predisposition toward a particular answer. Remain as neutral as possible.

3. Look for general promises.

These are promises given to all believers for all time. They are the foundation for the personal promises the Holy Spirit may choose to reveal. An example of a general promise would be Jesus' promise not to leave us as orphans (see John 14:18). Another would be the promise of grace and mercy whenever we approach God (see Heb. 4:16). One of my favorites is Isaiah 40:31 where God promises strength for those who are weary.

Exceptions

As I mentioned earlier, there is a debate among Christian leaders about whether or not God still speaks today. I believe He does. However, I don't believe He speaks as much as people claim He does. He has said so much already, we don't need a great deal more revelation.

There are times, however, when the Holy Spirit will take a passage and lift it out of its original context and apply it to our specific situation. This is the exception, not the rule.

I have met too many Christians who approach Scripture exclusively from a mystical standpoint. They never consider the context, the original audience, the speaker, or even which Testament they are reading. They don't necessarily have a hidden agenda. But they focus exclusively on finding God's personal message to them. This approach is dangerous.

Words of Encouragement

As I was saying, there are times when the Holy Spirit applies a select verse to our particular situation. For me, these occasions usually come when I need encouragement. One of the more dramatic instances occurred one morning on the way to church. I had been the pastor at First Baptist about two months. I was elected against the wishes of about two hundred people. At the time the church was much smaller than it is today, so a group of two hundred people was quite a faction. To make matters worse, the group was made up mostly of deacons, Sunday school teachers, and members of various committees. They had really made life difficult for my family and me. I was praying they would leave. But they seemed to be determined to stay until I gave up the fight and resigned.

During that conflict, the Holy Spirit graciously decided to send me a personal word of encouragement. Anna and I had just exited the expressway and were turning up Tenth Street toward Peachtree. As I made the turn, she said, "Charles, the Lord gave me a passage for you this morning." She opened her Bible and read,

> But Moses said to the people, "Do not fear! Stand by and see the salvation of the Lord which He will accomplish for you today; for the Egyptians whom you have seen today, you will never see them again forever. The Lord will fight for you while you keep silent."
>
> —*Exodus 14:13–14*

Well, if that passage was really meant for me, I knew immediately who the Egyptians were. But the thought of not having to deal with that group anymore seemed a little unrealistic at the time. I thanked her and didn't think about it again—until an hour later. That same Sunday morning, at 9:45, the entire group stood up in their Sunday school classes and walked out the door in protest of my appointment as pastor. From that morning on they met for worship in another building several blocks away. Their presence and influence were gone for good.

When my secretary walked in my office and told me what had happened, I was stunned. And then I thought about Anna's verses. Nothing in the world will ever convince me that it was coincidence. God knew I needed a boost, physical evidence that I was on the right track and the battle was worth fighting. From then on I never looked back.

The Bible is *God's* Word. He can use it any way He sees fit. When the need arises, the Holy Spirit will guide you to verses that in their original context have nothing in the world to do with your particular circumstances. But you will know when they are meant for you. The Holy Spirit has a wonderful way of making it clear. He knows how to make a verse bear witness with your human spirit. He knows how to make a verse leap off the page and into your life.

Read with the original context and audience in mind, but leave room for the Holy Spirit to lift something out of its historical context for the purpose of ministering to your specific needs.

Start Now!

I could say a lot more. There is no way to overemphasize the importance of the Bible when it comes to living a Spirit-filled life. If you are not in the habit of reading your Bible daily, start now! Put this book down and pick up your Bible. Buy a translation you understand. There is no reason to fear the modern translations. With the exception of the Living Bible (which I read almost daily), they were all translated from the original Greek and Hebrew, just like the King James Version. Regardless of the translation you prefer, make sure you read a little every day. In doing so you provide the Holy Spirit with unlimited access to your mind and heart, the access necessary for you to experience the wonderful Spirit-filled life.

For Further Reading

Many books have been written to help Christians understand their Bibles. Here are several that I have found to be particularly helpful:

- *30 Days to Understanding the Bible* by Max E. Anders
- *How to Read the Bible for All It's Worth* by Gordon D. Fee and Douglas Stuart
- *How to Study the Bible* by James Braga
- *How to Understand Your Bible* by T. Norton Sterrett
- *Talk Through the Bible* by Bruce Wilkinson and Kenneth Boa
- *Living by the Book* by Howard Hendricks

NOTES

1. Charles Ryrie, "Understanding the Bible," in *The Ryrie Study Bible* (Chicago: Moody Press, 1978), p. 1959.
2. Billy Graham, *The Holy Spirit* (Dallas: Word, 1988), p. 46.
3. Steven R. Covey, *Principle Centered Leadership* (New York: Summit, 1991), p. 290.

———— THINK ABOUT IT ————

- Why do you think we have to have some understanding of the Word of God before we can accurately identify the voice of God?
- How much time do you spend reading and studying God's Word? Is this enough?
- How would you explain someone's "feelings" of God's approval when their actions contradict God's teachings?
- Why is it dangerous to look for a special message from God by opening the Bible and reading a verse out of context?

CHAPTER 18

Marker 4: Wisdom

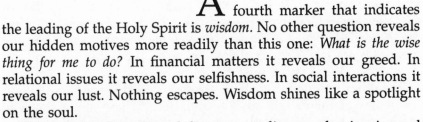

A fourth marker that indicates the leading of the Holy Spirit is *wisdom*. No other question reveals our hidden motives more readily than this one: *What is the wise thing for me to do?* In financial matters it reveals our greed. In relational issues it reveals our selfishness. In social interactions it reveals our lust. Nothing escapes. Wisdom shines like a spotlight on the soul.

The Holy Spirit leads and directs according to what is wise and unwise. It is following a discussion on wisdom that we find Paul's command to be filled with the Spirit:

> Therefore be careful how you walk, not as unwise men, but as wise, making the most of your time, because the days are evil. So then do not be foolish, but understand what the will of the Lord is. And do not get drunk with wine, for that is dissipation, but be filled with the Spirit.
> —*Ephesians 5:15–18*

There is no break in the discussion between his comments on wisdom and the command to be filled with the Spirit. Paul is not changing the subject. There is a vital and often-overlooked relationship between wisdom and the Holy Spirit, namely, the Holy Spirit guides the believer in the way of wisdom. To refuse to live wisely is to ignore the leading of the Holy Spirit.

I said earlier that the Holy Spirit is the mouthpiece of God to the mind and heart of man. With that in mind, take a fresh look at this familiar verse:

But if any of you lacks wisdom, let him ask of God, who gives to all men generously and without reproach, and it will be given to him.

—*James 1:5*

We are encouraged to ask for wisdom. God, through the person of the Holy Spirit, is more than willing to give us the wisdom we need for the decisions we face. We are encouraged to ask for wisdom rather than direction. Yet our tendency is to do just the opposite.

The Role of Wisdom

Many issues we are forced to deal with on a daily basis are not mentioned specifically in Scripture. Complicated situations arise, and there seems to be no biblical parallel to use as a guide. In these instances God expects us to ask, "What is the wise thing for me to do?" *Wisdom fills the gaps between the principles, promises, and commands of God.* Wisdom always takes all three into account and then asks, "What is the wise thing for *me* to do?"

The other unique thing about wisdom is that it operates beyond the realm of mere right and wrong. Somewhere along the way many of us have mistakenly come to believe that if the Bible does not specifically say something is wrong, it must be OK. Not so! Many things that the Bible does not specifically cite as wrong are detrimental to our spiritual as well as physical health.

Wisdom is often the tool the Holy Spirit uses to personalize God's will for our lives. What is wise for me may not be wise for you—and vice versa. I know a young man who has recently gotten out of involvement with the occult. To speed his recovery, he has put himself on an intensive mind-renewal program. He is memorizing Scripture by the chapter. He is in church every time the doors are open. And he listens to every Christian tape he can get his hands on.

In addition, there are some things he is not doing. He does not listen to any secular music. He does not go to certain parts of the city. And he does not return the phone calls of his old friends. Why? Well, here is what he told me:

It's just not wise for me to do those things right now. Eventually, I hope to go back and tell my friends what God has done in my life—but I'm not strong enough yet. On a couple of occasions I've been tempted to pick up the phone and call them. But something inside me said, "Wait." So I'm waiting. As far as the music goes, I don't have anything against secular music. It's just that I've got so much junk still floating around in my head. I don't want to risk putting more up there. Besides, Christian music helps keep me focused.

Here is a young man who understands the importance of wisdom. For him, it is a matter of survival. He has also discovered the relationship between wisdom and the Holy Spirit. The *something* that told him not to call his old friends was the Holy Spirit.

God has not called us to merely stay on the right side of the line dividing right from wrong. He has called us to walk wisely. Sometimes that means staying way back from the line. The Holy Spirit uses wisdom to keep us back from the brink of disaster. Most of us want to know how far we can go toward sin without actually sinning. Once we find out (or think we have found out), we move right out on the edge—and stay there until we go over. Consequently, there are habits we cannot walk away from. There are areas of weakness in our lives that never improve. And all because we ignore the Holy Spirit's promptings to walk wisely. The writer of Proverbs summed it up beautifully:

> He who trusts in his own heart is a fool,
> But he who walks wisely will be delivered.
> —*Proverbs 28:26*

A Three-Part Question

For maximum impact this penetrating question should be asked in three dimensions.

1. What is the wise thing to do in light of my past experience?

Phil works for a large firm out of St. Petersburg, Florida. His work requires him to be away from home two or three nights a week. When he came to see me, he was practically in tears.

"I have really gotten myself into a mess," he said. "I love my wife. We have a new baby. I'm a leader in my church. And at home everything is fine. But on the road things are different. You see, there are three or four of us from work who travel together.

The other guys aren't Christians. They can't wait to get away from their wives. Every week it's the same thing. They are like high-school kids on spring break. They just go wild.

"Every Monday I promise God I'm not going to participate. And every Monday night, there I am, right in the middle of them. It's killing me. It's hard to face my wife when I come home. She knows something is wrong, but I don't see any point in telling her. What am I supposed to do? I've got to work. And if I work, I've got to travel."

He was really shaken up. I asked, "Phil, tell me about these trips. Where do you stay? Who do you stay with? What are the circumstances surrounding the situation?"

"It's always the same. We work alone or in pairs during the day. Then we meet back at the hotel and go somewhere to eat together. After dinner it's downhill from there. When we first began working together, I would ask them to drop me off at the hotel. But they would kid me and eventually wear me down to the point that I would go along. Now I don't even ask. I know I should be stronger. But the fact is, I'm not."

I explained to Phil that God had called him to walk wisely. Sometimes that meant taking several steps away from the line dividing right from wrong. "Phil, apparently you have a difficult time overcoming the temptation to go with your buddies once you are in the car with them. Maybe the wise thing to do next trip is to eat dinner alone. Don't even hook back up with them until the next day."

"Is there something wrong with eating with them?" he asked.

"No," I replied. "But that's not the point. What is the wise thing for you to do in light of your past experience? It could be that the wise thing for you to do is to stay in a completely different hotel! Again, not because there is something *wrong* with staying in the same hotel as your buddies. But because of your track record with them, it may not be the wise thing to do."

He sat back in his chair. "That's pretty extreme."

"You're right," I said. "But then, you are in an extreme situation. And sometimes that calls for extreme measures."

"I know you are right," he said. "That is exactly what I ought to do."

I knew that the Holy Spirit was tugging at his heart, urging him to set a new standard. But I could not get him to make a commitment to follow through.

"I'll think about it," he said.

That was the last time I saw Phil. But I kept up with him through a mutual friend. Phil ignored my advice. Not too many months later he left his wife. Our mutual friend says that Phil has been over to see him several times and cries like a baby. He wishes he could go back and do it all over. But sometimes you just can't go back.

The Holy Spirit always takes our past experiences into account when giving us direction for our lives. He knows when we are settling ourselves up for moral disaster. Unlike Phil, we would do well to listen to the still small voice that quietly whispers, "Remember the last time . . . remember last time you went . . . remember last time you stayed . . . remember last time you agreed to do that . . . remember last time that happened . . . remember last time someone told you that . . ."

2. What is the wise thing to do in light of my present situation?

The second part of this three-part question focuses on what's going on NOW! Sometimes, because of the present state of your marriage, health, finances, or the economy, things that ordinarily would be OK are off-limits. This can be hard to take. After all, it was OK last time. Why not this time?

I know a man who gave up traveling for a little over a year because of a situation at home with his teenage daughter. He took a big cut in pay and lost some of his seniority. When asked why, he answered, "Well, it's not that I have anything against traveling. It's just not wise for me to be gone overnight in light of what my daughter is going through right now."

He understood that the issue was not one of right versus wrong, it was a wisdom issue. Eventually, the situation at home cleared up, and he was able to travel again.

Making decisions in view of our present situation can save us much heartache and regret. I once heard a student sharing a situation that he was faced with in college. He had been through a very intense week of final exams. He didn't get much sleep throughout the week because of all the studying and preparation for his tests. After his last exam was over, he was operating on pure adrenaline! He was physically, mentally, and emotionally spent. His buddies were going out that night to celebrate the end of exam week, and they invited him to go along. Although he was incredi-

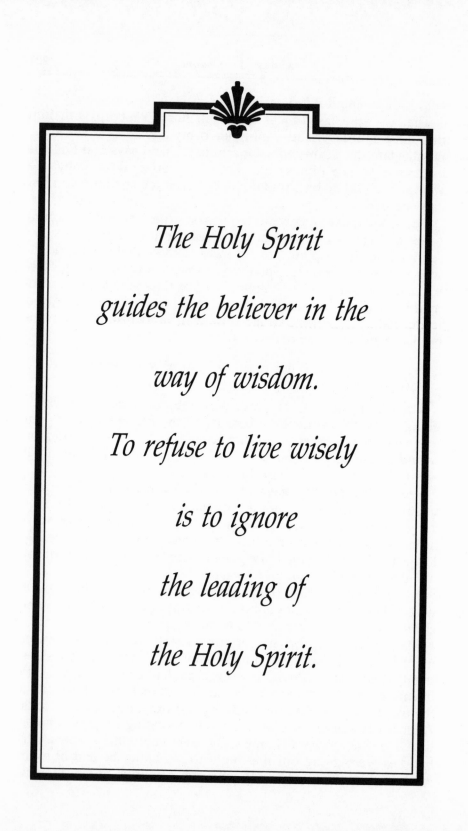

The Holy Spirit

guides the believer in the

way of wisdom.

To refuse to live wisely

is to ignore

the leading of

the Holy Spirit.

bly relieved to be finished and knew that going out would be fun, he realized that because of his particular state of mind, he would be much more apt to compromise his standards. He said no to his friends and didn't even allow himself to be tempted. He was being wise and evaluating his temptability based on his present situation.

Life changes quickly. What's good today may be detrimental tomorrow. And then it may be OK again the day after tomorrow. Very little is set in stone. God loves us and directs our lives according to what is happening around us. That is why it is so important for us to be sensitive to the initial promptings of the Holy Spirit.

3. What is the wise thing to do in light of my future plans and dreams?

We have a large number of single adults in our church. A recurring question that surfaces in my discussions with them concerns dating non-Christians. Usually, it is asked this way: "What does the Bible say about dating non-Christians?"

"That's easy," I say. "Nothing. In fact it doesn't say anything about dating at all, so maybe you shouldn't!"

After a brief look of panic, they realize I'm kidding. I answer this question by asking a series of questions. First, "Do you think that you will eventually marry someone you fall in love with?"

"Of course," they say.

I continue, "Do you think you will fall in love with someone you date for some length of time?"

"Probably."

"Do you want to marry a Christian?"

"Absolutely!"

"Well, if you are going to marry someone you fall in love with, and if you think it's likely that you will fall in love with someone you are going to date over a period of time, and if you are committed to marrying only a Christian, is it really wise to date a non-Christian?"

Reactions are usually mixed. Someone will almost always refer to the original question: "But where does it say that in the Bible?"

"The Bible," I say, "instructs us to walk wisely. In that context, the Bible does have something to say about dating non-Christians. It is unwise."

Be Careful

When Paul says "Be careful how you walk, not as unwise men, but as wise" (Eph. 5:15), he is instructing each of us to carefully examine everything that comes our way: every opportunity, every invitation, every date, every relationship, every trip, everything. Why? "Because," he says, "the days are evil." We live in an evil age. It's as if every organization and institution is out to destroy the things we as Christians hold sacred. Almost nothing in our society works to strengthen the family. No one seems to care whether married couples stay together. Just about everything on the airways teaches a philosophy of life that is diametrically opposed to what we stand for as Christians. To become like the world requires no effort at all. Just get out there and live. Sooner or later you will be just like them.

To survive, we must be wise! We cannot afford to walk blindly through life just taking things as they come. We must get in the habit of looking as far as we can down the road to anticipate trouble. We must get in the habit of taking evasive action. And most of all, we must stay a safe distance away from the line separating right from wrong.

Understand!

Just before he admonishes his readers to be filled with the Spirit, Paul commands them to do one other thing:

> So then do not be foolish, but understand what the will of the Lord is.
>
> —*Ephesians 5:17*

This verse puzzled me for a long time. How can you command someone to understand something? As I studied this verse, I realized what Paul was saying: "Face up to what you know in your heart God wants you to do!" This is a powerful command, especially in view of what he is about to say regarding the filling of the Spirit.

All of us have an amazing ability to sidestep God's will for our lives when it conflicts with *our* will for our lives. Given enough time, we can justify just about anything. To do so, however, is to grieve the Holy Spirit and to set ourselves up for disaster. When we know in our hearts that something is not right, we must face up to it. The longer we play games, the longer we rationalize, the longer we justify, the greater the risk.

Since the Holy Spirit moves in the realm of wisdom, His convicting work often begins several steps away from what is traditionally considered sin. Take, for example, the fellow I mentioned earlier who has just left behind the occult. When he reaches for the phone to call his old friends, the Holy Spirit whispers, "Don't do it." He could easily rationalize, "There is nothing wrong with calling them. What can it hurt? There is nothing in the Bible about calling old friends."

On one hand, he would be right. But on the other hand, he would be disobeying the prompting of the Holy Spirit. Notice, however, that the Holy Spirit would not be convicting him of something that we would normally consider a sin. After all, there may come a day when it is perfectly fine for him to call his old friends. And there would be no harm in my giving his friends a call. But that is not the point. The Holy Spirit would be convicting him at the wisdom level: "It's not wise to call your old friends."

Suppose he ignores the Holy Spirit's warnings and calls them anyway. Has he sinned? You better believe it. God has commanded us to be wise. And to act unwisely—especially after being warned by the Holy Spirit—is to sin. James asserted,

> Therefore, to one who knows the right thing to do, and does not do it, to him it is sin.
>
> —*James 4:17*

John Wesley's mother explained it to her son like this: "Whatever weakens your reason, impairs the tenderness of your conscience, obscures your sense of God, takes off your relish for spiritual things, whatever increases the authority of the body over the mind, that thing is sin to you, however innocent it may seem in itself."

Wisdom is not optional. It is not reserved for a special class of believers. It is for all of us. When the Holy Spirit convicts us at the level of wisdom, it is easy to rationalize. After all, what we are being tempted to do is usually not a sin in the normal sense of the word. But once the Holy Spirit warns us, at that moment it becomes sin for us.

I don't think I've ever counseled with anyone who didn't admit that their troubles began with a series of unwise decisions. Not sin necessarily. But things that led into the sin that eventually made its mark emotionally, financially, or physically. I have talked to hundreds of Christians who have admitted that in the midst of making what turned out to be unwise decisions, they had a persistent feeling that they were making a mistake. But since they couldn't find any verses about their particular situation, or they couldn't see what was wrong with it, they went ahead anyway. Now, they readily admit, they were being prompted by the Holy Spirit.

When Andy was thirteen, we hiked to the bottom of the Grand Canyon. About halfway down, we were met by a group of sight-seers riding mules. At that point the trail was only about three feet wide. The canyon went straight up on one side of the trail and straight down on the other. We leaned up against the side of the canyon as the mule train passed by. I noticed a strange thing. The mules were not walking nose to tail in a straight line. They were walking almost completely sideways. Their noses were actually hanging out over the edge of the ravine. Their riders looked scared to death. Most of them were leaning waaaaaay back in their saddles.

A lot of Christians are like those mules. They walk right on the line—with their noses on the other side. They don't see anything wrong with what they are doing. And they aren't aware of the convicting ministry of the Holy Spirit. It's no wonder. He is standing a few steps back whispering, "Hey, back here. Take a few steps back here. You can see fine from back here."

The Holy Spirit doesn't draw the line at the point separating good from evil. He always draws His line a safe distance back from the point of actual disaster. The convicting ministry of the Holy Spirit begins once we move outside the parameters of what is wise for us. If an option is outside the spectrum of wisdom, it is not God's will. The Holy Spirit is saying, "NO!" He loves us. He doesn't wait until we are on the edge of the cliff to warn us. He begins as soon as He discerns we are headed for the cliff. Sometimes I think He begins convicting me as soon as I even think about the cliff!

Please don't avoid the conviction of the Holy Spirit. As the apostle Paul says, face up to what you know in your heart God wants you to do. Don't play games. Don't avoid the issue. Heed the writer of Proverbs when he says, "He who trusts in his own heart is a fool." That is, the one who ignores the warnings of the

Holy Spirit just because he or she can't see anything wrong with something is foolish.

Also heed him when he says, "But he who walks wisely will be delivered" (Prov. 28:26). The one who heeds the initial promptings of the Holy Spirit—whether they make sense at the time or not—will be delivered from the pain and guilt and regret and broken relationships brought on by sin.

─────── **THINK ABOUT IT** ───────

Pray for wisdom.

Test each opportunity, invitation, business transaction, financial decision, and social interaction with these questions:

- Is this the wise thing for me to do?
- Is this the wise thing for me to do in light of my past experience?
- Is this the wise thing for me to do in light of my present situation?
- Is this the wise thing for me to do in light of my future plans and dreams?

If it isn't, stay away. By doing so, you will be right in step with the Holy Spirit. Choosing the path of wisdom is just one more way to ensure that you will experience the wonderful Spirit-filled life.

Conclusion

Much has happened in my life since that eventful day on the floor of my study back in 1964—some good, some bad. Through it all, God has continued to enlighten the eyes of my heart to the truth of who He is and who He is in me (see Eph. 1:18). I have walked through some valleys in which I found it difficult to abide in Him, and there have been months in which there was little or no fruit in my life.

God has been faithful to lead me back time and time again to the truth I discovered on that cold concrete floor twenty-eight years ago. The lessons have not always been easy. I have not always been quick to respond. But I will never forget. And I will never be the same.

The Spirit-filled life is a life of dependency on and sensitivity to the promptings of the Holy Spirit. Distinguishing Him from the messages around us is no easy thing. But it's essential for our survival. And it is essential to the survival of the church.

Within you is housed the power necessary to face whatever life throws your way, for you are a recipient of the very life of Christ. Through the person of the Holy Spirit, He longs to express His life through your personality, your lips, and your hands. You have been granted the incredible privilege of being His representative on earth. It's true; you may be the only Jesus some people ever know.

You are a unique blend of gifts and talents. There is a special niche in the family of God that only you can fill. Exercise your gift every chance you get. Stay closely involved with the body of Christ. As you exercise your gift in conjunction with theirs, you will experience the power of God.

Abide in Him. You are a lousy producer. We all are. But as you abide in Him, the quality of fruit He will produce in your life will amaze you. There will be the type of fruit that draws your unbelieving friends and neighbors into the kingdom. The fruit you bear will aid in keeping the body of Christ working in harmony together. Through the virtues of self-control and faithfulness, you will be protected from the schemes of the enemy.

Begin every day with a commitment to yourself to walk in the Spirit. Set—and leave—your mind on the things above. The mind set on the things of the Spirit results in life and peace. The mind set on the things of the flesh . . . well, you know where that leads. Think through your day. Go ahead and claim victory over your anticipated battles. Faith activates the power of the Spirit in your life. Get a head start.

The Holy Spirit will become as important to you as you allow Him to be. He won't force Himself on you. He sits back quietly and waits. Give Him control. He's not asking for rededication. He's asking for *surrender*.

Only when you raise the white flag is He able to assume control. Only then is He able to slide over into the driver's seat of your life. It's at the point of surrender that you begin to experience —and enjoy—the quality of life that I have come to know as the wonderful Spirit-filled life.

Spiritual Gifts

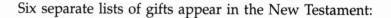

Six separate lists of gifts appear in the New Testament:

1 Corinthians 12:8–10
Word of wisdom
Word of knowledge
Faith
Healing
Miracles
Prophecy
Distinguishing of spirits
Tongues
Interpretation of tongues

1 Corinthians 12:28
Apostle
Prophecy
Teaching
Miracles
Healing
Helps
Administration
Tongues

1 Corinthians 12:29–30
Apostle
Prophecy
Teaching
Miracles
Healing
Tongues
Interpretation of tongues

Romans 12:6–8
Prophecy
Serving
Teaching
Exhortation
Giving
Leading
Mercy

Ephesians 4:11
Apostle
Prophecy
Evangelism
Pastor/Teacher

1 Peter 4:11
Speaking
Serving

The gifts in these lists can be broken down into two categories and two subcategories:

Motivational Gifts: These gifts serve as the primary motivation for their recipient's service. There are two categories of motivational gifts.

Equipping Gifts. These gifts are listed in Ephesians 4:11. They were given to certain believers to enable them to equip others to do the work of the ministry.

Service Gifts. These gifts are primarily service oriented.

Sign Gifts: These gifts validate the authenticity of God's messengers along with their message.

Motivational Gifts

Equipping Gifts

*Apostle**
Prophecy
Evangelism
Pastor/Teacher

Service Gifts

Administration
Exhortation
Faith
Giving
Service
Mercy
Leadership

Sign Gifts

Miracles
Healing
Tongues
Interpretation of tongues

---

* I believe the gift of apostle was reserved for the twelve men chosen by Jesus during His earthly ministry. Later, the apostle Paul was given this gift as well.

The Sign Gifts in Focus

The sign gifts continue to be a source of conflict and disagreement among believers. Although I don't claim to have a solution for the division, I do have some questions and observations that may help clear away some of the fog.

1. Why is it that so many people *seek* the sign gift of tongues when the apostle Paul clearly stated we should "eagerly desire the greater gifts"? When Paul lists the gifts in order of importance, tongues is last (see 1 Cor. 12:28).
2. Why will some people go to such great lengths to receive the sign gift of tongues but not the gift of service or giving or mercy?
3. Why don't people with the gift of healing go to hospitals?
4. Why is it that people who claim to have the gift of healing say the successful exercise of their gift depends on the faith of the recipient of their gift? A believer with the gift of mercy can show mercy on a faithless person. A man or woman with the gift of giving can give to a faithless person. Why does the gift of healing require something out of the recipient? And where in Scripture do we find that this particular gift requires special assistance from the one receiving the ministry?
5. In our experience, have the gifts of healing and tongues done more to validate or invalidate the message of the ones claiming to have these sign gifts? In the New Testament the *public* display of these gifts authenticated the one performing these feats as a messenger of God. I emphasize

the word *public* because of the contrast to where Jesus and His disciples performed their miracles and where modern-day miracle workers perform theirs.

6. Can a man or woman whose life is not characterized by the fruit of the Spirit perform signs and wonders by the power of the Spirit?

7. Which is a greater testimony to the power of God: healing a sick man within a matter of seconds or exercising self-control throughout a lifetime of temptation?

8. Why do so many people want to know whether or not I speak in tongues? Why doesn't anyone ask me what kind of father or husband (or better yet, grandfather!) I am? Why is it so important to certain people that I speak in tongues? And why do I get the impression that they think less of me when I inform them that I do not, have not, and don't plan to? After all, God has gifted me to fulfill a particular niche in the kingdom. Why would I insult Him by asking Him for another gift?

9. Do I believe God still heals? Yes. Do I believe He heals miraculously? Yes. Have I ever seen anyone miraculously healed? Yes. Have I ever laid hands on people and seen them healed? Yes. Do I have the gift of healing? No. I have never met or heard of anyone who has the gift of healing. By that, I mean I have never heard of anyone who could heal at will—like Jesus and His men.

For Further Study

Gifts of the Spirit

- Acts 8:20
- Romans 1:11
- Romans 11:29
- Romans 12:6
- 1 Corinthians 12:1–31
- 1 Corinthians 13:2
- 1 Corinthians 13:8
- 1 Corinthians 14:1
- 1 Corinthians 14:12
- Ephesians 4:7–8
- 1 Timothy 4:14
- 2 Timothy 1:6
- Hebrews 2:4
- 1 Peter 4:10

The Baptism of the Spirit

- Matthew 3:11
- Matthew 3:16
- Mark 1:8
- Luke 3:16
- John 1:33
- Acts 1:5
- Acts 11:16

- Romans 6:3
- 1 Corinthians 12:13
- Galatians 3:27

The Filling of the Spirit

- Luke 1:15
- Luke 1:41
- Luke 1:67
- Acts 2:4
- Acts 4:8
- Acts 4:31
- Acts 9:17
- Acts 13:9
- Acts 13:52
- Ephesians 5:18

The Fullness of the Spirit

- Luke 1:15
- Luke 4:1
- Luke 10:21
- Acts 6:3–5
- Acts 7:55
- Acts 11:24

Walking/Living by the Spirit

- Romans 8:5–13
- Galatians 5:16
- Galatians 5:25